A Cherokee Encyclopedia

A Cherokee Encyclopedia

Robert J. Conley

University of New Mexico Press | Albuquerque

11 10 09 08 07   1 2 3 4 5

LIBRARY OF CONGRESS CATALOGING-IN-PUBLICATION DATA

Conley, Robert J.
A Cherokee encyclopedia / Robert J. Conley.
    p. cm.
Includes bibliographical references.
    ISBN 978-0-8263-3951-5 (CLOTH : ALK. PAPER)
1. Cherokee Indians—Encyclopedias. I. Title.
E99.C5C694 2007
970.004'97003—dc22
                2007038318

Book design and typesetting by Kathleen Sparkes
Text type is Utpoia OTF.
Display type is Rotis family, OTF

To the
memory of
Talmadge

Contents

Preface

C herokee history has been marked by a number of migrations that have resulted in, among other things, the formation of different tribes from the same original people. For instance, little is known of a legendary migration led by Dangerous Man. His people are said to have migrated to the Rocky Mountains. They may be the original Mexican Cherokees, but that is conjecture. The first Cherokee group to be recognized by the U.S. government as a separate tribe from the Cherokee Nation was made up of the followers of Bowles, who left the old Cherokee country in 1794 and settled in Missouri for a time. The great earthquake of 1811 drove them out of Missouri, and, upon reaching Arkansas, they became known as the Western Cherokee Nation. Their existence as a separate Cherokee nation ended following the Trail of Tears. But some of them, including Bowles himself, had in the meantime gone to Texas, where both the Mexican government and the revolutionary government of Texas recognized them as the Texas Cherokees. These Cherokees were driven out of Texas in 1839 and dispersed under the Texas administration of Mirabeau B. Lamar. During the U.S. Civil War, Stand Watie proclaimed a Confederate Cherokee Nation. It ceased to exist, of course, with the end of the Civil War. When the majority of Cherokees, along with their government, the Cherokee Nation, were forcibly removed into what is now Oklahoma in 1838, a number of people managed to stay behind in the Southeast. Their descendants became known as the Eastern Band of Cherokee Indians. Finally, during the period of Cherokee Nation dormancy from 1907 until 1973, a group of full-blood Cherokees made application under the Oklahoma Indian General Welfare Act in 1936 and formed the United Keetoowah Band of Cherokee Indians in Oklahoma. Of all of these Cherokee nations, only three remain: the Cherokee Nation, the Eastern Band of Cherokees, and the United Keetoowah Band. In addition, there are people of Cherokee descent who cannot become affiliated with any of the three. This encyclopedia is intended to be a quick reference for many of the places, things, and people who are connected to these groups.

Acknowledgments

Special thanks are owed to the following individuals for their help in the preparation of this encyclopedia. Luther Wilson, director of the University of New Mexico Press, supported this project from the beginning; it would never have been done without him. Cheryl Glass, Travis Snell, Dan Littlefield, Dan Agent, David Fitzgerald, and many Cherokees and their family members very graciously provided me with information and photographs for their entries. There are too many to name here. Annie Barva did a meticulous and damn near perfect job of copyediting a difficult text. And finally, as always, my wife, Evelyn, has watched over my shoulder to keep me honest.

Introduction

-🌣-

Who knows how long the Cherokees have existed as a distinct people?
Tales from the oral tradition vary as to the Cherokees' origins. One
tale has them coming from an island off the coast of South America and
migrating north, presumably all the way to the Great Lakes area, and then,
following wars with other Iroquoian-speaking peoples, migrating south
again until they eventually settled in the area that we now know as the
Old South. Another tale has them coming in from the far north through a
land of ice and long nights. Of course, there are still those who would have
all American Indians coming from Asia across a Bering Strait land bridge.
Whatever the truth of their origins, once the Cherokees had been in the
Old South long enough, they made it their own, for there is also a tale from
the oral tradition, recorded by James Mooney, that tells of the creation of
the Smokey Mountains and the origins of life there.

Mooney also recorded a tale that he called "The Massacre of the Ani-
Kutani," which tells of a powerful priesthood that once existed among the
Cherokees and of its eventual overthrow by popular uprising. The tale
ends by saying the Cherokees never again allowed a central government
to develop among them. At the time the first Europeans encountered
the Cherokees in the sixteenth and seventeenth centuries, they found
them living in autonomous towns, each with its own government. These
towns—about two hundred of them, scattered over an area that today
is divided into the states of North Carolina, South Carolina, Tennessee,
Georgia, Alabama, Kentucky, Virginia, and West Virginia—were held

together only by a common culture, a common language, and clans. There was nothing like a central government.

The importance of the clan system in this scheme cannot be overemphasized. Cherokees have seven matrilineal clans. Descent was traced through the female line. Women owned their homes and their gardens. Children belonged to their mothers' clans. Most of what we would call law today was clan business. All seven clans were represented in each town, so if any Cherokee were to travel far in Cherokee country to a town he had never previously visited, he would find clan relatives living there.

The town government seems to have been made up of a war chief and a peace chief, each chief having his own advisory council. The simplified explanation of this system has it that the peace chief presided in times of peace and the war chief in times of war. In actuality, the peace chief was likely in charge of what we would call the internal powers of government and the war chief of the external powers. In other words, the peace chief was concerned with local matters including ceremonies, local disputes, and daily life. The war chief was responsible not only for war-related matters, but also for any dealings with people outside of the town—trade, alliances, disputes of any kind, and so on.

We know that the women played an important behind-the-scenes role in town government, but we do not know just exactly how that worked. It may have been as formal as a female mirror image of the perceived government by men. In other words, there may have been female advisors to the chiefs and female advisory councils. Or the relationship may have been less formal than that. The only thing we know for certain is that a woman known variously as the Beloved Woman, War Woman, and Pretty Woman had the power of life or death over captives. It is probable that she had other powers as well.

And we know that the Europeans were slow in figuring out just what the women had to do with decision making. At first, it seems they simply thought that the Cherokees were slow in making up their minds. At last, they discovered that the men had to go home after a meeting and talk things over with the women before they could render a decision. Englishmen thus said that the Cherokees had a "petticoat government" and that "among the Cherokees, the women rules [sic] the roost."

In addition, Europeans thought that if they made an agreement with one Cherokee town, all Cherokees should abide by that agreement. Why they should have felt that way even though each of the thirteen English colonies insisted on its own sovereignty, is anyone's guess. At any rate, in 1721, frustrated with their attempts at dealing with the Cherokees, Englishmen

Robert J. Conley

persuaded them to appoint a "trade commissioner," one Cherokee with whom they could deal and expect all Cherokees to abide by his promises. In exchange, the English appointed their own trade commissioner. The Cherokee appointment was "Wrosetasetow." (See "Wrosetasetow" for an attempt at deciphering this name.)

Up until the time of the appointment of "Wrosetasetow," Cherokee experience with the newcomers had been capricious and sporadic. In 1540, the notorious Hernando De Soto expedition passed through the Cherokee country, stopping probably at Guaxule (in present-day Georgia), Canasagua, and then on into the Creek, or Muskogee, country. Fortunately for the Cherokees, De Soto and his men were apparently on their best behavior during that time. The Cherokees gave them food and places to stay, and the Spanish went on their way. It was twenty-six years before the Cherokees were bothered again. In 1561, Spaniards under the command of Juan Pardo moved onto an area of the coast of South Carolina and established a fort called San Felipe. From there, expeditions went out into the country of the Cherokees and the Creeks. Again, the Cherokees received little trouble at the hands of the Spaniards. To this day, there are traces of Spanish gold mines in the old Cherokee country, but the Spaniards hid the fact of the mines from the rest of the world, and we have no documentation of what was going on. We can only assume a certain amount of Spanish influence on the Cherokees from this period.

Cherokees first met the English in 1654. The English of the Virginia colony had just concluded a long and bloody war with the Powhatans. A group of approximately six hundred Cherokees moved into the territory of Virginia, settling on the site of an abandoned Powhatan town. A battle followed in which the Cherokees soundly defeated the Virginians and their allies the Pamunkeys. Documentation of this skirmish and the events surrounding it is scarce. The Cherokees eventually abandoned the site.

James Needham and Gabriel Arthur from Virginia visited the Cherokee town of Echota (also known as Chota) in Tennessee, on the south bank of the Little Tennessee River, in 1673 in an attempt to establish trade relations. The trip turned out to be disastrous for Needham when he was murdered by Weesocks who were visiting the Cherokee town. Arthur, however, stayed at Chota for nearly a year before some Cherokees took him back to Virginia. In 1690, Cornelius Dougherty, an Irishman from Virginia, settled among the Cherokees as a trader. He started a mixed-blood Cherokee family and lived with the Cherokees for the rest of his life. The next year, South Carolina colonists murdered a number of Cherokees.

Several Cherokee chiefs went to Charleston with presents for the governor two years later, attempting to establish peace and form an alliance. The agreement was made, but the governor of South Carolina apparently continued to instigate wars with several Indian tribes, including the Cherokees, in order to obtain captives to sell into slavery. In 1715, in response to this aggression, the Yamassee attacked South Carolina in force. South Carolina managed to defeat the Yamassees at last, with the Yamassee survivors moving in with the Creeks or fleeing to Spanish protection in Florida. Chiefs from the Cherokees' Lower Towns in present-day South Carolina and northern Georgia went to Charleston again, suing for peace, and South Carolina sent Colonel George Chicken with a detachment into Cherokee country. He moved on into the Upper Towns, where he found the chiefs a bit more defiant. They wanted guns and ammunition to assist them in their wars with other tribes. An agreement was reached.

Then in 1721, Governor Francis Nicolson of South Carolina invited the chiefs of thirty-seven towns to Charleston. The governor wanted to simplify the business of dealing with Cherokees. He made a treaty with them that set up a system of trade, drew a boundary line between the territory of the Cherokees and that of the English, and appointed an agent to superintend their affairs. He also suggested the appointment of "Wrosetasetow" as head chief of the Cherokee Nation. The Cherokees agreed, and the appointment was made. It is doubtful that the Cherokees understood the role to which "Wrosetasetow" had been appointed in the same way that Governor Nicholson understood it, but it was the beginning of the modern Cherokee Nation.

This encyclopedia is presented as a quick reference to most things Cherokee: the several Cherokee "nations" that have appeared in history, people and places and things important to each of them, and individual Cherokees who have distinguished themselves in various walks of life and in different periods of Cherokee history. A few white men are listed in this book, all of whom were closely associated with Cherokees in a positive way. John Sevier, Andrew Jackson, Wilson Lumpkin, and others of their ilk have received more than enough coverage elsewhere, and I have no desire to give them more. Readers looking for entries such as "feathers, Cherokee use of," and specific Cherokee myths will be disappointed. I have not included those kinds of things. They can be looked up readily in James Mooney's *Myths of the Cherokee*, Charles Hudson's *The Southeastern Indians*, and other sources. It is inevitable that I have missed certain people and items. Some readers may be astonished that I have left out someone or something. I can only say that I have done my best to

Robert J. Conley

include entries for anything that the average reader might want to look up regarding Cherokees.

I have used the expressions *full-blood, half-breed,* and *mixed-blood* unashamedly. They are expressions still in use by Cherokee people and are useful and meaningful, if not always entirely accurate. And I have included many Cherokee "outlaws," in part because a majority of them were not really outlaws at all, but rather resisters, and in part because Indian Territory created a number of outlaws. Many of these outlaws, real or fabricated, are much more important to Cherokees today than are most of the chiefs. One final word: I have not limited the people included herein to those who are official members or citizens of one of the three federally recognized Cherokee tribes. Not all Cherokees have the proper paperwork to document their heritage. In general, I take people at their word. Let those whom Arigon Starr calls the "NDN Police" point their fingers.

A.

Abram of Chilhowie

In 1775, following the Cherokee sale of lands to the Transylvania Company, which Dragging Canoe opposed, Dragging Canoe organized raids against what he considered to be illegal squatter communities on Cherokee land. He assigned one of the three raiding parties to Abram of Chilhowie. Abram's party was to attack the white settlements at Watauga and at the Nolichucky River, running through North Carolina and Tennessee. Abram returned from his raid with a few prisoners, including Mrs. Bean and Samuel Moore, who was burned at the stake. Mrs. Bean was rescued by Nancy Ward, known to history as the "Ghigau," Beloved Woman. Abram was killed under a flag of truce in 1788 by a Franklin militia led by John Sevier.

Ada-gal'kala

Ada-gal'kala (Attacullaculla, Attakullakulla, the Little Carpenter) was born around 1712 and died in 1778. He was the recognized principal chief of the Cherokee Nation from 1762 until his death in 1778. He first appears in written records in 1730, when Sir Alexander Cuming took seven Cherokees with him to London. One of the seven was Ada-gal'kala, although he was not yet known by that name. As a young man, Ada-gal'kala was called "Okoonaka" (British spelling of the time), which translates as "White Owl." Englishmen called him "Owen Nakan." He was likely in his twenties at the time and was described as a small man, slight of frame. He was

Ada-gal'kala (far right). Engraving by Isaac Basire, London, 1730. Courtesy of the Smithsonian Institution.

certainly the youngest of the Cherokees in the group. Ada-gal'kala himself said in later years that he was the first to agree to make the trip. The others only consented afterward.

They left for England on the *Fox*, a man-of-war, on May 4, 1730, from Charleston, South Carolina, and landed at Dover on June 5. From there they went to London, where they were put up for a time at the Mermaid Tavern and later in an undertaker's basement in the Covent Garden section. On June 18, they saw the king at Windsor. Following that occasion, they were given new clothes, and in these English outfits they posed for a portrait that may have been painted by either Hogarth or Markham. In the portrait, Ada-gal'kala, on the far right, is holding a gourd rattle in his right hand, with his left hand resting on the haft of a knife hanging from his belt.

The seven Cherokees were taken to see all the sights of London, including a play, the Tower of London, the crown jewels, and a couple of fairs. On September 29, they signed the "Articles of Friendship and Commerce." Their interpreter, Eleazar Wiggan, gave them a translation of the document after the signing. When they discovered that they had acknowledged the king's right to the country of Carolina, they talked among themselves and considered killing Wiggan and the Cherokee who had been their spokesman, one "Oukayuda." At last, however, they decided that because they had no right to cede lands anyway, the agreement could not be binding. They would leave the matter in the hands of the authorities at home. The Cherokees departed for home from Portsmouth on the *Fox* on October 7. Ada-gal'kala had by this time learned to speak some English.

In 1736, the French sent emissaries to the Cherokees in an attempt to form an alliance. Ada-gal'kala was instrumental in convincing the

Robert J. Conley

Cherokees to reject them. Then around 1740, he was captured by the Ottawas, who were allied to the French, and taken to Canada. During his captivity, Ada-gal'kala came to be treated as an Ottawa, for whatever reason, becoming good friends with Pontiac. He also met any number of Frenchmen, including the governor of New France.

When Ada-gal'kala returned to the Cherokee country in 1748, he found the South Carolina traders cheating the Cherokees. "Ammouskossittee" was now the Cherokee "emperor," and Guhna-gadoga was in effect running things for him. Ada-gal'kala became a trusted advisor of Guhna-gadoga. The South Carolina traders' behavior and his own eight or so years among the Ottawas had turned Ada-gal'kala toward the French, and he visited with the French-allied Shawnees in Ohio and the Senecas in New York. He returned to the Cherokee country with a rumor that Governor James Glen of South Carolina was trying to entice the Creeks and Catawbas to attack the Cherokees. But the Cherokees attacked South Carolina settlers and settlements instead, and South Carolina imposed a trade embargo.

Many of the Cherokee towns, however, were still strongly in favor of the English, and they agreed to South Carolina's terms for resuming trade. One of those terms was that "the Little Carpenter" be delivered up to them for having incited all the trouble. Ada-gal'kala and some of his allies went to Virginia, where they attempted to establish trade with that colony because South Carolina was not fulfilling its obligation. Virginia was hesitant to start trouble with South Carolina, but South Carolina's attitude did soften somewhat. When Lower Town Cherokees visited Charleston, Governor Glen asked only that they "oblige" Ada-gal'kala to make a trip to Charleston to explain his behavior. It is instructive to note the absence of an "emperor" from all these shenanigans and the nonexistence of any real concept of "nation" in the Cherokee towns' behavior.

By this time, Ada-gal'kala was already known by his new name. We do not know when that came about or why. "Ada-gal'kala" can be translated as "Leaning Wood," and the British had come to call the man "the Little Carpenter," presumably playing on his name and the fact that he was known to be able to "craft a bargain [skillfully]." His reputation was already firmly established.

Ada-gal'kala may have been pro-French, but he probably also discovered that the French were unable to establish trade with the Cherokees and that the Cherokees' best interests lay with the British colonies. In an attempt to convince the British that he was not working in French interests, he raided against "French Indians," killing eight Frenchmen and taking two prisoners. With the evidence of his triumph, he went to

Charleston to meet with Governor Glen. His visit was successful, bringing a promise that trade conditions would be improved and a great many presents given. He told the governor that he was the spokesman for the Cherokee Nation.

Glen's promise of improved trade was not fulfilled, and in 1754, with the threat of a war between France and England in the air, Virginia attempted to enlist the aid of the Cherokees. The meeting was friendly but unfruitful, so in the next year the Cherokees were again meeting with South Carolina. This time Ada-gal'kala persuaded Governor Glen to meet with him on the banks of the Saluda River, half the distance from Charleston. At this meeting, the governor again promised improved trade. He also promised a fort to be built in the Cherokee country for the protection of the women and children while the men were away at war. He said that he would send Ada-gal'kala and some other Cherokees to England. In exchange, Ada-gal'kala gave up Cherokee land and declared himself and his people "children of the great King George." He said that his voice was "the voice of the Cherokee Nation." The fort was not built.

Virginia became desperate in 1755, when General Edward Braddock's army was defeated by the French. They asked for another meeting with the Cherokees, and at that meeting Virginia agreed to trade with the Cherokees and to build a fort. The Virginians built their fort in the Overhills in Tennessee. There were still pro-French Cherokee towns as well as persistent rumors from those towns that the British were preparing to march against the Cherokees. More meetings were held with both South Carolina and Virginia, and the wily Ada-gal'kala continued playing one against the other.

He had, however, developed a taste for rum, and on one occasion he went very drunk into Fort Prince George in South Carolina and made a motion as if he would strike Captain Raymond Demere, the fort's commander, in the face with a bottle. Several of the Indians there took Ada-gal'kala away. The next day he apologized profusely to Demere for his behavior while drunk, blaming everything on the liquor.

The South Carolina fort was at last built and called Fort Loudon. Ada-gal'kala once again led a raid against the French and afterward visited Charleston, where he presented the governor with scalps. He complained again about some traders' behavior, and one trader was placed on probation. The new governor did not, however, approve of the promised Cherokee visit to England. Back in Chota in Tennessee, Ada-gal'kala found that a Cherokee named Old Hop (see "Guhna-gadoga") had been entertaining the French in his absence. He told Captain Demere that

Robert J. Conley

Old Hop was a fool who could do nothing without his help. And when Cherokees complained about the traders, he said that it was because they had allowed the French to come among them.

By 1758, Ada-gal'kala had become the most influential leader of the Cherokees. Old Hop still held the title, but everyone seems to have known the truth. Influential though Ada-gal'kala may have been, no one could exert absolute control over the Cherokees. Many Cherokee towns still acted as independently as ever. Although Ada-gal'kala met with the Virginians and even went on an expedition or two with them, other Cherokees were fighting with Virginians. Some Cherokees also killed South Carolina settlers. South Carolina governor William Lyttleton responded by restricting trade with the Cherokees once more. In 1759, Ada-gal'kala went on an expedition in Illinois against the French, presumably to show his unfailing support of the British.

In Ada-gal'kala's absence, Ogan'sto', the great war leader, and a number of other Cherokees went to Charleston to ask that the latest trade embargo be lifted. Governor Lyttleton had them surrounded and taken prisoner. Then he marched with a force of seventeen hundred men to Fort Prince George in South Carolina, taking the hostages along with him. When Ada-gal'kala returned from Illinois and heard what had happened, he marched to Fort Prince George with a British flag carried before him. Lyttleton met with him and demanded that the Cherokees who had killed Virginians be captured and turned over to him for punishment. Ada-gal'kala agreed, but said it would be very difficult, if not impossible. He managed to come up with two of the guilty Cherokees, and Lyttleton released two hostages.

Ada-gal'kala then persuaded Lyttleton that he could not convince the Cherokees to cooperate with him in the matter of the guilty Cherokees without the help of Ogan'sto', who was one of the most powerful men in the nation. He managed to secure the release of Ogan'sto' and a few others. Ogan'sto', however, remained strongly anti-English for the rest of his life. Then an outbreak of smallpox frightened the governor back to Charleston. Ogan'sto' lured the commander of Fort Prince George out of the front gate and had him fired on and killed. Inside the fort, angry soldiers murdered all of the Cherokee hostages. Around this same time, Old Hop died and was succeeded by his nephew.

Ada-gal'kala, possibly seeing events coming over which he could exercise no control or possibly attempting to escape the dreaded smallpox, took his family to the woods to live in isolation. Ogan'sto' laid siege to Fort Loudon. When Major Archibald Montgomery was sent to the aid of the besieged in the fort, Ada-gal'kala traveled there to see what he himself could do to resolve the situation. When Montgomery was ambushed and lost 140 men, he said that he had accomplished his mission and left the country. Fort Loudon was still surrounded.

When Captain Demere at last surrendered and abandoned the fort, the Cherokees discovered that he had betrayed them by destroying guns and ammunition, contrary to an agreement the two parties had reached, and so they attacked the retreating British troops. Ada-gal'kala ransomed his friend John Stuart and led him to safety. He later brought out ten more survivors of the Fort Loudon siege. With Ogan'sto' ready to take the Cherokees over to the French side, Ada-gal'kala became even more important to the British.

In retaliation for Fort Loudon, the British sent a force out of Charleston against the Cherokees. Led by Colonel James Grant, the troops went to Fort Prince George, where Grant had a meeting with Ada-gal'kala. Grant was not to be dissuaded from attacking the Cherokees, however, and before he was through, he had destroyed fifteen Cherokee towns, and many acres of corn and had driven hundreds of Cherokees into the mountains. Grant met with Ada-gal'kala once more to talk of peace. This time he was ready to come to some agreement, but he demanded that four Cherokees be turned over to him to be executed in front of his army. Ada-gal'kala met with Governor William Bull of South Carolina, and the governor agreed to strike out the clause about killing four Cherokees. The peace was concluded.

In 1761, Ada-gal'kala asked Governor Bull to make John Stuart the British Indian superintendent, but the governor replied that he did not have that authority. He did use his influence, though, and Stuart was appointed the following year. Then, with the news of the death of Uka Ulah that year, Stuart acknowledged Ada-gal'kala as the (sixth) principal chief of the Cherokee Nation because everyone knew that he was the real leader of the Cherokees anyway. The title *principal chief* was, of course, in recognition of the fact that there were many Cherokee chiefs, at least two for each town. This British appointment may or may not have been a rubber stamp for general Cherokee opinion. It was, however, a major step in the direction of modern nationhood and the role of a chief executive. At one point in his career, Ada-gal'kala even referred to himself as the president of the Cherokee Nation.

The year 1763 marked the end of the war between France and England. In 1767 and again in 1770, Ada-gal'kala gave up some Cherokee land to Stuart. White settlers were swarming onto Cherokee land. Seventy families settled along the Watauga River, running in North Carolina and

Robert J. Conley

Tennessee, where they became known as the Wataugans. Under British law (the Proclamation of 1763), they were forbidden to purchase Indian land, so they formed a plan to lease it. Stuart's assistant, Alexander Cameron, agreed, and so did Ada-gal'kala. The land was leased for eight years.

In 1774, Ada-gal'kala seems to have made a private deal with the Transylvania Company, owned by Judge Richard Henderson and Captain Nathaniel Hart of North Carolina. Henderson and Hart, aided by Daniel Boone, proposed to purchase twenty million acres or so from the Cherokees, forming middle Tennessee and central Kentucky. Ada-gal'kala went to visit Henderson and Hart to inspect the goods to be traded. On January 1, 1775, with six wagonloads of goods, they headed for Sycamore Shoals on the Watauga River in northeastern Tennessee. The deal was concluded in March in spite of strong protestations from Ada-gal'kala's own son, Dragging Canoe, from Cameron, and from Governor Dunmore of Virginia. The British objections were based on English law: Indian land could be purchased only by the king. The sale went through along with another private sale for the land that had been leased by the Wataugans.

When Dragging Canoe protested to Superintendent Stuart, he was assured that the sale would be nullified as illegal. He was told to be patient, but then the American Revolution broke out. A group of Cherokees went to visit Stuart and pledged their loyalty to Great Britain. Dragging Canoe became the war leader of the pro-British Cherokees. Stuart fled Charleston for his life and went to Florida. Ada-gal'kala went to visit him there, pledged his loyalty, and repented of his role in the Sycamore Shoals affair.

The Americans, as the rebels were now called, attacked the Cherokee towns with a vengeance, and Ada-gal'kala and Ogan'sto' met with them to talk of peace. It was Dragging Canoe, they said, who was causing all the trouble, and because his towns had been burned by the Americans, he was no longer in the Cherokee Nation. He had moved into the Creek country and built new towns. He and his followers were being called Chickamaugas because they had built along Chickamauga Creek, a tributary of the Tennessee River. Colonel William Christian of Virginia said that the Cherokees could have peace only if they handed over both Cameron and Dragging Canoe. Ogan'sto' agreed. Any response by Ada-gal'kala was not recorded. The two old men, sometimes allies, sometimes enemies, managed to get Christian to guarantee their neutrality in the war.

In 1777, the Cherokees gave up more land, and Ada-gal'kala agreed to provide warriors to aid Virginia and North Carolina when called on. He died the next year, at somewhere between sixty-six and seventy-eight years of age. (See also "Dragging Canoe" and "Ogan'sto'.")

Adair, George

George Adair was born at Braggs, Cherokee Nation, Indian Territory, in 1887 and educated in Cherokee Nation public schools. He married Edna F. McCoy at Nowata, Oklahoma, in 1907. On September 19, 1917, he enlisted in the U.S. Army and went to France with the 36th Division. He was pulled off the firing line and put to work with other full-blood Cherokees in the telephone service, where they transmitted military orders in the Cherokee language, thereby foiling any Germans who might be intercepting the messages. The Navajos in World War II were not the first code talkers!

Adair, William Penn

William Penn Adair was born in Georgia in 1830. His family moved west in 1837 before the Removal, becoming part of the Western Cherokees, later to be called the Old Settlers. He attended Cherokee Nation schools in what is now Oklahoma and later went east to study law. He was elected to the Cherokee Nation's Senate from Flint District in 1855, 1857, and 1859. At the start of the Civil War, he joined Stand Watie's Confederate Cherokees and was colonel of the 2nd Regiment of Mounted Volunteers. At the war's end, he spent much of his time in Washington, D.C., representing the interests of the Southern Cherokees. His wife, Sarah Ann McNair, died during the war, and in 1868 he married Susannah McIntosh Drew. He was elected to the Cherokee Nation's Senate again in 1871, this time from the Saline District. He was an uncle to the later famous Will Rogers, who at birth in 1879 was given the name "Colonel William Penn Adair Rogers." Colonel Adair died in 1880.

Adams, K. S. "Bud"

K. S. Adams, known as "Bud," was born in 1923. He served in the U.S. armed forces during World War II in the Pacific theater. After the war, he became a "wildcatter" in Texas and eventually made his fortune in the petroleum business. In 1959, he was instrumental in starting the new American Football League and became owner of the Houston Oilers. In 1968, he moved his team into the Houston Astrodome, making them the first professional football team to play in a domed stadium. In 1996, he moved the team to Nashville, Tennessee, and renamed it the Tennessee Titans. A registered member of the Cherokee Nation, Adams has been very supportive over the years of the Cherokee National Historical Society, having funded the nineteenth-century Cherokee village called Adams's Corner, located at Tsalagi, on the grounds of the Cherokee National Historical Society in Tahlequah, Oklahoma.

Agan'stat', see "Ogan'sto'"

Agent, Dan

Dan Agent received his bachelor's degree in journalism from the University of Tulsa in 1969 and his master's in American studies with an American Indian literature emphasis from Northeastern State University in Tahlequah, Oklahoma, in 1992. He served in the U.S. Army as an information specialist from 1966 to 1968.

Agent has been the editor of the *Cherokee Phoenix* (formerly the *Cherokee Advocate*) since November 1999. Prior to that, he was the public-affairs and marketing specialist for the Institute of American Indian Arts Museum; director of public affairs and marketing and editor of the *Cherokee Advocate*; public-affairs specialist and public-information officer for the National Museum of the American Indian at the Smithsonian; writer-reporter-photographer for the Cherokee Nation's Communications Department; as well as news photographer and cinematographer for the NBC affiliate in Tulsa, KTEW-TV (now KJRH-TV).

Agent received fellowships to attend the Salzburg Seminars in Salzburg, Austria, in 2003 and again in 2004. He is the recipient of, among other awards, the Tulsa Local Hero Award in 2005; the Cherokee Medal of Honor in 2001; the Certificate of Award from the Smithsonian Institution for the publicity campaign for the opening of the Heye Center at the National Museum of the American Indian in New York City in 1994; and the National Conference of Christians and Jews Mass Media Award in 1978. Under his editorship, the *Cherokee Phoenix* has received three Awards of Excellence from the Native American Journalists Association.

Agent's publications are too numerous to mention, but include articles in *Native Peoples Magazine*; the *Cherokee Phoenix*; the *Progressive Media Project* (Madison, Wisconsin); *News Watch* (San Francisco); and the *Smithsonian Runner*.

Ahuludegi, see "Jolly, John"

Alberty, Eliza Missouri Bushyhead

When Reverend Jesse Bushyhead's removal party was trapped in southern Illinois waiting for the icy waters of the river to thaw, his daughter was born on January 3, 1839. Because she was born in Missouri, she was named Eliza Missouri Bushyhead. Eliza graduated from the Cherokee Female Seminary in 1856 and taught school for a time. She married David Rowe Vann in 1858. Vann died in 1870, and Eliza married Bluford West Alberty in 1873. Together they became stewards at the Cherokee Male Seminary. In 1885, they bought the National Hotel in Tahlequah, Cherokee Nation, where the registry included the names James G. Blaine, General U. S. Grant, General William Sherman, Philip Sheridan, Bret Harte, and Bill Nye. She died on November 6, 1919.

Ama-edohi

"Moytoy," as he was called by the English, but whose Cherokee name was most probably Ama-edohi of Tellico in Tennessee, was the English choice for the next trade commissioner following the death of "Wrosetasetow," but this time, perhaps because "Wrosetasetow" had not lived up to their expectations, they decided to call the person in this position the Cherokee "emperor." They wrote his name down as "Moytoy." In 1730, in an attempt to solidify British-Cherokee relations, Sir Alexander Cuming was sent on a "secret mission" to the Cherokees from the king of England. The story that has been told and gone down in history is totally outlandish. Its main sources are Cuming himself and Ludovic Grant, a trader who was present part of the time and wrote about it. The Cherokees, they say, were leaning toward the French, and Cuming went into the Cherokee town of Nikwasi and so impressed everyone there that they fell down on their knees to the king of England and gave themselves up to his sovereignty. They also, at Cuming's insistence, named "Moytoy" of Tellico as their "emperor." The truth of what happened there will never be known. Perhaps Cuming was a charismatic man, and perhaps he did convince the Cherokees present to appoint "Moytoy" in the place of "Wrosetasetow." It could be that "Wrosetasetow" was not working out the way the English had hoped. They certainly did not write about him after his appointment. Or he might have died. We just do not know.

What we do know is that in 1730 "Wrosetasetow" was replaced rather dramatically by "Moytoy." From that point on, the English recognized a Cherokee Nation with a head of state, whom they for a time called the "emperor." It is almost certain that the Cherokees did not recognize either appellation. They most likely thought of "Moytoy" as a kind of trade commissioner. Before the arrival of Cuming, "Moytoy," whose Cherokee name or title was almost for sure "Ama-edohi," which can be translated as "Water-goer" or "Water-walker," was town chief of Tellico. The name was almost certainly a title held by someone in every Cherokee town, for there were "Moytoys" of other towns as well. So this particular Ama-edohi was a man of some local importance at least before he was thrust into a role of national importance. (Another possible translation of the name was given by John P. Brown in 1938, who wrote, "The name Moytoy means, in Cherokee, Amo-Adaw-ehi, Water Conjurer, or Rainmaker.")

"Moytoy's" role in British trade is attested to by the fact that several of the early mixed-blood families seem to have been started by a European trader and one of "Moytoy's" daughters. We can safely assume that these marriages were sanctioned by "Moytoy" as one way of strengthening the trade relations.

"Moytoy's" first official act as "emperor" seems to have been to select, or at least approve the selection of, seven "chiefs" to make a trip to England. The "emperor" himself did not make the trip because his wife was ill. The "chiefs" took along a "crown," five eagle tails, and four scalps. They presented their gifts to the king of England and signed a new treaty acknowledging the sovereignty of England over the Cherokees and promising to trade only with the English, to ally themselves with no one but England, to allow no white people other than the English to settle among them, and to deliver up any fugitive slaves who might fall into their hands. They were given guns, ammunition, red paint, and promises of love and perpetual friendship. It is certainly doubtful that the Cherokees at Whitehall knew what they had signed, however.

In 1736, the Cherokees were visited by a strange little man who called himself Christian Gottlieb Priber. He seems to have learned the Cherokee language and adopted Cherokee dress. He fell into the Cherokee lifestyle and got on well with everyone. He styled himself the secretary of state to "Emperor Moytoy" and corresponded with the governor of South Carolina under that title. The English believed him to be a Jesuit priest working for the French. That seems doubtful because they also claimed that he had drawn up a new system of government for the Cherokees, which included free love and children as community property. Priber was also supposed to have been working on a book of Cherokee grammar. He was seized by the English in 1741 and died in prison. His manuscripts were presumably destroyed. It is unfortunate that all we know of Priber comes from the English, who hated and feared him. Having lived with the Cherokees for five years, he must have had some influence and must have been well acquainted with Ama-edohi, the "emperor" of the Cherokees.

In 1738, while Priber was still living in Tellico, an outbreak of smallpox swept away approximately half of the Cherokee population. The terrible disease had come into the Carolinas on slave ships and had spread throughout the Cherokee country within a year. Many people died of the disease. Some who survived it, upon seeing their disfigurement from it, killed themselves. Cherokee traditional doctors, baffled by the dreadful sickness, threw away their healing paraphernalia.

In 1740, a trade route was laid out from Augusta, Georgia, to the Cherokee towns on the Savannah River, and a party of Cherokees led by Golana, the Raven (of what town we do not know), joined with Governor James Oglethorpe of Georgia in an expedition against the Spanish at Saint Augustine. The following year Ama-edohi agreed to go to war with the enemies of South Carolina. He was killed in battle.

"Ammouskossittee"

Ammouskossittee was called the Cherokee "emperor" by the British from 1741 to 1753. (It might also be said that he was the third principal chief of the Cherokee Nation, although at this time the Cherokees did not really have a central form of government.) His name has also been spelled "Amascossite" and "Ammonscossittee," and he was a son of Ama-edohi. (John P. Brown says that the name is Amo-sgasite, or "Dreadfulwater.") Nothing has apparently been recorded regarding the passing of the title from father to son, but it is interesting to note that descent was being passed along according to British practices, through the male line rather than the female, as was the custom among the Cherokees. The British seem to have been busy trying to maintain their influence by continuing to make appointments or, at the least, to have some say in who was designated "emperor." "Ammouskossittee" was only thirteen years old when he became "emperor," and the decisions for the nation were apparently made by a group of advisors, including the warrior Ostenaco and Guhna-gadoga, "Ammouskossittee's" uncle. Several Cherokee town chiefs were displeased by the naming of the young boy to the high position.

Early British attempts at spelling Cherokee names range from comical to terribly frustrating. At times, the same name is spelled so differently from one source to another that it is barely If at all recognizable as the same name. To add to the frustration, the same Cherokee was often known by more than one name or would change his name from time to time. Thus, Edmund Atkin, in his "Report and Plan of 1755," making reference to the agreement

Robert J. Conley

signed in England by the six Cherokees, says that "Moytoys son the present Emperour Ousteaika Shaleloske" had reaffirmed the terms of the agreement many times. Atkins's editor, Wilbur R. Jacobs, says in a footnote that Atkins was probably referring to "Autossity Ustonecka," also known as "Outacite" or "Outacity" (Mankiller), who was one of the three Cherokees to visit London in 1763. If Atkins was referring to "Ammouskossittee," this man could not be the same Cherokee who visited London in 1763. During the tenure of "Ammouskossittee," the Cherokees were involved in the conflict between England and France that was being played out in America as well as in Europe. In 1751, "Ammouskossittee," now twenty-three years old, headed for Charleston to attend a conference on trade, but on the way he became ill and turned around to go home, leaving others to conclude the negotiations. The following year he made a trip to Virginia to attempt to establish trade relations with that colony. The governor of Virginia would not commit himself, and "Ammouskossittee's" party was attacked by northern Indians and very nearly wiped out as they made their way home. The young man's luck did not change, either. Shortly after his arrival back home, he was badly beaten by a pack-horse driver following accusations about the "emperor's" wife. In addition, rumors spread that he had tried to sell the Cherokees' northern hunting grounds to Virginia. His reputation was completely ruined. When "Ammouskossittee" died in 1753, the mantle was passed along to his uncle Guhna-gadoga, so there was little change, if any, in the way things were done. The British had apparently realized who had been the real "power behind the throne."

Anderson, Troy

Troy Anderson is a Master Artist of the Five Civilized Tribes Museum in Muskogee, Oklahoma. Of Cherokee descent, Anderson has won many awards, including the Grand Award Masters Show from the Five Tribes Museum and others from the Cherokee Heritage Museum and the Cherokee Nation. He received a resolution of commendation from the Arkansas General Assembly and designed the Trail of Tears Sesquicentennial Commemorative Medallion.

Ani-gatagewi

One of the seven Cherokee clans, the Blind Savanna or Wild Potato Clan. James Mooney says that the name cannot be translated, though. The most popular translation seems to be "Wild Potato."

Ani-gilohi

One of the seven Cherokee clans. The name "Ani-gilohi" is often translated as "Twisters" or "Long Hairs." The Kilpatricks say that it means, "They have just become offended."

Ani-kawi

One of the seven Cherokee clans: the Deer Clan.

Ani-Kituwagi

The Keetoowah people, meaning people from the town of Keetoowah, the mother town of the Cherokees in the old Southeast. Cherokee people refer to themselves by this name. See also "Keetoowah."

Ani-Kutani

The name of an ancient Cherokee priesthood. According to a tale from the Cherokee oral tradition recorded by James Mooney, the Ani-Kutani became tyrannical and abusive of their powers. A popular democratic revolution wiped them out, and a powerful central government was never allowed to grow up again.

Ani-sahoni

One of the seven Cherokee clans: the Blue Clan, or possibly the "Clan of a Large Extinct Feline."

Ani-tsisqua

One of the seven Cherokee clans: the Bird Clan.

Ani-waya

One of the seven Cherokee clans: the Wolf Clan.

Ani-wodi

One of the seven Cherokee clans: the Paint Clan.

Ani-yunwiya

A name Cherokees formerly used to refer to themselves. It is usually translated as the "Real People," sometimes the "Original People." It consists of the plural prefix ani along with yunwi, meaning "person," and the intensive ya. As Cherokees began to use the name "Cherokee," Ani-yunwiya came to mean "Indians."

Robert J. Conley

Annesley, Bob

Bob Annesley was born in 1943, in Norman, Oklahoma, and is an artist of Cherokee descent. Annesley won his first major award in painting at the age of fourteen and had his first one-man show at eighteen. He studied art at the University of Oklahoma and Oklahoma City University. He began painting and sculpting full-time in 1973, and since then has won more than one hundred major awards in national competitions. In 1976, he was given a one-man retrospective show at the Cherokee National Museum, the first artist ever so honored. In 1986, he was named Master Artist by the Five Civilized Tribes Museum. His works are in the permanent collections of the Royal Academy of Fine Arts in London, the Five Civilized Tribes Museum, the Cherokee National Museum, the Southern Plains Indian Museum, the Buffalo Museum, the Oklahoma University Museum of Art, and the U.S. Department of Interior's Indian Arts and Crafts Board. He lives and works in Houston, Texas.

Ark

The Cherokee Ark, called the Sacred Ark, was a wooden box, nearly square, wrapped in buckskin. The most sacred things of the old religion were kept in it. Two priests carried it along with them on special trips and watched over it constantly. William Penn Adair claims to have seen it in 1756, but he was unable to ascertain its contents. The Delawares captured it probably sometime around 1780 or 1790, and many Cherokees blamed all of the subsequent Cherokee troubles on the loss of the Sacred Ark.

Arkansas Cherokees

The Western Cherokees are sometimes called the Arkansas Cherokees because they moved to Arkansas and settled there until the U.S. government forced them to move across the line into the new Cherokee Nation (in what is now Oklahoma) at the time of the Removal. See "Western Cherokee Nation" and "Old Settlers."

Arnette, Carroll

Carroll Arnette (Gogiski) was born in Oklahoma City in 1927. He served in the U.S. Marine Corps in 1946 and 1947. In 1951, he received a bachelor's degree from Beloit College, magna cum laude, and in 1958 his master's from the University of Texas. He taught literature and writing at Nasson

College and was professor of English at Central Michigan University. Arnette wrote more than three hundred poems and short stories. In 1974, he won a National Endowment for the Arts fellowship. His published works include *Like a Wall* (1969); *Night Perimeter: New and Selected Poems 1958–1990* (1991); *South Line: Poems* (1979); and *Tsalagi: Poems* (1976).

Artists, Cherokee

The long list of Cherokee artists includes contemporary painters, sculptors, traditional craftspeople (basket makers, potters, ceramists), doll makers, jewelry makers, makers of traditional weapons, and makers of musical instruments. Some artists have their own entries in this book. For a variety of reasons, not all could be listed, so others are acknowledged here. Some names do not appear, and for that I apologize.

From North Carolina: Davy Mitchell Arch, Jackie Bradley, Goingback Chiltoskey, Bill Crowe, Birdie Crowe, Gilbert Crowe, Richard Crowe, Virgil Crowe, Betty Dupree, Emmaline Garrett, Christina Goings, Ed Goings, George Goings, Louise Goings, General Grant, Tom Hill, David Hornbuckle, Jenean Hornbuckle, Marie Junaluska, Virgil Ledford, Ernie Lossiah, Lucille Lossiah, Ramona Lossie, Betty Maney, Katrina Maney, Louise Bigmeet Maney, Melissa Ann Maney, Shirley Jackson Oswalt, Freeman Owle, Lloyd Carl Owle, Joel Queen, Polly Rattler, Robert Reed, Richard Saunooke, Emily Smith, J. Bud Smith, Amanda Swimmer, Emma Taylor, Shirley Taylor, and Reuben Teesatuskie.

From Oklahoma: Mary Adair, Gary Allen, Roger Cain, Wynona Dreadfulwater, Tom Fields, Kenneth Foster, Demos Glass, Lucille Hair, Catherine Hastings, Al Herrin, Evelyn Stone Holland, Daniel Horsechief, Mary Horsechief, Dorothy Ice, Sharon Irla, Ken Masters, Dewayne "Fishinghawk" Matthews, America Meredith, Harry Oosawhee, Marie Proctor, Shirlene Proctor, Traci Rabbit, David Scott, Knokovtee Scott, Bessie Russell, Kathy VanBuskirk, Perry VanBuskirk, William Varnell, Sam Watts-Kidd, and Terry Lee Whetstone.

Attacullaculla, see "Ada-gal'kala"

Awiakta, Marilou

Storyteller and writer Marilou Awiakta is a Cherokee who lives and writes in Tennessee. Her work has been featured on three PBS programs. Her publications include *Abiding Appalachia: Where Mountain and Atom Meet*; *Rising Fawn and the Fire Mystery*; and *Selu: Seeking the Corn-Mother's Wisdom*. She received the Tennessee Distinguished Writer's Award in 1989. She is a member of the Wordcraft Circle of Native Writers.

Ayunini

A highly respected Eastern Band of Cherokees medicine man, Ayunini, or "Swimmer," was one of James Mooney's main informants when he was gathering Cherokee materials on the reservation in North Carolina in the 1890s for his works for the Bureau of American Ethnology: *The Sacred Formulas of the Cherokees* (1891); *Myths of the Cherokees* (1900); and, finally, *The Swimmer Manuscript: Cherokee Sacred Formulas and Medicinal Prescriptions*, finished and published by Frans M. Olbrechts in 1932.

Mooney wrote of Ayunini,

First and chief in the list of storytellers comes Ayunini, "Swimmer," from whom nearly three-fourths of the whole number were originally obtained, together with nearly as large a proportion of the whole body of Cherokee material now in possession of the author. The collection could not have been made without his help, and now that he is gone it can never be duplicated. Born about 1835, shortly before the Removal, he grew up under the instruction of masters to be a priest, doctor, and keeper of tradition, so that he was recognized as an authority throughout the band and by such a competent outside judge as Colonel [William Holland] Thomas. He served through the [Civil War] as second sergeant of the Cherokee Company A, Sixty-ninth North Carolina Confederate Infantry, Thomas Legion. He was prominent in the local affairs of the [Eastern] [B]and, and no Green-corn dance, ballplay, or other tribal function was ever considered complete without his presence and active assistance. A genuine aboriginal antiquarian and patriot, proud of his people and their ancient system, he took delight in recording in his native alphabet the songs and sacred formulas of priests and dancers, as well as the names of medicinal plants and the prescriptions with which they were compounded, while his mind was a storehouse of Indian tradition. To a happy descriptive style he added a musical voice for the songs and a peculiar faculty for imitating the characteristic cry of bird or beast, so that to listen to one of his recitals was often a pleasure in itself, even to one who understood not a word of the language. He spoke no English, and to the day of his death clung to the moccasin and turban, together with the rattle, his badge of authority. He died in March, 1899, aged [*sic*] about sixty-five, and was buried like a true Cherokee on the slope of a forest-clad mountain. Peace to his ashes and sorrow for his going, for with him perished half the tradition of a people.

Robert J. Conley

B.

Baldridge, Orvel

Orvel Baldridge, a citizen of the Cherokee Nation, was born August 4, 1955, in Newton, Kansas, to Orvel Baldridge and Juanita Sanders. He went to school in Kansas and in 1972 joined the U.S. Marine Corps. A student of Tae Kwon Do under Mr. Wilson Vann, he has achieved his second dan and is working on his third dan.

He began acting at the Cherokee Heritage Center's outdoor drama in Tahlequah, Oklahoma, and went on to play R. P. McMurphy in a Tahlequah Community Theater production of *One Flew over the Cuckoo's Nest*. Numerous stage roles followed. Baldridge received training in acting from Morgan Sheppard and Karen Dugan in Hollywood, from Northeastern State University in Tahlequah, and in workshops from Mike Perkins in Tahlequah and Jane Lind in Tulsa.

Baldridge has been an extra or a featured player in several television productions, including episodes of *Walker, Texas Ranger*. He has also appeared in several video productions and in television commercials. He worked as an extra in the films *Last of the Mohicans*; *Dragon*; and *Indecent Proposal*, and he was a featured actor in *Doe Boy*; *Where the Red Fern Grows* (the 1999 version); and *Tushka*. He was also coproducer on the latter film, which has been screened at film festivals around the world, including the Sundance Film Festival and the Munich International Film Festival, and has won two major awards.

Baldridge is the owner and president of the Native American Indian Talent and Casting Agency (NAITCA) in Tahlequah, which he established in 1992 to develop and market American Indian talent. The organization has nearly five hundred members and has expanded to include writers, cinematographers, artists, and language consultants. NAITCA has sponsored film-acting workshops for its clients, and clients have been placed in television and film roles. He is also the founding father of the International Cherokee Film Festival.

Ballard, Cherokee

Born and raised in Oklahoma, Cherokee Ballard is a popular newscaster on television station KOCO in Oklahoma City. On April 19, 1995, she covered the events of the Oklahoma City bombing. She and the staff of KOCO won a Peabody Award for their coverage of the events that day. In June 1998, Ballard was diagnosed with non-Hodgkins lymphoma. As a result of that experience, she produced and starred in the television series *Cherokee's Journal: Lessons in Living with Cancer*, receiving numerous awards for it. She has also received the Oklahoma Association of Broadcasters Award for Investigative Reporting and the Excel Award from the International Association of Business Communicators. She was named Honorary Chair of the American Cancer Society's Relay for Life, and she serves as a member of the Native American Journalists Association board of directors. In 2001, Ballard received a Cherokee Medal of Honor.

Ballard, Lucien

Lucien Ballard was born in Miami, Oklahoma, on May 6, 1908. He attended college briefly at the University of Oklahoma and then at the University of Pennsylvania, after which he made a trip to China. When he returned to the United States, he worked for a time as a lumberjack and a surveyor. In 1928, he went to Hollywood to visit a girlfriend who was working at Paramount Studios as a script clerk. Ballard was soon hired on at Paramount, first loading trucks, then acting as a camera assistant. By 1935, he was working with director Josef von Sternberg. His first film credit was for *The Devil Was a Woman* (1935), and he and Von Sternberg received the Best Cinematography Award at the Venice Film Festival. After working on several films together, Ballard and Von Sternberg had a falling out, and Ballard went to Columbia Pictures, where he worked as cinematograher on B pictures and two-reel comedies, including several Three Stooges titles.

In 1944, when Ballard was cinematographer for director Henry Hathaway on *The Lodger*, he met and married Merle Oberon. The marriage lasted until 1949. Ballard made several more pictures with Hathaway—among them, *Diplomatic Courier* (1952); *Prince Valiant* (1954); *The Sons of Katie Elder* (1965); *Nevada Smith* (1966); and *True Grit* (1969). He worked with Bud Boetticher on *The Magnificent Matador* (1955); *Maverick* (1957, for television); and *Buchanan Rides Alone* (1958); and with Sam Peckinpah on *The Westerner* (1960); *Ride the High Country* (1962); *The Wild Bunch* (1969); *The Ballad of Cable Hogue* (1970); *The Getaway* (1972); and *Junior Bonner* (1972). In 1969, he received the National Society of Film Critics Award for

Best Cinematography for his work on *The Wild Bunch*. Over a fifty-year career, Ballard worked on more than 130 films.

Ballard was married twice after Merle Oberon, and in 1988 he was killed by an automobile while he was riding his bicycle near his home.

Ballplay, see "Stickball"

Belt, Tom

A full-blood Cherokee originally from the Rocky Ford community in Oklahoma, Tom Belt has worked as a community liaison specialist for the Cherokee Nation. He was vice president of the Original Cherokee Communities Organization. He married Roseanna Sneed from Cherokee, North Carolina, and moved with her to Cherokee, where he taught the Cherokee language in Cherokee schools for a number of years. He then became a counselor for the United National Indian Tribal Youth, Inc. (UNITY) program at Cherokee. Much quoted and much consulted in recent years, Belt has been employed as an "elder in residence" by the Cherokee Studies Program at Western Carolina University in Cullowhee, North Carolina, and is now a Cherokee-language instructor in that program. One of his major concerns at the present time is preservation of the Cherokee language. A fluent speaker of Cherokee, he helped to write a series of textbooks for Cherokee students at Cherokee, North Carolina.

Benge, Bob

Also known as "the Bench," Bob Benge was a mixed-blood Indian with red hair who was one of the followers of Dragging Canoe. During the time of war between the Cherokees and the English colonists in the 1770s, Benge was much feared along the frontier. In 1794, still fighting after the death of Dragging Canoe and the end of the American Revolution, Benge was killed. (See also "Chickamaugas" and "Dragging Canoe.")

Big Mush

Following the killing of Richard Fields in Texas in 1827, presumably for his part in the ill-fated Fredonia Rebellion (an attempt to establish a new republic called Fredonia), Big Mush (Gatunwali) was elected peace chief, and Bowles was elected war chief of the Texas Cherokees. Both Bowles and

Big Mush had refused to go along with Fields on the Fredonia scheme in the first place. Big Mush was a signer of the 1836 treaty with the Provisional Government of Texas. He was killed by Texans, along with Bowles and others, in 1839 on the Neches Plain near Tyler, Texas.

Bird, Traveller

Traveller Bird was born on the Cherokee reservation in North Carolina in 1930. His book *Tell Them They Lie: The Sequoyah Myth* was published by Westernlore Press in 1971. Bird claims that virtually everything previously written about the famous Cherokee named Sequoyah was erroneous. His evidence unfortunately seems to be nonexistent, and the book is not very convincing.

Black Coat

Black Coat was one of the Western Cherokees in Arkansas. He participated in the Cherokee war against the Osages. He was with the group that captured the Osage girl Maria James, taking her into his own home and treating her as if she were his daughter. A white man persuaded Black Coat that he could make the little girl a better home, but then the man sold her into slavery. She was rescued with the help of the governor of Arkansas and placed in Dwight Mission. She married, but upon the death of her husband went to work for Dwight Mission. In her old age, she returned to the Osages. Black Coat, married to Sarah Hildebrand, was second chief of the Western Cherokees. He died in 1835.

Black Fox

During his first term as tenth principal chief of the Cherokee Nation from 1805 to 1808, Black Fox made himself notorious by signing the Treaty of January 7, 1806, by which the Cherokee Nation gave up seven thousand acres of Tennessee and Alabama. In exchange, Black Fox received a lifetime annuity of $100. The earliest printed law of the Cherokee Nation was passed during this time to suppress horse stealing, and in 1808 Chief Black Fox signed a law abolishing the old blood feud.

During Black Fox's first term as principal chief, Reverend Gideon Blackburn, who had established a Presbyterian mission school in the Cherokee Nation in 1803, suggested that the Cherokees revise their laws and write them down. In 1808, the first Cherokee constitution was written and adopted by the Cherokee Council. The new government was patterned after that of the United States. Companies of Lighthorse police were authorized.

By this time, however, the U.S. government was already at work planning for the removal of all eastern Indians to new locations west of the Mississippi River. President Thomas Jefferson had signed the Georgia Compact in 1802, in which he had promised to Georgia that the United States would get the Indians out of Georgia as soon as it could be "peaceably" accomplished, and the government was forcing the Indians to go to government factories (i.e., trading posts) for their trade goods. The government had instructed these factories to keep the Indians in debt. Thus, when the bill became too big for the Indians to handle, the government would take land in payment.

The government continued to acquire tracts of Cherokee land, and in 1806, desirous for even more and already pushing for removal, they bribed some of the old Chickamauga leaders and invited them to a treaty council in Washington City. The treaty, selling large tracts of land to the U.S. government, was signed in December that year. However, the Cherokee Nation had become seriously divided, with the Lower Towns being conservative and the Upper Towns "progressive." The Upper Towns were ready to negotiate for removal, whereas the Lower were adamantly opposed to it. It is interesting to note that the Upper Towns were made up largely of members of the old Chickamauga group.

Doublehead, who supposedly had been bribed to sign the treaty, was executed by the Ridge (later known as Major Ridge) and Alex Saunders. A delegation of men from the Lower Towns deposed Black Fox and recognized Pathkiller as principal chief. The U.S. government tended to side with the Upper Towns, of course. Because of a movement to separate the Cherokee Nation into two nations, the Lower Towns relented the following year at a National Council meeting. In an effort to show national unity, the council reinstated Black Fox in 1809, with Pathkiller as second chief. When Black Fox died in 1811, Pathkiller was made principal chief.

Blackbird, Lena

Lena Blackbird learned to make traditional Cherokee crafts when she went to work at the ancient village of Tsalagi (the Cherokee Heritage Center) in Tahlequah, Oklahoma, where she worked for twelve years. She received training in basket weaving from Diana Scott and Nadine Wilburn. She also made clay beads for necklaces. Her beads became valuable and sought after by collectors. At the Five Civilized Tribes Museum in Muskogee, Oklahoma, she won several first- and second-place awards for her necklaces. In 1996, at the Art under the Oaks competition in Muskogee, Oklahoma, she entered a basket, the first she had ever entered in any show, and won the grand prize. At the Cherokee National Museum's 2001 Trail of Tears Art Show, she received a special merit award for her honeysuckle basket. In 1998, she was named a Cherokee National Living Treasure, and in 2001 she received a Cherokee Medal of Honor.

Blanket

Cephas Washburn tells us that Blanket, a Western Cherokee, was a younger brother by about twenty years to Ta-ka-e-tuh, which would make him around eighty years old at the time Washburn met and interviewed him. Blanket told Washburn Christian tales similar to those his brother had told, thus convincing Washburn that they were from the ancient traditions of the Cherokees. (See "Ta-ka-e-tuh.") Blanket also described a Cherokee wedding to Washburn in which the bride and groom exchange gifts (a leg of venison from the groom and a basket of corn from the bride), which are then wrapped in one blanket. And he told a story of a man who had killed a rattlesnake and was then killed in turn by the rattlesnake's kinsman. Washburn said he was never satisfied with his interviews of Blanket because Blanket was "too much of a wag," always turning everything into a joke.

Bloody Fellow

One of the followers of Dragging Canoe in the late eighteenth century, Bloody Fellow (Iskagua) wrote a letter to John Sevier, the self-proclaimed president of the short-lived state of Franklin, after a Franklinite murdered a Cherokee, in which he said, "White men on Nolichucky are planting crops on lands over French Broad River. As soon as the leaves grow a little, if your government does not make them move off, I will come with a party and kill every man, woman, and child that shall be found over the river." Later, following a raid on one of the illegal settlements, Bloody Fellow left a note for Sevier on one of his victims that said, "I did not wish for war, but if the white people want war, that is what they will get." Following the death of Dragging Canoe in 1792, Bloody Fellow went with a Cherokee deputation to see President George Washington. A treaty was negotiated whereby the annuity of $1,000 paid by the United States to the Cherokees was raised to $1,500. Washington was so impressed by Bloody Fellow that he gave him a U.S. flag, a brigadier general's uniform, a medal, and a new name—Iskagua, or "Clear Sky." (The name is from Shawnee, not Cherokee.) (See also "Chickamaugas" and "Dragging Canoe.")

Blue Circle, see "Southern Rights Party"

Blue, Monte

Monte Blue was born in Indian-apolis, Indiana, in 1890. He grew up in an orphans' home and held a variety of odd jobs before becoming a mainte-nance man for a film studio. He worked his way up to script clerk and eventually stuntman. Finally, he worked as an actor in D. W. Griffith's *Birth of a Nation* (1915). Thereafter, he was much in demand as an actor and amassed a small for-tune. He retired from filmmaking and took a trip around the world. When he returned home, he found that bad investments had left him nearly broke, so he went back to acting. He discovered, though, that his box office appeal had nearly vanished along with his money. He thus worked in B films, mostly Westerns, playing any part he could get. He retired from films once more and became an advance agent for the Hamid-Morton Circus. He died in Milwaukee of a heart attack in 1963 while on the road for the circus. His films include *Intolerance*; *Thundering Herd*; *Wagon Wheels*; *Wanderer of the Wasteland*; *Young Bill Hickok*; and *Hangman's Knot*.

above and left:
Monte Blue, 1934.
Ken Jones Collection.

Blythe, David

David Blythe, a store owner in Cherokee, North Carolina, was the eleventh principal chief of the Eastern Band of Cherokee Indians from 1915 to 1919.

Blythe, Jarrett

Born May 30, 1886, Jarrett Blythe, the son of mixed-blood James Blythe and the daughter of Chief Nimrod Smith, was the sixteenth principal chief of the Eastern Band of Cherokees from 1931 to 1947. His father was bilingual and had been one of the informants for the work James Mooney did on the Cherokee reservation in North Carolina for the Bureau of American Ethnology in the 1890s. He was the first Cherokee to serve as the resident federal agent. After Jarrett Blythe became chief in 1931, he enthusiastically welcomed and supervised the New Deal programs under the administration of President Franklin Roosevelt and Indian Commissioner John Collier, but he was vigorously opposed in this support by Fred Blythe Bauer, a cousin who had been raised with him as a brother, who denounced the programs as communistic. In 1935, although Blythe was reelected as chief, Bauer won the office of vice chief. For the next four years, Blythe and Bauer fought on almost every issue that came before the tribe. Then, in 1939, Bauer opposed Blythe in the election for chief, but Blythe won. The 1930s saw a tremendous increase in tourism at Cherokee, North Carolina, owing to a new highway and the establishment of the Great Smoky Mountains National Park. World War II, however, caused a drop in tourism. Blythe held the tribe together during the war years and disappearing New Deal programs. He chaired a committee to convince every family on the reservation to raise a victory garden. He achieved the purchase of the Boundary Tree Tract in 1943 to establish a luxury motel. In addition, under his administration, the Eastern Band began producing its outdoor pageant *Unto These Hills* and built "Oconaluftee," a replica of an early Cherokee town. Blythe was also the founder of the Cherokee Historical Association. In 1946, North Carolina was finally forced to allow Cherokees to register to vote. About that same time, tourism began to rise again. Chief Blythe initiated a small business loan fund for Cherokees on the reservation. Out of office beginning in 1947, Jarrett Blythe returned to politics in 1955, winning the office of chief once again. He continued his efforts at quality education for Indian people and for expanded industry and tourism.

Blythe served his sixth and final term as chief during the years

Robert J. Conley

1963–67. His health was declining, and at the end of this term he retired for good at the age of eighty. J. Ed Sharpe says that "perhaps more than any other Cherokee in recent history he won the hearts of his people with his solid reputation for honesty, generosity, and application of Christian principles to every component of his many faceted life." Jarrett Blythe died in 1977 at ninety years old.

Boudinot, Elias (Buck Uweti)

A son of Uweti and brother of Stand Watie, Buck Uweti was sent north to school at Cornwall, Connecticut, with his cousin John Ridge, where both of them married white girls from Cornwall. They had to flee for their lives from Cornwall because of these marriages. Buck Uweti changed his name in honor of a benefactor, Elias Boudinot. Back home in the Cherokee Nation in the mid-1820s (at this time still located in the Southeast), Boudinot launched a series of public lectures throughout Philadelphia and New York, raising enough money to establish a Cherokee newspaper, the *Cherokee Phoenix*. Its first issued came out on February 21, 1828. Published in both Cherokee and English, the *Phoenix* undertook a major campaign to educate audiences regarding the progress Cherokees had made toward "civilization." It was part of a conscious effort on the part of Cherokees to gain sympathy for their cause in the face of rising pressure for Cherokee removal from their lands in the South to the West. Elias Boudinot was the paper's first editor. Boudinot was assisted in these efforts by the missionary Reverend Samuel Worcester. Boudinot was a staunch ally of Principal Chief John Ross in their resistance to removal pressures, particularly from Georgia, until the Cherokees' hopes seemed to be crushed by President Andrew Jackson's refusal to enforce the Supreme Court decision in *Worcester v. Georgia* in 1832. At that point, Boudinot, his cousin John Ridge, and Ridge's father, Major Ridge, decided that the best course was to give in to the pressures and make the move west. Without the sanction of the majority of the Cherokee people, they and their followers signed the Treaty of New Echota, a treaty calling for the removal of all Cherokees from their ancient homelands to new land in the West. Chief Ross fired Boudinot from his position as editor of the *Phoenix*, but in the meantime Boudinot had become the first Cherokee novelist by writing and publishing *Poor Sarah*; or, *The Indian Woman* in 1833. He made the move west along with others of what came to be called the Treaty Party, and following the Trail of Tears he was enticed out of his home in 1839 by three men who claimed to need his assistance in obtaining medical supplies from Reverend Worcester. Halfway between his home and that of Reverend Worcester, the men hacked him to death with hatchets for his part in the signing of the Treaty of New Echota.

Boudinot, Elias Cornelias

Elias C. Boudinot was the son of Elias Boudinot and Harriet Gold Boudinot. He was born in Rome, Georgia, in 1835. As a small child, he moved to Arkansas with his parents. He was only four years old when his father was killed for his part in signing the Treaty of New Echota, also known as the Removal Treaty. (See "Elias Boudinot.") He studied engineering at Manchester, Vermont, and then worked for an Ohio railroad. Returning to Arkansas, he studied law in Fayetteville under A. M. Wilson and was admitted to the bar in 1856. He was editor of the *Weekly Arkansan* of Fayetteville and of the *True Democrat* of Fort Smith. When the Civil War broke out, he assisted the Cherokee Stand Watie in raising a regiment of Confederate Cherokees. He was commissioned a major and later promoted to lieutenant colonel. At the war's end, he took an active part in the negotiations for the Treaty of 1866, representing what were now called the Southern Cherokees and generally making himself a thorn in the side of Chief John Ross.

Boudinot recommended the allotment of Cherokee lands in severalty and the opening of the Unassigned Lands to white people. Unpopular among his own people, he lived most of his life in Arkansas. He and Stand Watie were partners in a tobacco company, hoping to sell tobacco without it being taxed, but the U.S. government took them to court, and the court ruled in its favor.

Boudinot had long been a friend of the celebrated sculptress Vinnie Ream Hoxie, and he urged the town of Downingville, Oklahoma, to change its name to Vinita in her honor. He met with success. He spent much of his time in Washington, D.C., consorting with railroad officials and promoting deals in opposition to Chief Ross. In 1885, he married Clara Minear, and they settled near Fort Smith, where he died in 1890.

Boudinot, Frank

Frank Boudinot, a son of Elias Boudinot and Harriet Gold Boudinot, was taken, along with his brothers, by his white mother back to her hometown in Connecticut. He became a professional actor, using "Frank

Starr" as his stage name. When the Civil War broke out, he joined the Union army, serving with distinction and rising to the rank of a commissioned officer. He was wounded in action and later died from the effects of that wound.

Boudinot, Frank J.

Following the impeachment and removal from office of Chief W. C. Rogers in 1905, the Cherokee National Council chose Frank J. Boudinot to replace him. Boudinot never served as chief, however, because the president of the United States reinstated Rogers, refusing to recognize the council's actions. Frank was born in the Cherokee Nation in 1866, son of William P. Boudinot and Carrie Fields Boudinot, grandson of Elias Boudinot. He was educated in Cherokee Nation schools, at a high school in Flint, Michigan, and at Indian University (later Bacone College) in Oklahoma. He was editor of the *Cherokee Advocate* for a time. He attended law school at the University of Michigan at Ann Arbor in 1894. He was one of four attorneys who represented the Cherokee Nation before the Dawes Commission in 1896 in the Cherokees' fight against individual allotment of their lands, and he was admitted to practice before the U.S. Supreme Court that same year. He married Anna Stapler Meigs, a granddaughter of Chief John Ross. He died in 1945 and was buried in Washington, D.C.

Bowles

Bowles is also known as Bowl, the Bowl, John Bowles, Colonel Bowles, and Chief Bowles. His Cherokee name, Diwali, refers to a kind of mushroom, but it can also literally refer to a bowl. Bowles first comes to the attention of history as the chief of Running Water, one of Dragging Canoe's Chickamauga towns in Tennessee. In 1792, Dragging Canoe died. In 1794, Cherokees gathered at Tellico Blockhouse in Tennessee to receive payment they were due from a 1785 treaty. Bowles and the people of Running Water stopped along the banks of the Tennessee River on their way home. Several boats filled with white people and trade goods stopped along the way. The Indians bought glass beads, mirrors, and a great deal of whiskey from them, but then ran out of money.

When the Cherokees sobered up, Bowles went back aboard one of the boats and offered to pay for the whiskey, but wanted to give back the trade goods for a full refund. The white men refused and ordered him off the boat. The Cherokees wanted to fight, but Bowles wanted to try diplomacy one more time. He took two of his calmest men with him to the boat, where he explained to the traders that unless they agreed to his wishes, there would be a fight. The white men seized boat poles and attacked the three Indians, killing one and knocking another into the river. Bowles escaped. He returned with the rest of his warriors, and they killed all the white men, but did not harm the women, children, or slaves.

Afraid that whites and Cherokees alike would be furious with them for breaking the Treaty of 1785, Bowles and the rest of his Chickamaugas did not go home. They kept going west until they reached Missouri, which at the time was French territory. They stopped there and built new homes. From time to time, they were joined by other Cherokees. They lived in Missouri until 1811, when a great earthquake leveled mountains and made the Missouri River run backward. Following this terrible disaster, Bowles and his people moved into what is now western Arkansas, settling between the Arkansas and White rivers. Other Cherokees had preceded them to that area.

This group of Cherokees was soon known as the Western Cherokee Nation. The U.S. government treated them as a nation separate from the Cherokee Nation. It began to use them as a means of enticing other Cherokees to abandon their eastern homelands and move west. Some did. Some were talked into it by government agents, and others just tired of the pressures at home and moved west for relief. Some doubtless made the move to join family who were out west.

The Western Cherokees found themselves at war with the Osages, though, who claimed the land on which the Cherokees had settled and lands on which the Cherokees were hunting. The U.S. government, through the army officers at Fort Gibson (in present-day Oklahoma), tried hard to put an end to the war, for it was hurting efforts back east to recruit more Cherokees to move west. Bowles served as chief of the Western Cherokees until 1813. In 1819, when U.S. agents told the Western Cherokees to move their homes to the opposite side of the Arkansas River, Bowles angrily moved all the way down into Texas.

When Bowles went into Texas in 1819, he took with him sixty men and their families. They settled first at the Three Forks of the Trinity but soon moved to near Nacogdoches. They built their homes beneath the tall pine trees, cleared fields to plant corn, and planted orchards of peach trees. They were joined by other Cherokees as well as by Shawnees, Delawares, Kickapoos, Choctaws, Biloxis, Alabamas, and Koasatis. An election was soon held, and Richard Fields was chosen chief. Following the death of Fields as a result of his involvement in the Fredonia Rebellion in 1827, Bowles was chief once again. He was also made a lieutenant colonel in the Mexican army and given a fine military hat. He continued to press for title to the lands on which they lived. The group now had 150 families, about eight hundred people. They owned six hundred horses and three thousand cattle and hogs, but title was not forthcoming.

In 1835, Sam Houston was in Texas, and talk of rebellion was everywhere. The poor Fredonians had apparently been just a little ahead of the times. On November 13, 1835, the provisional Texas government met and signed a "solemn declaration" of perpetual friendship to the Cherokees and promised them their land. One of the signers was Sam Houston. Then in February 1836, Houston and others went to Bowles's town, and there they signed a treaty with the Cherokees. It, too, promised perpetual peace and friendship and clear title to the Cherokee lands. The Texans did not ask for the Cherokees' help in fighting the war with Mexico that was taking place at the time. They asked only for the Cherokees' neutrality.

Following the successful conclusion of the revolution, Sam Houston was elected president of the Republic of Texas. He tried but could not get the Texas Senate to ratify the treaty with the Cherokees. Houston sent Bowles on a mission to western tribes seeking peace with them, and Bowles was successful until he visited the Comanches. There he was very nearly killed, but managed to escape. Nearly a year after Houston had presented the treaty to the Senate, they declared it null and void. Houston ordered that the Cherokee lands be surveyed and the boundary line established. Then Houston was replaced as president by Mirabeau B. Lamar, who wanted the Indians expelled from Texas.

In 1839, President Lamar sent the Texas army to Bowles's settlements to demand that the Indians remove themselves from Texas. During several days of negotiations, the Texans tried to get the old chief to sign a treaty. He refused, but at last he got his people together, and they moved out in the middle of the night, heading for the northern border. When the Texans awoke to find them gone, they mounted up to go after them, attacking and burning Indian villages wherever they found them. When they at last caught up with the Cherokees, they shot Bowles's horse out from under him during battle. He stood up and started to walk away, but was shot in the back. When he rose to a sitting position, a Texan came up behind him and shot him in the head from close range. When Bowles died, he was carrying a sword that Sam Houston had given to him. He was also carrying his copy of the treaty signed by Houston and was wearing his Mexican military hat. He was eighty-three years old. The Texas Cherokee Nation was no more. The survivors of the slaughter scattered, some going up into the Cherokee Nation in present-day Oklahoma, some making their way to Mexico.

Bradley, Henry

Henry Bradley was born September 28, 1883, a half-brother to Chief Jarrett Blythe. He attended the Cherokee Indian School in North Carolina and then Carlisle Indian Boarding School at Carlisle, Pennsylvania. When he returned to the Cherokee reservation in North Carolina, he married Nancy Tahtahyeh, a full-blood Cherokee, with whom he had nine children. Bradley was a song leader at Rock Springs Baptist Church and led other groups at Geyger Memorial and Soco Valley Church. He joined the U.S. Army and was stationed with federal troops along the Mexican border in 1916 and 1917. Thereafter, he was a farmer and a logger. In 1947, after having served as a councilman from Painttown, North Carolina, and as vice chief, he was elected chief of the Eastern Band of Cherokees. While Bradley was chief, the Museum of the Cherokee Indian was founded in a log building in 1948. The collection of artifacts was small, but it was a beginning. Following his term as chief, which ended in 1951, Bradley again served a two-year term as a council member before retiring from tribal politics. He died on November 18, 1965.

Breath

When the Chickamauga town of Nickajack in Tennessee was attacked in 1794, the shots were heard four miles north in Running Water Town. Warriors from Running Water Town, led by a Cherokee called the Breath, rushed to Nickajack to assist in the battle. Both towns were destroyed by the attacking Americans, and the Breath was killed in the fight.

Brewer, Oliver Hazard Perry

O. H. P. Brewer, usually called Colonel Perry Brewer, was, of course, named for Commodore Oliver Hazard Perry. He was the son of John Brewer and Elizabeth (Taylor) Brewer. He was born in 1829 in the old Cherokee Nation in the South. After the Removal in 1838, Perry Brewer attended Cherokee Nation schools in what is now Oklahoma, including the Cherokee Male Seminary. He went on from there to schools in Arkansas. In 1849, he accompanied other Cherokee gold seekers to California. He returned to the Cherokee Nation in 1851, but made a second trip to the West Coast in 1852. After two or three years, he returned home again.

In 1856, Brewer married Delia Vann, who was the daughter of "Rich Joe" Vann and had been educated in Cherokee schools, at Dwight Mission in Arkansas, and at Mount Holyoke Seminary for Girls in Massachusetts.

Robert J. Conley

Their home was northwest of Webbers Falls in the Cherokee Nation. Although a farmer, he was elected to the Cherokee Senate in 1859. At the start of the Civil War, Brewer became first lieutenant of the Confederate army's Company C of the Cherokee Regiment under Captain Daniel Ross Coodey. By the war's end, he had been promoted to lieutenant colonel.

During the war, Brewer's family had sought refuge in Preston, Texas, and at the end of the war he moved them to Paul's Valley in the Chickasaw Nation (in what is now Oklahoma). After bringing in a crop and making a good profit, he bought some cattle and returned to his old home in the Cherokee Nation.

Brewer was elected superintendent of education of the Cherokee Nation in 1871 and reelected in 1876. He was selected as president of the Cherokee Board of Education in 1881 and was appointed to the Cherokee Nation's Supreme Court in 1890. He died while in office in 1891.

Brewer, Oliver Hazard Perry, Jr.

Born March 21, 1871, O. H. P. Brewer Jr. was the son of O. H. P. Brewer and Delia Vann Brewer. He was born near Webbers Falls, Indian Territory. His father had been a colonel in the Confederate army, chief justice of the Cherokee Nation's Supreme Court, and president of the Cherokee Board of Education.

Young Brewer, known as "Chute," attended Cherokee Nation schools and the Cherokee Male Seminary and graduated from the University of Arkansas in 1893. When his father died, he took over the family's plantation and ran it for seven years. He was elected to the Cherokee Nation's Senate and served as chairman of the Cherokee Nation Board of Education. In 1906, he was a delegate to the Constitutional Convention for the coming state of Oklahoma.

In 1913, Brewer was admitted to the bar. That same year he was appointed postmaster of the Muskogee, Oklahoma, post office, a position he held until 1921. He was elected county judge of Muskogee for three terms, during which time he was appointed "chief for a day" on May 26, 1931. He was elected district judge of the Fifteenth Judicial District in 1934. He continued in that office until his death at eighty in 1951. He never married.

Bronson, Ruth Muskrat

Ruth Muskrat was born in 1897 in the Delaware District of the Cherokee Nation, Indian Territory. She attended boarding school at Tonkawa,

Oklahoma, and received scholarships to the University of Oklahoma, the University of Kansas, and Mount Holyoke Seminary for Girls. She was the first Indian woman to graduate from Mount Holyoke. In 1922, she was the first Indian representative to the annual World's Student Christian Federation convention in Beijing, China. In 1923, she was a member of the Committee of 100, made up of one hundred reformers who met in Washington, D.C., and established as a volunteer citizens' forum on planning issues. While there, she met President Calvin Coolidge. She worked as a teacher at the Haskell Institute in Lawrence, Kansas, where she met and married John F. Bronson. She became an administrator for the Bureau of Indian Affairs' student loan program and in the early 1940s became involved with the National Congress of American Indians and helped establish its Washington, D.C., office. She retired in 1943, and a year later her book *Indians Are People Too* was published. In 1957, she went back to work, this time for the Indian Health Service. She was sent to the San Carlos Apache reservation in Arizona, where she worked in health education. She retired in 1962 and settled with her husband in Tucson, Arizona. She died there in 1982 at the age of eighty-five.

Brown, Catharine

Catharine Brown was born in Wills Valley in Alabama around 1800. She was educated at Brainerd Mission and, upon completing her education there, established her own mission school at Creek Path in what is now Alabama, where she taught for many years. Her letters, written around 1818, reveal the ambiguities and difficulties of what it meant to be an acculturated Cherokee in this period. They have been preserved by Rufus Anderson in *Memoir of Catharine Brown* (1831).

Brown, David

David Brown was the son of John Brown and Tsa-luh, Walter Webber's mother by a previous marriage. In the autumn of 1823, the Cherokee National Council had a silver medal made and inscribed to Sequoyah for his contribution of the Cherokee syllabary. Sequoyah was back in Arkansas, and the medal was delivered to him there by David Brown, "a prominent half-breed preacher." By 1825, Brown had completed a translation of the New Testament using the syllabary. His father-in-law was George Lowrey.

Brown, John

John Brown married Tsa-luh, the mother of Walter Webber by a previous marriage. He was one of the signers of the 1827 Constitution at New Echota, Georgia. By 1829, he had moved to Arkansas and was to accompany Sam Houston and Walter Webber to Washington, D.C., to protest the behavior of some of the U.S. Indian agents. He served as chief of the Western Cherokees in 1839. Details about the Western Cherokees' government during the time just following the forced removal of the Cherokee Nation are sketchy, but we do know that Chief W. C. Rogers, who had replaced John Jolly, was not chief for long. He was replaced by John Brown, who struggled to keep the government of the Western Cherokee Nation together. Principal Chief John Ross of the Cherokee Nation was working to reabsorb the Western Cherokees into the larger body of the Cherokee Nation. The Western Cherokees were already being called the "Old Settlers," presumably in an attempt to minimize the legitimacy of their government. Chief Brown and his close associates absolutely refused to talk with Chief Ross, so at last a group of "Old Settlers," including Sequoyah and second chief John Looney met and deposed Brown, and Looney was made chief of the Western Cherokees. In 1846, John Brown was a member of the delegation that went to Washington, D.C., to present the Old Settlers' claims.

Buffington, Thomas Mitchell

Thomas Mitchell Buffington was born October 15, 1855, in the Goingsnake District of the Cherokee Nation (in what is now Oklahoma). His father was Reverend Ezekiel Buffington, his mother Louisa Newman, and he had four brothers and four sisters. He was one-eighth Cherokee but, according to John W. DeVine, could speak Cherokee. Thomas attended tribal schools. He became a farmer, eventually setting up his own farm in the Delaware District near where Vinita, Oklahoma, is today. In 1878, he married Susan Woodall, and when she died in 1891, he married Emma Gray. In 1889, he was elected judge of the Delaware District. In 1891, he resigned and was elected to the Cherokee Senate, where he became president. When both the principal chief and the second chief died within a few days of one another, Buffington became chief until the National Council could meet to appoint someone. He resumed his duties in the Senate when the council appointed Colonel Johnson Harris.

When Buffington's Senate term expired, he moved to Vinita and was elected mayor. Then he ran for the position of principal chief on the Downing Party ticket and was elected over Wolf Coon on August 7, 1899. The Curtis

Thomas Mitchell Buffington,
c. 1891. Public domain. Courtesy
of the Cherokee Honor Society.

Act had been passed the previous year,
requiring the allotment of Cherokee
lands to individual Cherokees, abol-
ishing the tribal courts and laws, and
making any council act subject to
the approval of the U.S. government.
Buffington seems to have cooperated
with the Dawes Commission on all
of these things. Perhaps he knew it was all going to happen anyway and
simply wanted to help make the changes as smooth as possible. However,
biographer John W. DeVine says that Chief Buffington worked hard to get
the best deal he could for the Cherokees under the circumstances and
that the chief always talked with newsmen and white officials in Cherokee
through an interpreter. According to DeVine, Chief Buffington—dressed in
"Indian regalia," accompanied by his interpreter, and carrying a horseshoe
in his hands—went to see President Theodore Roosevelt to haggle over some
details of the allotment process. When the interview was over, DeVine says,
Buffington stood up and said in English, "Mr. President, the treaty has to be
approved as we have written it—or else." He bent the horseshoe straight and
dropped it on the floor. Chief Buffington did get his "treaty" with the Dawes
Commission approved by the president. In 1902, because of the impover-
ished state of many of the Cherokee full-bloods, he went to Washington,
D.C., again to discover whether the Cherokee National Council had the
power to appropriate funds for the relief of the full-bloods. Finding out that
it did, he requested the council to appropriate $10,000 for that purpose.
When his term was over, he did not run for reelection, but returned home to
Vinita, where he engaged in stock raising, the oil business, and local politics
as the town's mayor. He died in Vinita in 1938 at eighty-three years old.

Bushyhead, Dennis Wolfe

Dennis Wolfe Bushyhead was the eldest son of Reverend Jesse Bushyhead
and Elizabeth Wilkinson, a half-breed from Georgia. Dennis had been
born in the old Cherokee country on Mouse Creek near the present town

Dennis Wolfe Bushyhead, c. 1880. Public domain. Courtesy of the Cherokee Honor Society.

of Cleveland, Tennessee, on March 18, 1826. He was born into the Wolf Clan. He attended the Candy Creek Mission in Tennessee and Reverend Evan Jones's Valley River Mission School in North Carolina. He was twelve years old when he moved west over the Trail of Tears in the contingent led by his father in 1839. Following the Removal, he attended Reverend Samuel Worcester's Park Hill Mission for a year before going to college in New Jersey in 1841. He joined a delegation of Cherokees headed by Chief John Ross for the inauguration of General William Henry Harrison as president of the United States. He graduated in 1844 and moved back to the Cherokee Nation in what is now Oklahoma, where he went to work in the mercantile establishment of Lewis Ross.

In 1847, Bushyhead became clerk of the Cherokee National Committee, one of the two houses of the National Council, but he abandoned his position and his nation to seek gold in California in 1849. He went with a party that included Sam Mayes (the father of Joel Bryan and Samuel Houston Mayes) and his own brother Ned Bushyhead. Ten of the Cherokees in this group died of cholera along the way. Bushyhead and the other survivors joined another group of gold seekers and continued the journey. When smallpox broke out at a mining camp in California, Bushyhead helped care for the victims and amazingly escaped the disease, but afterward he moved to San Francisco to join a group of Cherokees who were planning to return home by steamer. Bushyhead looked the steamer over, decided that it was unsafe, and stayed behind. The steamer went down, and all who were on it were killed. He ended up remaining in California, placer mining with indifferent success until 1868. His brother Ned became a highly respected law officer in California.

When Dennis Bushyhead returned to the Cherokee Nation, he took over a mercantile business in Fort Gibson that had been operated by his brother Jesse, recently deceased, and then was elected treasurer of the Cherokee Nation in 1871 and 1875. Bushyhead was a strong supporter of former chief John Ross and an adherent of the Ross Party, from which he formed the National Party.

In August 1879, Bushyhead was elected principal chief of the Cherokee Nation, then reelected at the end of his first term. Perhaps it helped politically that he had been out of the Cherokee Nation for the duration of the Civil War. He had no political enemies. No one knew where he stood. According to John Meserve, Bushyhead's tenure as chief "was entirely free from domestic dissension, and a judicious poise was maintained with the Federal authorities."

He married Elizabeth Alabama Schrimsher, Will Rogers's aunt, and when she died, he married Eloise Perry Butler, grandniece of Commodore Oliver Hazard Perry and a teacher at the Cherokee Female Seminary.

Bushyhead negotiated the lease of the Cherokee Outlet to the Cherokee Strip Livestock Association for $100,000 a year for five years. In 1881, when a group of Creek Freedmen killed a Cherokee near Wagoner, a party of one hundred Cherokees, former Confederate soldiers, joined to seek revenge. Chief Bushyhead, Assistant Chief William Penn Adair, and the Indian agent met this company of Cherokees at Fort Gibson and convinced them not to take the law into their own hands. Then Chief Bushyhead met with the Creek chief, who had the culprits arrested and turned over to the Cherokee Nation. The murderers were tried, convicted, and hanged at Tahlequah in the Cherokee Nation.

In 1887, Chief Bushyhead was ineligible to run for another consecutive term. Rabbit Bunch was his second chief then and became the National Party's nominee. Joel B. Mayes was the Downing Party's nominee. The election results showed that Mayes had won. Cherokee law required that the National Council certify the election results, but when the council adjourned without having done so, Bushyhead remained in office. When the Cherokee Female Seminary burned that year, Chief Bushyhead called a special session of the council to ask for an appropriation for a new building. It was because of that special session that Ned Christie was in Tahlequah when Deputy U.S. Marshal Dan Maples was killed. Christie was blamed for the killing, and a four-year manhunt followed. (See "Christie, Ned.")

Although the 1887 election had been held in October, Bushyhead was still in office in January 1888 when armed members of the Downing Party, headed by Hooley Bell, stormed the Capitol Building in Tahlequah, broke down the door to the chief's office, and removed Chief Bushyhead, installing Mayes as chief. The next day a plaster cast of a foot with a missing big toe appeared in the window of one of the stores on the main street of Tahlequah. When curious passersby inquired, they were told that it was the foot of Hooley Bell, who had broken off his toe when he kicked down the chief's door. Even after this rather inglorious departure from office, Bushyhead did not abandon politics, but served as a Cherokee delegate to Washington, D.C., in 1889 and again in 1890. He died in Tahlequah in 1898 at seventy-two years old and was buried in the Tahlequah City Cemetery. An interesting note to his story is that when Chief Bushyhead took office, the Cherokee Nation was in debt, but when he left office, it was free of debt.

Bushyhead, Jesse

Jesse Bushyhead, a descendant of John Stuart (Bushyhead), was born in 1804 in Tennessee. He attended Reverend Evan Jones's Valley River Mission School in North Carolina and assisted Reverend Jones in the translation of the Bible. He was ordained a Baptist minister in 1830. Reverend Bushyhead and his family were imprisoned at Camp Hetzel in North Carolina in 1830 and held for the Removal. He was captain of one of the contingents of immigrants over the Trail of Tears. His daughter Eliza was born on the trail. They left the old country on September 3, 1838, and arrived in the new on February 27, 1839. Following the Removal, he worked hard at reconciling the Cherokee Nation and the Western Cherokee Nation. In 1841, he was clerk of the National Council. He became chief justice of the Cherokee Nation's Supreme Court before his death in 1844.

Bushyhead, Ned

Ned Bushyhead was born in Tennessee in 1832, the son of Reverend Jesse Bushyhead and Eliza Wilkerson Bushyhead. He moved west over the Trail of Tears as a child with the contingent led by his father. In 1840, he was apprenticed as a printer and was later employed as a printer in Fort Smith, Arkansas. In 1850, he accompanied his brother Dennis Wolfe Bushyhead to the California goldfields. For a time, he worked a claim near Placerville in El Dorado County, then moved on to Toulumme County. In 1853, apparently tired of searching for gold, he became a printer in Calaveras County, where he started a newspaper, the *San Diego Union*, with a partner, Ned Gatewood. His brother Dennis returned to the Cherokee Nation in 1868, but Ned remained in California, where he and Gatewood moved their newspaper to San Diego. In 1873, he sold his interest in the paper for $5,000. He became a deputy sheriff of San Diego County in 1875, married Helen Corey Nichols in 1876, and was elected sheriff in 1882. A local newspaper wrote, "No better man could have been selected. Thoroughly honest, cool, brave and intrepid in time of danger, patient, wary and sagacious when on the trail of a criminal; courteous and gentle—generous almost to lavishness, he is a true type of a thorough American gentleman." In 1889, Ned Bushyhead became a partner in another printing firm and chief of police of the City of San Diego. Another local paper printed the following comment: "Ned Bushyhead is one of nature's noblemen. He is as square as a die, as true as Toleda steel, as brave as Paladin, as generous as a child. He never knew the meaning of fear." Ned Bushyhead died in 1907, and his body was returned to Tahlequah, Oklahoma, for burial according to his own wishes.

Byrd, Joe

A bilingual Cherokee, Joe Byrd was the first full-blood principal chief of the Cherokee Nation since Chief Lewis Downing in the mid-nineteenth century. Born in Muldrow, Oklahoma, in 1954 and raised in Nicut, Byrd is the son of Stand Watie Byrd and Lillian Byrd. He attended Northeastern State University on a basketball scholarship, receiving his bachelor's degree in education in 1978 and his master's in guidance counseling in 1979. He worked in bilingual education and as a coach at Bell Community Public School and as a guidance counselor at Stilwell High School. Byrd served two terms on the Cherokee National Council. Then in 1995, when Chief Wilma Mankiller chose not to run again, he decided to make a bid for the office of principal chief.

When the election was held, no one received the necessary majority, so a runoff election was called for between the top two vote getters: George Bearpaw, who was Chief Mankiller's choice, and Joe Byrd. Chad Smith had come in third. Before the runoff was held, it was determined that Bearpaw was ineligible because of an earlier felony conviction he had not revealed on his application. Chad Smith and his supporters maintained that the ballot should be changed from "Bearpaw and Byrd" to "Smith and Byrd," but the Judicial Appeals Tribunal (the Cherokee Nation's Supreme Court) decided that the time was too short and the expense of printing new ballots would be too much. The judges determined that the election would go on as scheduled with the ballots printed as they were, but no votes for Bearpaw would be counted. In other words, the tribunal handed the election to Joe Byrd.

In 1997, when several council members made repeated requests for contracts and other financial records regarding public business, Chief Byrd did not comply. Although the tribunal ordered him to produce the records, he

Joe Byrd, 1995. Author's collection.
Photo by D. L. Birchfield.

did not. The tribal prosecutor then requested the chief justice issue a search warrant. With the warrant in hand, tribal marshals went to Chief Byrd's office to secure the records. The Byrd administration characterized the incident as a surprise raid on the chief's office, and Chief Byrd fired the marshals.

The rest of Byrd's administration was marked by turmoil, with Byrd calling in the Bureau of Indian Affairs police to stand between him and the Cherokee Nation's judicial branch. National news was made when the Cherokee Nation marshals attempted to move back into the old Cherokee capitol, where they had been housed. They were met at the back door by Chief Byrd's "security guard." A scuffle suddenly ensued, and people were thrown from the back porch. Bureau police, deputy sheriffs from two counties, and the Oklahoma State Highway Patrol were all present. But perhaps the most enduring image of these troubled times was the Cherokee Holiday parade, when all eyes were not on the parade, but on the armed guards on the rooftops in downtown Tahlequah, Oklahoma. The problems were not resolved until the next election, when Chad Smith, with running mate Hastings Shade, defeated Byrd. Over the next four years, Byrd insisted that all of the trouble during his administration had been caused by "conspirators" and that his reputation had been smirched by lies and allegations. In 2003, he ran for the office of principal chief again but was defeated soundly by Chad Smith in the first vote. In spite of his troubled administration, Chief Byrd remains a very popular man among many Cherokees.

C.

Cabbagehead, William

Renowned for his fine jewelry, William Cabbagehead was also a maker of traditional Cherokee crafts such as blowguns, darts, and ball sticks. He worked for a time at the "ancient village" of Tsalagi (the Cherokee Heritage Center) in Tahlequah, Oklahoma. The following story was told about him. One day as tourists were being guided through the ancient village, one white man was being abusive, especially to the Cherokee women dressed in deerskins and working in the village. The costumed Cherokee workers were not supposed to speak to the tourists. One woman finally looked up Bill Cabbagehead and told him about the tourist. Bill spotted the man in a crowd in front of one of the houses and went around behind it. Putting a dart in his blowgun and aiming it almost straight up, he fired it, and it went in a high arc over the building and came down, striking the offending tourist in the neck. About that time, Bill came around the house and walked up to the man, plucking the dart from his neck. "So that's where that thing went," he said. They had no more trouble with the man.

Calhoun, Walker

Walker Calhoun was born in Big Cove on the Cherokee reservation in North Carolina in 1918. A nephew of Will West Long, he attended the boarding school at Cherokee and served in the U.S. military during World War II. Calhoun grew up speaking Cherokee and learned about Cherokee music and dance from his famous uncle. In the 1980s, he formed a family group, the Raven Rock Dancers, and revitalized the traditional stomp dance of the Eastern Band of Cherokees. He received the Sequoyah Award at a joint meeting of the Eastern Band of Cherokees and the Cherokee Nation in

Robert J. Conley

1988, the North Carolina Folk Heritage Award in 1990, the National Folk Heritage Award from the National Endowment for the Arts in 1992, and the Mountain Heritage Award from Western Carolina University in 2004. A respected traditional elder of the Eastern Band of Cherokee Indians in North Carolina, Calhoun has recorded traditional Cherokee songs.

Casinos

Not only are Indian casinos big business for Indian tribes, but they are also extremely controversial, and it is getting more and more difficult to discuss anything about Indians anywhere without the talk turning to casinos. All three federally recognized Cherokee tribes now operate casinos. The Eastern Band of Cherokees was first with its Cherokee Harrah's Casino in Cherokee, North Carolina, on the reservation. The United Keetoowah Band operates a casino in Tahlequah, Oklahoma, and the Cherokee Nation now has six casinos—one just outside Tahlequah, one at Fort Gibson, one at Sallisaw, one at East Siloam Springs, one at Claremore, and the Cherokee Casino and Resort in Catoosa, a suburb of Tulsa—the newest and biggest for the Oklahoma Cherokees. The casinos provide a tremendous amount of revenue for the tribe. In addition, casino money is donated to the state, where it is used for education and roads. Thus, the casinos may be responsible for making the states allies of Indian tribes in support of tribal sovereignty.

Ceremonies, see "Worldview"

Chalakee

A Choctaw word denoting the Cherokees that found its way into the old southeastern trade jargon and was eventually accepted by the Cherokees in the form "Tsalagi" and in English as "Cherokee."

Charley, see "Tsali"

Cheera-ta-he-gi

Cheera-ta-he-gi, Possessor of the Sacred Fire, is said to have been chief of the Lower Towns in 1714.

Cherokee

The anglicized version of the name "Chalakee." (See "Chalakee.")

Cherokee Advocate

The Cherokee Nation's official newspaper, established in Tahlequah in 1844, the *Cherokee Advocate* was the second newspaper owned by the Cherokee Nation and the first it owned in its new home in the west (now Oklahoma). Its first editor was W. P. Ross, nephew of Chief John Ross. It was known as the *Cherokee Nation News* for a while, but once again became known as the *Cherokee Advocate* in February 1977.

Cherokee Bill, see "Goldsby, Crawford"

Cherokee Celebrities

For a variety of reasons, not all celebrities who are Cherokee or who have claimed to be Cherokee or have been publicized as Cherokee have their own listings in this book. Some of them include the following: Tom Mix, Walter Brennan, Art Acord, Vice President John Nance Garner, Bob Barker, Oral Roberts, Elvis Presley, Sally Richardson, Keely Smith, Jimi Hendrix, Dotty West, Cher, Kim Basinger, James Brown, Rita Coolidge, Kevin Costner, Shannon Elizabeth, James Garner, Val Kilmer, Eartha Kitt, Burt Reynolds, Tina Turner, Dennis Weaver, Loretta Lynn, Crystal Gayle, Peggy Sue, Mel McDaniel, Johnny Cash, Waylon Jennings, Willie Nelson, Chuck Norris, Demi Moore, James Earl Jones, Quentin Tarantino, Tommy Lee Jones, President Bill Clinton, Litefoot, Tom Allard, Wayne Newton, Sonny Landham, Thomas King, Valerie Red-Horse, Cherokee Rose and Silena, Michael Jacobs, Terry Lee Whetstone, and Marvin Rainwater. Many other names can be added to this list.

Cherokee Culture

Cherokee culture is much too complex to attempt to detail here, so this entry offers only a nutshell description. Cherokees historically lived in autonomous, semipermanent towns scattered over all or parts of what is now North and South Carolina, Tennessee, Georgia, Alabama, Virginia, and West Virginia. Each town had a population of approximately two hundred. When the population of a town grew too large, part of it would move

Robert J. Conley

and establish a new town. Towns might be moved every ten years or so to locate fresh garden sites and to allow the old ones to replenish themselves. A town consisted of family dwellings, buildings for grain storage, a town house (or council house), a communal garden, individual family gardens, a ceremonial ground, and, on the outskirts, ball fields.

The family homes consisted of a summer house and a winter house, or *osi*. The main house, or summer house, was rectangular, constructed of sticks, daubed with mud, and painted white. The roof was thatched and covered with grasses. Some homes were actually two stories high. The osi was much smaller and dome shaped or conical, and it may have served double duty as a sometime sweat lodge. It was used to sleep in during the winter because it could be kept much warmer than the summer house.

The town house was much larger, built of logs, and seven-sided, one side for each of the seven Cherokee clans. (See the entries starting with "Ani-" for the clans.) It served as a gathering place for official meetings and, when not thus in use, as a place for smoking and visiting in informal gatherings. Early European visitors to the Cherokee towns found the town houses almost unbearable because they were generally filled with smoke, both from the fire that burned in the middle of the room and from the smoke of the many pipes puffed there.

The towns were organized around matrilineal clans, as was Cherokee life in general. Rules or laws were not enforced by the town government, but rather by clans. If a member of one clan offended another clan, the offended clan had the duty of retribution. The right, or obligation, of the slain person's clan to claim a life from the offending clan has been widely misinterpreted as "clan revenge."

This practice was actually one of many ways of maintaining balance and harmony in the world. Many of the Cherokees' ancient ceremonies and rituals were designed with that same purpose. Priests were initially in charge of the ceremonial calendar, but later each town's peace chief was.

Each town had a peace chief and a war chief, sometimes called the white chief and the red chief. In terms of contemporary political science, they might appropriately be called the "chief of internal affairs" and the "chief of external affairs." The peace chief was in charge of all internal town matters, and the war chief of not just war, but also trade and other alliances. The arrival of Europeans greatly affected the workings of this age-old governmental system.

Although we do not know the details, women, too, had a powerful political voice. Europeans initially had trouble figuring out why the

Cherokees took so long to make up their minds. At a meeting, they would not make a decision, but would instead call for another meeting in a few days because they had to go home to discuss the matter with the women. When the Europeans figured out what was happening, they said that the Cherokees had a "petticoat government." One of the few details we do know is that women occasionally rose to the role of War Woman or Beloved Woman, the Cherokee word for this role having been written down by Englishmen as "Ghigau." A woman so designated had the power of life and death over captives and other political powers.

In addition, there were medicine people, who were usually, but not always, men. Individuals with various physical and spiritual problems went to them.

Even though Cherokee culture has been greatly altered over the years, much of the old culture surprisingly remains to this day, mostly in conservative Cherokee communities. A number of Cherokee communities have "stomp grounds," or ceremonial grounds, where people gather to sing and dance throughout the night and play a form of stickball the next morning. There are still much relied on medicine people who deal with actual injuries and sicknesses as well as with spiritual or psychological problems. Many old habits persist, although people may not know why they do certain things. For example, when children marry, they often tend to establish their own homes near their mothers. Children often run with a problem to a mother's sister as readily as to their mother. Traditional foods are still gathered and cooked, although some things have become "traditional" in more recent times. The best example is probably the Cherokee hog fry, which is often called "traditional" even though hogs are not native to North America. They were brought in by the Hernando De Soto expedition in 1540 and eventually allowed to run wild. So even before the American Revolution, Cherokees were curing hams. They did such a fine job of it that colonials would go to the Cherokee country to buy hams because these hams were so much better than what could be obtained in the colonies.

Cherokee Fall Festival

Also known as the Cherokee Fair, the Cherokee Fall Festival began in October 1914 in Cherokee, North Carolina, largely as a means of promoting the sale of Cherokee-made crafts. By the 1920s, the Eastern Band of Cherokees was staging traditional dances during the fair. It continues today as an annual event, drawing Cherokees and tourists from all over.

Robert J. Conley

Cherokee Female Seminary

The Cherokee Female Seminary opened on May 7, 1851, in the Cherokee Nation (in what is now Oklahoma). The curriculum was designed by Miss Mary Chapin, principal of Mount Holyoke Female Seminary (now College) at South Hadley, Massachusetts, and it included Latin, algebra, botany, vocal music, geography, grammar, and arithmetic. No emphasis was placed on Cherokee culture, and the seminary students were considered the Cherokee elite. The first principal was Miss Ellen Whitmore, a native of Marlboro, Massachusetts. Constructed of brick and stone, the building was 185 feet long and 109 feet wide, and part had two stories and another part had three. It was closed in 1856 because of lack of funds and not reopened until after the Civil War. In 1887, the building burned but was rebuilt in a new location. Upon Oklahoma statehood in 1907, it was taken over by the state and became a normal school, which eventually developed into Northeastern State University. The old Female Seminary building, now called Seminary Hall, still stands on the university campus and is in use.

Cherokee Heritage Center

Established by the Cherokee National Historical Society on lands outside of Tahlequah, Oklahoma, once the site of the Cherokee Female Seminary, the Cherokee Heritage Center, known popularly as Tsalagi, includes a re-creation of an early eastern Cherokee village, called the ancient village; an outdoor theater for the annual presentation of a historical pageant; and the Cherokee National Museum, including the National Archives. The theater opened in 1969, the museum in 1975. The Cherokee National Historical Society and the Cherokee Heritage Center were planned by Chief Bartley Milam, but were not put into effect until the administration of Chief W. W. Keeler. Once separate from but heavily supported by the Cherokee Nation, the Heritage Center has now been taken over by the Cherokee Nation under the administration of Chief Chad Smith.

Cherokee Historical Association

Established in Cherokee, North Carolina, under the administration of Chief Jarrett Blythe in the 1930s, the Cherokee Historical Association was dedicated to "preserving Cherokee culture and history." Its first jobs were constructing an outdoor theater and acquiring and producing a play,

Unto These Hills, which premiered in 1950. The play was written by Kermit Hunter, a white man, and directed by Harry Davis of the University of North Carolina. The musical score was composed by Oklahoma Cherokee Jack Kilpatrick. *Unto These Hills* is still being presented with both Cherokee and non-Cherokee actors and support staff. Tourism was thus brought to Cherokee in a big way.

Cherokee Holiday

The Cherokee Holiday is celebrated every year in Tahlequah, Oklahoma, on Labor Day weekend, commemorating the September 6, 1839, adoption of the new Cherokee Nation Constitution, which incorporated the old Western Cherokee Nation back into the Cherokee Nation. The celebration includes a parade through downtown Tahlequah, a state-of-the-nation address by the nation's principal chief, the selection and crowning of Miss Cherokee, a softball tournament, a golf tournament, a cornstalk shoot (archery contest), a blowgun competition, demonstrations of traditional Cherokee games and crafts, and a powwow. Dozens of vendors' booths selling everything from food to arts and crafts are set up all around town.

Cherokee Honor Society

The Cherokee Honor Society was organized in 1999 by Murv Jacob and Deborah Duvall to recognize and honor individuals of Cherokee descent who have made significant contributions to society. At the first Cherokee Medal of Honor Awards, Wes Studi, Rita Coolidge, John D. Loudermilk, Tom Allard, Valerie Red-Horse, Jim Halsey, Barbara McAlister, Colonel Martin Hagerstrand (a white man), and Bill Glass Jr. were honored with medals. In the years that followed, recipients of the Medal of Honor have included Keely Smith, Mel McDaniel, Crystal Gayle, her sister Peggy Sue, Louis Ballard, Joe Thornton, Joan Hill, Luther Wilson, Lucille Hair, Joey Browner, Jason Stone, James Earl Jones, Lena Blackbird, Bill Rabbit, Archie Dunham, Diane Glancy, Cherokee Ballard, Dan Agent, Tommy Lee Jones, Marie Wadley, Wilson Vann, Jerry Eliot, Robert J. Conley, Lorene Drywater, Robin Coffee, Carl Barnes, Jean Hager, Leo Feathers, Dr. Jerald C. Walker, Francene Geers-Sampson, Virginia Stroud, Perry and Kathy Van Buskirk, Talmadge Davis, Janet L. Smith, Betty Jo Smith, Choogie Kingfisher, J. C. Elliott, and Mark Farner.

Cherokee Indian Baptist Association

The Cherokee Indian Baptist Association, founded in 1869, is an organization of Cherokee Baptist churches. At one time, it had as many as one hundred member churches. It has held annual meetings at the Cherokee Indian Baptist Assembly Grounds near Tahlequah, Oklahoma, for more than 130 years and is still active today.

Cherokee Insane Asylum

The Cherokee Insane Asylum was built six miles south of Tahlequah in the Cherokee Nation, Indian Territory, after the Civil War and originally given the name Cherokee Asylum for the Deaf, Dumb, Blind, and Insane. The ravages of the Civil War had brought about the physical and mental conditions that necessitated the establishment of this institution.

Cherokee Language

The Cherokee language is an Iroquoian language related to the languages of the Seneca, Cayuga, Oneida, Onondaga, Mohawk, and others. Although most of the Iroquoian speakers were located historically in the region of the Great Lakes in Canada and New York, the Cherokees were in the Southeast, surrounded mostly by Muskogean-speaking peoples.

Cherokee was spoken in three major dialects identified with three major areas of Cherokee settlement: the Upper or Overhills, the Middle or Keetoowah, and the Lower Valley or Eastern. The Eastern dialect, characterized by an *r* sound where the others have an *l* sound ("Tsaragi" as opposed to "Tsalagi") has disappeared. The remaining major dialectal difference is now between North Carolina and Oklahoma, although in Oklahoma there are minor differences from one Cherokee community to another.

Since 1823, when Sequoyah made his Cherokee syllabary known, the Cherokee language has been a written language. (For more on this topic, see "Cherokee Syllabary" and "Sequoyah.")

Today the Cherokee language is spoken by perhaps ten thousand people in Oklahoma and a few thousand more in North Carolina; however, it is not the primary language spoken in many homes, so the next generation may show a drastic drop in the number of speakers. In order to combat this trend, Cherokee-language classes are being taught in schools and communities throughout "Cherokee country." The Cherokee Nation in Oklahoma, the Eastern Band of Cherokee Indians in North Carolina, and the United Keetoowah Band of Cherokee Indians in Oklahoma are involved in this effort.

Some of the many talented, bilingual Cherokee speakers who are also teachers of the language today include Harry Oosahwee, Tom Belt, present United Keetoowah Band chief George Wickliffe, Hastings Shade, Adalene Proctor Smith, Durbin Feeling, Martin Cochrane, Ed Jumper, Sam Still, Levi and Virginia Carey, David Scott, Marie Junaluska, Bobbie Gail Smith, and Myrtle Driver.

Cherokee Male Seminary

The Cherokee Male Seminary and the Cherokee Female Seminary were the first institutions of higher education west of the Mississippi River, in what is now Oklahoma. The Male Seminary opened May 6, 1851, a day before the Female Seminary opened, and was built to the same plan. (See "Cherokee Female Seminary.") Like the Female Seminary, the Male Seminary was closed from 1856 until after the Civil War. Graduates of the Male Seminary included Joel Bryan Mayes, William Wirt Hastings, Samuel Houston Mayes, and Emmet Starr. The building burned in 1910.

Cherokee Nation

The Cherokee Nation slowly evolved in the old Cherokee country in the Southeast with the development of the role of a "head person": from trade commissioner to "emperor" to president and finally to principal chief. With this evolution came written laws, a constitution, and recognition by the U.S. government through treaties. Not just the people but the government was relocated in the Removal to the West in 1839, and the Cherokee Nation was continued in what is now Oklahoma following the Trail of Tears. The U.S. government began a slow and systematic dismantling of the Cherokee Nation following the Civil War and by 1907, the year of Oklahoma statehood, had nearly done the job, leaving the Cherokee National Council with the power to adjourn and the U.S. president with the power to appoint a Cherokee principal chief. In 1973, President Richard Nixon and the U.S. Congress gave elections back to the Cherokee people, and the Cherokee Nation began a revitalization program. At this writing, the Cherokee Nation has a tribal registration list of more than 240,000 members and is operating a thriving tribal government. Its principal chiefs have been:

"Wrosetasetow," 1721-35. Though not actually principal chief,
"Wrosetasetow" was a kind of trade commissioner in

dealing with the British, and, as such, his appointment to that position marks the beginning of a movement toward the position of principal chief.

Ama-edohi (Moytoy), 1736–41. The British called him "emperor," but his position was probably much the same as that of "Wrosetasetow."

Ammouskossittee, 1741–53. Son of Ama-edohi, whose position was evolving more toward that of principal chief.

Guhna-gadoga, 1753–60. Ammouskossittee's uncle.

Ukah Ulah, 1760–61. Guhna-gadoga's son.

Ada-gal'kala, 1762–78. Moved into the vacant position with the help of England's superintendent of southern Indian affairs John Stuart. Referred to himself as "president of the nation."

Ogan'sto', 1778–85

Tassel, 1785–88

Little Turkey, 1788–1804

Black Fox, 1804–11

Pathkiller, 1811–27

William Hicks, 1827

John Ross, 1828–66

William Potter Ross, 1866–67

Lewis Downing, 1867–72

William Potter Ross, 1872–75

Charles Thompson, 1875–79

Dennis Wolfe Bushyhead, 1879–88

Joel Bryan Mayes, 1888–91

Thomas Mitchell Buffington, 1891

Colonel Johnson Harris, 1891–95

Samuel Houston Mayes, 1895–99

Thomas Mitchell Buffington, 1899–1903

William Charles Rogers, 1903–17

A. B. Cunningham, November 8–25, 1919

Ed M. Frye, June 23, 1923

Richard B. Choate, October 25, 1925

Charles J. Hunt, December 27, 1928

Oliver Hazard Perry Brewer Jr., May 26, 1931

William Wirt Hastings, January 22, 1936

Jesse Bartley Milam, 1941–49

William Wayne Keeler, 1949–75

Ross O. Swimmer, 1975–85

Wilma P. Mankiller, 1985–95
Joe Byrd, 1995–99
Chad Smith, 1999–present

For more information on these people, see individual listings.

Cherokee National Council

Like the U.S. Congress, the legislative branch of the Cherokee Nation's government, the National Council, was originally bicameral, consisting of two houses: the National Committee and the National Council. Following the near destruction of the Cherokee Nation at Oklahoma statehood in 1907 and something like sixty-three years of presidentially appointed chiefs, the National Council was reestablished in the 1970s and set up as a unicameral legislative body. The contemporary council is made up of fifteen members elected from the nine voting districts of the Cherokee Nation and two at-large members who represent the absentee voters.

Cherokee National Historical Society

Established in Tahlequah, Oklahoma, in 1963 under the administration of Chief W. W. Keeler, the Cherokee National Historical Society was first envisioned by Chief Bartley Milam. The purpose of the organization was to serve as the umbrella for the development and operation of the Cherokee Cultural Center, or Cherokee Heritage Center, and to raise funds for the center's continued operation. (See "Cherokee Heritage Center.")

Cherokee Nation News

The official newspaper of the Cherokee Nation from March 7, 1968, to January 7, 1977. Its first editor was Ralph Keen. In 1977, its name was changed to the *Cherokee Advocate*.

Cherokee Nation Supreme Court

A superior court was authorized by the Cherokee National Council in 1822. It was to meet during council sessions to review cases appealed from the district courts. It came to be called the Cherokee Supreme Court, and a Supreme Court building was erected at New Echota, Georgia. The Supreme Court had reviewed 246 cases by 1835, when it was closed

Robert J. Conley

because of Georgia's agitation for removal of the Cherokees. Following the Trail of Tears, a new brick, two-story Supreme Court building was constructed across the street from the capital square in Tahlequah, the new capital city of the Cherokee Nation in what is now Oklahoma. The Cherokee Nation currently operates with what is called the Judicial Appeals Tribunal instead.

Cherokee Nation v. Georgia

In March 1831, attorney William Wirt (a white man) took a case to the U.S. Supreme Court for an injunction against the state of Georgia for its many violations of the sovereignty of the Cherokee Nation. As a sovereign nation, Wirt argued, the Cherokee Nation could not be subjected to Georgia's laws. The Court's decision was that it did not have jurisdiction to hear the case, Chief Justice John Marshal declaring that "an Indian tribe or nation within the United States is not a foreign state in the sense of the constitution, and cannot maintain an action in the courts of the United States. . . . [T]his is not the tribunal which can redress the past or prevent the future." He further defined Indian tribes as "domestic, dependent nations."

Cherokee National Prison

Established in Tahlequah, the capital of the Cherokee Nation in Indian Territory, after the Civil War, the Cherokee National Prison is a two-story building constructed of stone. At Oklahoma statehood in 1907, it became the Cherokee County Jail. During the administration of Chief Wilma Mankiller, it was returned to the Cherokee Nation, and the building is still in use today.

Cherokee National Youth Choir

The Cherokee National Youth Choir, sometimes referred to as the Cherokee National Children's Choir and sometimes simply as the Cherokee Choir, was established in 2000 by the Cherokee Nation in Oklahoma. Its ranks are filled through auditions, and it performs in the Cherokee language. The singers in the choir are children from grades six to nine. Since its inception, under the direction of Mary Kay Henderson, it has performed at the Native American Music Awards (NAMMYs); at "ground zero" in New York City following the disaster on September 11; and in Washington, D.C., at the Department of Interior, at the Smithsonian, at the opening of the Museum of the American Indian, and in the East Room of the White House before President George W. Bush. In 2003, Harvard University's Kennedy School of Government named the choir as one of sixteen tribal programs to receive the Honoring of Nations Award for exemplary tribal government programs. In 2005, it received a NAMMY for the Best Gospel Album of the year and two additional nominations. The Cherokee National Youth Choir has to date released three CDs, accompanied on one of them by Cherokee singer Rita Coolidge.

Cherokee Neutral Lands

The Cherokee Neutral Lands formed a tract of land in Kansas conveyed to the Cherokee Nation for the sum of $500,000. It was twenty-five miles wide and ran for fifty miles along the western border of Missouri for a total of eight hundred thousand acres. This additional land was provided for in the Treaty of New Echota in 1835 because the treaty "would afford insufficient land for the Cherokees." It was segregated from the rest of the Cherokee land and had never been occupied by a significant number of Cherokees. The Treaty of 1866 called for it to be sold.

Cherokee, North Carolina

A town on the Qualla Boundary (Cherokee reservation) in North Carolina where the Eastern Band of Cherokee Indians' headquarters are located. It is also a major tourist destination, initially because of its annual production of *Unto These Hills*, its old-time Cherokee village, its museum, and its many shops, but now also because of its casino.

Cherokee One Feather

The official newspaper of the Eastern Band of Cherokee Indians, the *Cherokee One Feather* first appeared in January 1968.

Cherokee Orphanage

The Civil War left many orphans in the Cherokee Nation in what is now Oklahoma, and in 1873 the Cherokee Nation purchased the Lewis Ross home near Salina for use as an orphanage. It was known as the Salina Cherokee Orphan Asylum. The building burned in 1903, leaving only the stone springhouse, which stands today in a park in Salina. It was listed in the National Register in 1983. After the original orphanage burned, another was constructed south of Tahlequah, Oklahoma, where Sequoyah High School is now located.

Cherokee Outlet

Following the Trail of Tears, the Treaty of New Echota assigned the Cherokee Nation six million acres of land to the west of the nation (in present-day Oklahoma) as "a perpetual outlet west" in addition to the nation proper. The Treaty of 1866 forced the Cherokee Nation to allow the United States to settle "friendly tribes" there. In 1880, the remaining land of the Cherokee Outlet was leased by an organization of Texas cattlemen known as the Cherokee Strip Livestock Association for $100,000 per year, but in 1892 the U.S. government put a stop to that and forced the Cherokee Nation to sell the outlet to the association. It was opened to white settlement in September 16, 1893, in what has been called "the most spectacular of all land runs," with one hundred thousand land-hungry participants.

Cherokee Phoenix

The first newspaper owned and published by the Cherokee Nation. It made its initial appearance on February 21, 1828, with Elias Boudinot as editor. Making use of the syllabary presented to the Cherokee people by Sequoyah in 1821, it was published in Cherokee and English, making it not only the first newspaper operated by an Indian tribe, but also the first bilingual newspaper in the United States. When Boudinot and the Treaty Party (those who signed the Treaty of New Echota, or the Removal Treaty) parted political company with Chief John Ross, Boudinot resigned as editor. He was replaced by Elijah Hicks, who unfortunately lacked Boudinot's experience, so the *Phoenix* limped on only until May 31, 1834, when Georgia authorities seized the press, and it ceased publication.

Cherokee Strip

The Cherokee Strip was a strip of land in Kansas two and one-half miles wide running the length of the Kansas border from its eastern boundary to the eastern edge of what is now the Oklahoma Panhandle. It was given to the Cherokee Nation by the Removal Treaty, but it was taken away by the Treaty of 1866.

Cherokee Syllabary

The Cherokee syllabary was presented to the Cherokee people in Arkansas in 1821. Sequoyah had people in Arkansas write letters in Cherokee to friends and family in the Southeast, then traveled to deliver the letters and present the syllabary to the Cherokee National Council there. It was accepted almost immediately, and most Cherokees became literate in their own language in a brief time. The Cherokee Nation had print type cast and began to publish a bilingual newspaper, the *Cherokee Phoenix*, and the missionaries went to work with a zeal to publish hymn books, translations of the New Testament, and other religious tracts. Cherokees wrote letters back and forth east and west.

Cherokee syllabary. Public domain. Courtesy of the Cherokee Honor Society.

Whether Sequoyah actually invented the syllabary is controversial. Some believe that it was an ancient system that had fallen into disuse and that Sequoyah somehow managed to salvage it and make it available to the people. Either way, it was a great gift. The syllabary consists of eighty-five symbols. Although sometimes referred to as the Cherokee alphabet, it is, in fact, a syllabary. With the exceptions of symbols for each of the six Cherokee vowel sounds and one for the sound of the letter *s*, each symbol stands for a complete syllable. For example, "Tsalagi," the Cherokee word for "Cherokee," is written in syllabary with three symbols rather than seven letters, *Tsa la gi*.

Cherokee Weavers, see "Sequoyah Indian Weavers Association"

Chickamaugas

During the American Revolution, when Dragging Canoe and his followers were fighting against the colonists (soon to be called Americans) and siding

Robert J. Conley

with the British, their towns were burned by colonial Virginians led by Colonel William Christian. They moved to new locations along Chickamauga Creek near the home of British deputy commissioner of Indian affairs John McDonald in Tennessee and rebuilt their towns there. The Cherokee Nation repudiated their actions, so this group became known as "secessionist" and were call Chickamaugas. (See also "Dragging Canoe.")

Chiefing

A practice on the Qualla Boundary (Cherokee reservation in North Carolina) wherein the Eastern Band of Cherokee men dress up in the clothing of plains Indians to attract tourists to pay them to be allowed to photograph them.

Chief for a Day

A "chief for a day" was a principal chief of the Cherokee Nation appointed by the president of the United States, but only for a day. The Curtis Act of 1898 had all but destroyed the Cherokee Nation. Its courts had been abolished. Elections had been taken away. Property had been confiscated, and the land was being allotted to individual Cherokees, with the "surplus" going to white settlers. It was supposed to have been the end of the Cherokee Nation, and, indeed, after the death of Chief W. C. Rogers, there was no Cherokee chief for two years. No one felt a need for one. In the United States, however, land title is extremely important, and in 1919 the federal government felt the need for a Cherokee chief again—at least long enough to sign some papers. The law that had all but dismantled the Cherokee Nation contained a clause allowing the U.S. president to appoint a chief of the Cherokee Nation. Between 1907 and 1973, eight such "chiefs for a day" were appointed—or, if we count the reinstatement of Chief Rogers, nine. In fairness, it should be said that the last two such appointments, of Chief Jesse Bartley Milam and Chief William Wayne Keeler, were for much more than a day. The presidentially appointed chiefs were:

W. C. Rogers, 1905-17 (elected in 1903, impeached and removed from office in 1905, and appointed chief in 1905)
A. B. Cunningham, November 8-25, 1919
Ed M. Frye, June 23, 1923
Richard B. Choate, October 25, 1925
Charles J. Hunt, December 27, 1928
Oliver Hazard Perry Brewer Jr., May 26, 1931

William Wirt Hastings, January 22, 1936

Jesse Bartley Milam, 1941–49

William Wayne Keeler, 1949–71. (In 1971, the Cherokee Nation held its first election since before Oklahoma statehood in 1907, and Keeler was elected, serving another four years until 1975.)

For more information on these people, see their individual listings.

Chih-kil-leh

According to Cephas Washburn in his *Reminiscences of the Indians*, it was Chih-kil-leh who talked Degadoga into ending the war against the Osages sometime around 1832. Washburn says that Chih-kil-leh, one of the Western Cherokees in Arkansas, was a very powerful and eloquent speaker. The name "Chih-kil-leh" (Washburn's spelling) is most likely from chi-ki-le-le or ji-gi-li-li, "chickadee."

Chisholm, Jesse

Jesse Chisholm was born in 1805 or 1806 in Tennessee, the son of Ignatius Chisholm, a mixed-blood Cherokee. By 1813, Jesse and his father are known to have been living in Arkansas with the Western Cherokees, where Ignatius had the reputation of a scoundrel. Jesse lived along the Arkansas River with his father until about the age of twenty. He may have learned the trading business from Ignatius. He then made his way to Fort Gibson (in what is now northeast Oklahoma). In 1834, he accompanied the Dodge Expedition out of Fort Gibson into what is now western Oklahoma to meet with Comanches and Pawnees. Jesse Chisholm and five other Cherokees assisted Captain Dutch, the head scout. Artist George Catlin also went along. It was on this expedition that Catlin painted his portraits of Dutch and created his rendition of a Wichita village. Jesse Chisholm could speak the Caddo language and served as interpreter at times. On this expedition, many of the soldiers became ill. Upon their return to Fort Gibson, Catlin, afraid that he would fall ill, mounted his horse and rode alone back to St. Louis. Dutch, Jesse Chisholm, and the other Cherokees did not suffer from the undefined illness.

Thereafter, Chisholm became a trader. He did business with many of the plains Indian tribes and is said to have become fluent or at least conversant in fourteen different languages. He was often used by the U.S. government as a go-between to tribes otherwise hostile to the United States.

When Sequoyah disappeared in Mexico in 1842, the Cherokee Nation sent Jesse Chisholm in search of him.

Chisolm eventually settled with his family at the mouth of the Little Arkansas River. On his trading expeditions, he ranged over all of what is now Oklahoma, down into Texas, up into Kansas, and east over into Missouri and Iowa. He established the cattle trail that was to become famous as the Chisholm Trail in 1865. He died on March 4, 1868, probably of food poisoning.

Choate, Richard B.

Richard Choate was a delegate to the Sequoyah Convention in July 1905. He was appointed principal chief of the Cherokee Nation on October 25, 1925, but only for that day. (See "Chief for a Day.")

Christie, Ned

Ned Christie was born December 14, 1852, in the Rabbit Trap community in the Cherokee Nation. He was the son of Watt Christie and Lydia Christie. Watt was a blacksmith, and Ned became a blacksmith and a gunsmith. In 1838, Watt had traveled the Trail of Tears with his father, also named Ned. During the Civil War, Watt served with the Indian Home Guard, also called the "Pin Indians," on the Union side. Ned was thirteen years old when the war started. When the war was over, Watt gave Ned his pair of .44 caliber cap-and-ball Colt revolvers, and Ned converted them to fire bullets.

In 1885, Ned was elected to the Cherokee National Council under the administration of Principal Chief Dennis Bushyhead. Ned could speak both English and Cherokee and was an outspoken proponent of Cherokee sovereignty. On the evening of May 4, 1887, Ned was in Tahlequah, the capital of the Cherokee Nation, for a council meeting. After a day's work, he went for some whiskey with John Parris. They met some other men and drank for a time, then Ned said he was going home. On his way, he passed out in the woods.

On this same night, Deputy U.S. Marshal Dan Maples was crossing a footbridge across the creek from Tahlequah to his camp on the north side when a man, almost certainly Bub Trainor, shot and killed him from a hiding place in the woods. Ned Christie was accused of the killing, so he left town and went home.

In 1889, Deputy Marshal Heck Thomas, Deputy Marshal L. P. Isbel, and Bub Trainor went to Ned Christie's home to arrest him. In the fight,

Isbel was wounded, Ned's house was set on fire, and Ned was shot in the face—the bullet smashing his nose, taking out his right eye, and traveling under the skin around to the back of his head. His son Arch was shot in the chest. Thomas and Trainor had to abandon the scene in order to get the wounded Isbel to help. Both Ned and Arch recovered from their wounds, and Ned swore that he would never speak English again. They rebuilt their house, this time constructing it with double log walls and filling the space between the walls with sand. It came to be known as Ned Christie's Fort.

A few other attempts were made to arrest Ned at his home. The results were always the same. He would wound one of the posse, and the others would have to take the wounded man back to town for treatment. In the meantime, the rumors flew, and Ned Christie was accused of every crime that took place within miles of his home.

On November 3, 1892, the final assault took place. A twenty-three-man posse headed by Deputy Marshal Paden Tolbert approached Ned's house. They fired hundreds of rounds of ammunition into the house all day long and into the night. They also shot flaming dowel rods at the house in an attempt to set it on fire and fired a cannon until they split the barrel. The fight continued throughout the night. In the morning, they managed to plant some dynamite under a wall and blow it apart, setting the house on fire. When Ned came running out of the house, he was killed by members of the posse. (See also "Bushyhead, Dennis Wolfe.")

Chunkey, see "Gatayusti"

Clans

The Cherokee family is a matrilineal clan, meaning that descent is traced strictly through the female line. Marriage of individuals within the same clan is forbidden. When a man marries a woman, he goes with her to live among her clan. Children belong to their mother's clan. It is probably the safest and most secure family system ever devised for women and children, but the early intermarriage with whites in the eighteenth century began to erode the traditional Cherokee family structure. Although the clans are not lost, they no longer function the way they used to, and many Cherokees no longer know their clans. In addition, because of the current tribal government practice, heavily influenced by the U.S. federal government, of determining tribal membership (or citizenship) based on blood degree, regardless of whether that blood comes from the mother or father,

Robert J. Conley

many Cherokees do not have a clan and cannot have one except through adoption by a clan.

The seven Cherokee clans are: Ani-kawi (Deer), Ani-waya (Wolf), Ani-wodi (Paint), Ani-tsisqua (Bird), Ani-gilohi (Long Hairs), Ani-sahoni (Blue), and Ani-gatagewi (Wild Potato). It is said that long ago there were seven more, but they were lost somewhere along the line.

According to Rennard Strickland, Cherokees recognized four kinds of deviations from the cultural norm. One constituted an offense against the clan and was "avenged by individual members of the offended clan." He says further that the clan was "the major institution exercising legal powers." For example, clan members of a murdered man were obligated to kill a man of the murderer's clan.

Claphan, Sammy Jack

Sammy Jack Claphan was born in Stilwell, Oklahoma. In 1970, he tried out for the Stilwell Indians High School football team, and in his sophomore year he had a starting job on the offensive and defensive lines. He lettered in football, basketball, wrestling, and track. As a senior, he was named Northeast Oklahoma Athletic Association (NOAA) All Conference, All State, and Parade All American in football. He was also NOAA Conference Player of the Year in basketball.

Upon his graduation from high school in 1974, he entered the University of Oklahoma on a football scholarship. By 1976, he had earned a starting job as a special teams lineman and offensive guard. He was picked by the Cleveland Browns in the second round of the draft in 1979, but a preseason injury kept him off the Cleveland roster. In 1980, he was picked up by the San Diego Chargers and the next year had a starting position as a special teams lineman. He stayed with the Chargers for seven years.

Sammy Jack Claphan (right) with Robert J. Conley (left) and Wes Studi, Tahlequah, Oklahoma, 1999. Conley and Studi are standing on chairs. Author's collection.

Returning to Oklahoma, he became assistant coach at Midwest City Carl Albert High School before going back to Stilwell in 1996 as line coach for its high school team. In 1998, he became head coach of the team for a time. He taught special education at Stilwell High School until his death from a heart attack in 2001.

Clark, Admiral J. J. (Jocko)

Joseph James Clark was born November 12, 1893, in Chelsea, Indian Territory (present-day Oklahoma). He attended the U.S. Naval Academy, becoming its first Native American graduate in 1918. Known as "J. J." or "Jocko," Clark went into the navy upon his graduation and made it his career. In 1944, he was promoted to rear admiral. It is said that during the battle of the Philippine Sea, Clark's planes were prominent, and his ships were always closest to the enemy. In 1945, he was made vice admiral. He was commander of the 7th Fleet during the Korean War and became famous for quick attacks that he called "Cherokee Strikes." He was decorated with the Navy Cross, the Distinguished Service Medal, the Silver Star, the Legion of Merit, the Navy Commendation Medal, and the Korean Order of Military Merit. When he retired in 1953, he was a full admiral. He died in New York City in 1971 and is buried in Arlington National Cemetery.

Coffee, Robin

Robin Coffee was born in Lawrence, Kansas, in 1953, where his parents were attending Haskell Indian School. In 1963, Robin moved to Tahlequah, Oklahoma, where he attended Sequoyah High School. It was there that he discovered his love for writing poetry. For years, he did not display any interest in pursuing publication by major publishers, but was content to publish his own books: *Voices of the Heart* (1990); *The Eagle's Path* (1991); *Sacred Seasons* (1995); *Visions of the Winter Sleeping Seed* (1998); and *The Eagle and the Cross* (2000). Luther Wilson, director of the University of New Mexico Press, overheard Robin reading some of his poems in Tahlequah and made him an offer, which Robin accepted. The result is Robin's 2005 University of New Mexico Press book *A Scar Upon Our Voice*.

Confederate Cherokee Nation

When the U.S. Civil War broke out, Principal Chief John Ross was determined to keep the Cherokee Nation neutral. In March 1861, the Arkansas

Robert J. Conley

secession convention met and elected Cherokee Elias C. Boudinot its secretary. Boudinot encouraged Stand Watie, his uncle, to defy John Ross and raise a regiment of Confederate Cherokees. Watie already had a band of men around him called the Knights of the Golden Circle who then changed their name to the Southern Rights Party. The Confederacy warmly welcomed Stand Watie and his followers, gave them arms and ammunition, and made Watie a colonel. Stand Watie won the battle of Wilson's Creek in Arkansas. Cherokees were divided over these developments. John Ross, fearful of a Confederate victory and desperate to keep the Cherokees united, signed a treaty with the Confederacy on October 7, 1861.

Reverend Evan Jones wrote a letter to U.S. Indian commissioner W. P. Dole explaining Ross's dilemma and declaring that Ross was actually loyal to the United States. On July 7, 1862, Colonel William Weer of the U.S. Army wrote a letter to Chief Ross requesting an interview, which was delivered to Ross under a flag of truce. Ross's answer was a refusal. Captain H. S. Greeno was ordered to Park Hill in the Cherokee Nation (in present-day Oklahoma) to arrest John Ross at his home. Ross was taken to Washington, D.C., and then to Philadelphia. He repudiated the Confederate treaty he had signed and was assured by President Lincoln that the treaty would never be held against him or the Cherokee Nation. Ross stayed in Philadelphia for the duration of the war.

In August 1863, Stand Watie called a council at Tahlequah in the Cherokee Nation and was elected principal chief. Chief Ross and his followers did not see this election as legal, nor did the U.S. government recognize it, but it might be said that Stand Watie was principal chief of the Confederate Cherokee Nation until the end of the war and General Watie's surrender.

Conley, Evelyn L. Snell

Evelyn L. Snell, the daughter of Swimmer Wesley Snell and Patricia Roberts Snell, in Tahlequah, Oklahoma, born in 1949 into the Wolf Clan, became a noted community worker. After her graduation from Morningside College in Sioux City, Iowa, she worked for a time as a home-school liaison for the Sioux City School District, resigning that position to take on the directorship of the failing Sioux City American Indian Center. During that time, one of the Sioux City television stations selected her as "Person of the Week." Returning to Tahlequah with her husband, Cherokee author Robert J. Conley, Evelyn became the director of the Cherokee United Way and began work with Cherokee communities. When Chad Smith

Evelyn Conley, 1988.
Author's collection.

was elected principle chief, she went to
work for Deputy Chief Hastings Shade
and continued her community work.
When Shade left office, she left her job
as well, but she has continued working
with Indian communities as a consultant. On three occasions, she was part
of a group of women addressing the United Nations on issues concerning
women worldwide.

Conley, Gene

Donald Eugene Conley was born on
November 10, 1930, in Muskogee, Oklahoma, to a Cherokee mother. Gene's
family moved to Richland, Washington,
when he was eleven years old. He has
been called one of the greatest athletes
in the history of sports.

Gene attended Washington State
University, where he played baseball and basketball for three years.
In 1951, he signed on with the Boston
Braves as an amateur free agent. Then
in 1957, with the Milwaukee Braves,
he pitched the winning game of
the World Series. He struck out Ted
Williams and played against Jackie
Robinson. A right-hander, he played
eleven seasons in the major league,
three with the Boston Red Sox, one with the Boston Braves, five with the
Milwaukee Braves, and two with the Philadelphia Phillies.

Gene Conley with the
Milwaukee Braves, 1957.
Courtesy of Gene and
Katie Conley.

In addition, he played six seasons of professional basketball in the
National Basketball Association (NBA)—four with the Boston Celtics and
two with the New York Knicks. While Gene was playing with the Celtics,
they won three NBA titles in 1959, 1960, and 1961. Gene thus became the only

70 | Robert J. Conley

Gene Conley with the Boston Celtics, 1959. Courtesy of Gene and Katie Conley.

professional athlete to win championships and have rings in two different sports. He played his final game (baseball) on September 21, 1963, and was released by the Red Sox on April 25, 1964.

After that, with his wife, Katie, he ran his own business, the Foxboro Paper Company, in Foxboro, Massachusetts, for thirty-five years. Then the two retired to Florida. Gene and Katie have been married for fifty-four years. They have two daughters, one son, and seven grandchildren. Katie wrote a book about Gene's life called *One of a Kind*.

Conley, John

John Franklin Conley was born in Oklahoma on March 16, 1943. Following a stint in the U.S. Army, he went to work in construction and rose to the rank of foreman. He retired in 2005. An armorer in the service, he has been a black powder gun enthusiast and collector for years. He owns an impressive collection of more than sixty black powder guns, both rifles and pistols, some of them originals and some modern replicas, and he keeps all of them in working order. He has also taken part in numerous "competitive shootings" in Oklahoma, Texas, and Arkansas over the years, earning more than two hundred medals, including first place in Flintlock Rifle at the Oklahoma State Championships at Arcadia, Oklahoma, in 1989; first place in Flintlock Rifle Aggregate at the Wichita Falls Memorial Shoot in Texas in 1990; first place in Men's Revolver at the Oklahoma State Championships at Arcadia in 1995; first place in Men's Pistol at the Salt Fork Renegades at Altus, Oklahoma, in 1995; second place in the Oklahoma State Musket Aggregate in 2006; third place in the Oklahoma State Musket Aggregate in 2007; and second place in the Arkansas State Championship Pistol Aggregate in 2007. John lives with his wife, Allene, outside of Pink, Oklahoma.

Conley, Robert J.

Born in Cushing, Oklahoma, on December 29, 1940, Robert J. Conley is the son of Robert Parris Conley and Peggy Marie Jackson Conley. After finishing high school in Wichita Falls, Texas, he attended Midwestern University (now Midwestern State University) in Wichita Falls, finishing with a bachelor's degree in 1966 and a master's in 1968. He worked as a teacher of English at Northern Illinois University and Southeast Missouri State University before being hired as coordinator of Indian culture at Eastern Montana College (now Montana State University at Billings). He left Eastern Montana to work for the Cherokee Nation as a proposal writer and later as assistant programs director. Then he worked as director of Indian studies at Bacone College in Muskogee, Oklahoma, and director of Indian Studies at Morningside College in Sioux City, Iowa. After nine years at Morningside, he quit to work full-time as a writer. Conley has published forty-one novels under his own name and twenty-one novels written under house names. He has also written a collection of short stories, a collection of poetry, and three nonfiction books, and has had numerous poems, stories, and articles published in magazines and anthologies. He married Evelyn Snell in 1978, and they live together in Norman, Oklahoma.

Robert J. Conley, 2006.
Photo by Roger Hall.

Conley, Lieutenant Robert T.

Lieutenant Robert T. Conley was a senior lieutenant in Company F of Love's Regiment of Thomas Confederate Legion during the Civil War. (See "Thomas Legion.") When General Jubal A. Early formed a company of sharpshooters from the ranks of the legion in 1862, Conley was placed in command of the group of twenty-five men who became known as Conley's Sharpshooters. For his part in the battle of Snicker's Ferry, Conley was cited for bravery. In 1865, Colonel George Kirk and his Union troops were turned back by Conley's Sharpshooters at Soco Gap. In the last battle of the Civil War to be fought in North Carolina, Conley's Sharpshooters were about three miles north of Waynesville. Union colonels Kirk and William C. Bartlett had been

Robert J. Conley

ordered to "clear the mountains" of Southern "guerillas." Bartlett's troops had taken Waynesville and were headquartered there. His soldiers were camped at White Sulphur Springs. Conley was ordered to circle Waynesville and hook up with Colonel James R. Love. In doing so, he ran into Bartlett's troops and set up a line of battle. Conley, only twenty-three years old at the time, later wrote, "I charged them with my skirmishers, driving them from the spring and killing one of them, named Arwood, who now lies buried in the Federal part of the cemetery at Asheville. Arwood was, doubtless, the last man killed by a regular command east of the Mississippi River. I yet have his gun as a relic." This shot is said to have been the last shot of the Civil War fired in North Carolina. Conley was said to have always been the first man in and the last man out. Following the close of the war, Conley engaged in several different business ventures with men who had served with him. He moved to Talladega, Alabama, around 1870 and later to Mumford, Alabama, where he died in 1892, leaving a widow and six children.

Constitution of the Cherokee Nation

The first Cherokee Nation Constitution was adopted in 1827. It divided the Cherokee government into three parts: an executive branch (the principal chief), a legislative branch (in a bicameral National Council), and a judicial branch (the Supreme Court). It divided the Cherokee Nation into eight judicial districts, each with a judge, a marshal, and a local council. Each pair of two districts had a company of Lighthorse and a circuit judge. The national capital was established at New Echota, Georgia.

On September 6, 1839, following the Trail of Tears, a new constitution, based on the old, was adopted at Tahlequah, the new capital of the Cherokee Nation in what is now Oklahoma. It continued in force until it was replaced on October 7, 1975. A constitutional convention was called again in 1999, and another new constitution was written. It has not been approved by the Bureau of Indian Affairs, but the Cherokee Nation maintains that it does not need such approval and is operating under the new constitution, having amended it twice, most recently in 2007.

Cook, Bill

William Tuttle Cook was born in the Cherokee Nation, north of Fort Gibson (present-day Oklahoma), December 19, 1873, to James Cook, a white man, and a Cherokee mother known only as Mrs. Morton, a widow. Bill and his younger brother, Jim, led a restless life. When James Cook died in 1878,

Bill's mother moved to near Fort Smith, Arkansas, with the two small boys. A little more than a year later she returned to her old home and married again. They moved twice more, first to Fort Gibson and then around 1880 to Fourteen Mile Creek (both in present-day Oklahoma), where Bill's mother died. When the stepfather made away with all her property, the boys were taken by a cousin, but then placed in the Cherokee Orphan Asylum after only a year.

When Bill Cook was fourteen years old, he left the orphanage and found work in the Creek Nation, also in Indian Territory. Then he went to work on a ranch, learning to drink, shoot, and play cards with the cowboys. He was soon selling whiskey in Indian Territory. When he was found out, he fled to New Mexico in 1892, where he worked on a ranch for a few months. However, he returned to the Cherokee Nation and was arrested on the whiskey charge. He spent forty days in jail. In 1893, he worked for a time as a posse member for the federal court. By the summer of 1894, though, he had formed an outlaw gang and robbed the bank at Chandler.

That same year Bill's brother, Jim, was charged with horse stealing in the Cherokee Nation. He fled to the Creek Nation, where he joined up with his brother. In June, in the company of Crawford Goldsby, later known as Cherokee Bill, the Cook brothers went to Effie Crittenden's Halfway House and sent Effie into Tahlequah to collect their Cherokee Strip payments. A fight followed when a posse arrived there to arrest the three men. During the fight, Jim was shot seven times. (For more on this fight, see "Crittendon, Zeke and Dick.") When the three men fled the scene, Bill and Goldsby took Jim to a doctor in Fort Gibson, but officers were on their trail, and they had to abandon him there. He was captured, tried by the Cherokee courts, and sentenced to seven years in the Cherokee National Prison. He escaped and was recaptured several times. Following his last escape, the Cherokee authorities abandoned the case.

Throughout the rest of the year, the Cook Gang robbed stores and banks, and by the end of the year a reward of $250 was offered for each member of the gang. In January 1895, Bill was arrested in Texas but escaped following a fight. The Texas sheriff followed Bill into New Mexico, where he was joined by a sheriff from that state, and they continued the pursuit together. They later captured Bill near Roswell. He was returned to Fort Smith, Arkansas, sentenced to forty-five years in prison, and sent to Albany, New York, where he died some years later.

Cook, Jim, see "Cook, Bill"

Robert J. Conley

Cowee Town

The name "Cowee Town" is probably, according to James Mooney, from the name "Kawi yi" and might mean "the Place of the Deer Clan." It was the name of two different towns, one in northern South Carolina and the other ten miles south of present-day Franklin, North Carolina. The latter was one of the oldest and largest of Cherokee towns, with about a hundred houses. It was burned in 1783 by the Americans.

Crittenden, Dick, see "Crittenden, Zeke and Dick"

Crittenden, Zeke and Dick

Zeke and Dick Crittenden were half-Cherokee brothers who were semi-notorious in and around Wagoner, Indian Territory (present-day Oklahoma). They were part of the posse that went to Effie Crittenden's Halfway House and attempted to capture Bill and Jim Cook and Cherokee Bill (Crawford Goldsby). When Cherokee Nation treasurer E. E. Starr began passing out per capita payments from the Cherokee Strip money in the summer of 1894, the outlaws were at the Halfway House. Afraid they would be arrested if they went into Tahlequah to get their share, they sent Effie Crittenden, estranged wife of Dick Crittenden, into Tahlequah with notes each had signed to pick up their money for them. In Tahlequah, Effie was paid, but officials had taken note of the signatures. A posse of eight men was formed, headed by Sheriff Ellis Rattlinggourd and including Zeke Crittendon, Dick Crittenden, and Sequoyah Houston. On July 18, the posse rode out to the Halfway House. The outlaws heard the posse's approach, and someone started shooting. Jim Cook was wounded seven times, and Sequoyah Houston was killed. Sheriff Rattlinggourd and all of the posse except the two Crittendens fled. Afraid to expose themselves to the fire from the Halfway House, Zeke and Dick stayed and continued the fight until after dark, when Cherokee Bill and the Cooks managed to get away.

In January 1895, when Cherokee Bill was at last captured, he was brought into Nowata, Indian Territory, and turned over to officials there. Deputy marshals stopped in Wagoner with Cherokee Bill on their way to Fort Smith, Arkansas, and the federal court. In Wagoner, a photograph was taken. Zeke and Dick managed to get themselves included in the picture, which has often been published and labeled "The Capture of Cherokee Bill." According to S. W. Harman in *Hell on the Border*, Cherokee Bill would never have been photographed standing next to Ike Rogers, who had betrayed him. Instead, he stood next to Dick Crittenden. The story is that he threw his arm around Dick and said, "Here's a fellow who once stood up and fought like a man. I'll have my picture taken with him." He then tried to get hold of Dick's revolver, but Dick stopped him, and the picture was taken.

Ed Reed, son of the notorious outlaw Belle Starr, served as a deputy U.S. marshal for about three years. Zeke and Dick Crittenden, former deputy marshals themselves, were among a number of people opposed to his appointment because of his background and family connections. On October 24, 1895, in Wagoner, Zeke and Dick, who had apparently been drinking and shooting up the town, fired at Reed, who fired back, killing both of them. They are buried head to head in the cemetery at Hulbert, Oklahoma, a single marker serving for both men.

Crockett, David

Although best known as an Indian fighter, Davy Crockett, a white man, well deserves a mention in this book. In 1830, when the U.S. Congress passed President Andrew Jackson's removal bill by a narrow margin, Davy Crockett was a senator from Tennessee. With a strong speech made on the Senate floor, Crockett severed his political ties with the president and ended his political career because of this vote. He left Tennessee, only to be killed in Texas defending the Alamo. Crockett's later description of his speech to the Senate regarding the removal bill says that

> [I was] without disguise, the friend and supporter of
> General Jackson, upon his principals [*sic*] as he had laid them
> down, and as "*I understood them*," before his election
> as President. . . . I worked along with the Jackson party
> pretty well. . . . His famous, or rather I should say his
> in-*famous*, Indian bill was brought forward, and I
> opposed it from the purest motives in the world. Several
> of my colleagues . . . told me . . . that I was ruining myself.
> They said this was a favorite measure of the President,
> and I ought to go for it. I told them I believed it was
> a wicked, unjust measure, and that I should go against
> it, let the cost to myself be what it might; that I was
> willing to go with General Jackson in everything that
> I believed was honest and right; but, further than this,
> I wouldn't go for him or any other man in the whole

creation; that I would sooner be honestly and politically
damned, than hypocritically immortalized. . . . I voted
against this Indian bill, and my conscience yet tells
me that I gave a good honest vote, and one that I believe
will not make me ashamed in the day of judgement.
I served out my term. . . . When it closed, and I returned
home, I found the storm had raised against me for sure.

Crowe, Amanda

Amanda Crowe was born in 1928 in the Qualla Cherokee community in
North Carolina. She was drawing and carving already at the age of four and
selling her work at age eight. She received her master of fine arts degree
from the Chicago Arts Institute in 1952 and then studied in Mexico at the
Instituto Allende in San Miguel under a John Quincy Adams fellowship. She
had been away from home for twelve years when the Cherokee Historical
Association invited her back to teach art and woodcarving at Cherokee
High School in Cherokee, North Carolina. She accepted and taught there
for nearly forty years. Highly renowned for her woodcarving, she received
the North Carolina Folk Heritage Award and exhibited at the Art Institute
of Chicago, the Mint Museum in Charlotte, the Atlanta Art Museum, and
the Denver Museum of Art. Her work is in the permanent collections of the
Smithsonian Institution and the U.S. Department of Interior.

Crowe, John

John Crowe was born October 7, 1917, to Molly Crowe and Wesley Crowe. He
lived in the Bigwitch community in North Carolina all his life and attended
Cherokee schools, graduating from Cherokee High School. During World
War II, Crowe served in the U.S. Army in Europe. Upon his return to
Cherokee, North Carolina, he spent four years teaching building construction in vocational training. In 1950, he married Olly Wolfe. For a time, he
was in charge of the building and maintenance for the *Unto These Hills* production and the Oconaluftee Indian village. He served on the council of
the Eastern Band of Cherokee Indians before being elected to the office of
vice chief. When Chief Noah Powell died in office in 1973, Crowe became
chief. He continued the work Powell had begun on the new high school
in Cherokee. In 1974, Chief Crowe was authorized by the Tribal Council to
proceed with the construction of a new building for the Cherokee National

Museum. He participated in the ground-breaking ceremony on August 9 of that year. In 1976, Chief Crowe said there was no reason for Indians to celebrate the U.S. bicentennial. He remained in office until 1983.

Cunningham, Andrew Bell

Born May 1, 1869, in Delaware District of the Cherokee Nation, near Vinita (in present-day Oklahoma), A. B. Cunningham was the son of Jeter Thompson Cunningham, a Confederate Cherokee soldier, and Keziah Camille Moore. His father was a farmer, but when Andrew was old enough to go to school, the family moved into Vinita so that he could attend the free public school. Andrew was ready to graduate from the Cherokee Male Seminary when it was closed owing to a lack of funds. In spite of not graduating, he became a schoolteacher. In 1895, when a disastrous fire destroyed eighteen businesses, eight residences, and thirteen offices in Tahlequah, the capital of the Cherokee Nation, Andrew Cunningham and Claude Shelton raised $1,000 as a reward for the capture and conviction of the person who started the fire. Two years later Cunningham was elected sheriff of Tahlequah District. He was appointed by Chief Thomas Mitchell Buffington as executive secretary of the Cherokee Nation and continued to serve in that capacity under Chief W. C. Rogers. After Oklahoma became a state in 1907, Cunningham served as mayor of Tahlequah. Two years after the death of Chief Rogers, the U.S. government found that it needed the signature of a Cherokee chief on some documents, so the Interior Department appointed Cunningham as principal chief for eighteen days, from November 8 to November 25, 1919. Cunningham was twice married, first to Sammie Gunter, who died in 1913, and then to Viola Ritchie Harris. He died on September 12, 1928. He had no children.

Curtis Act

The Curtis Act of 1898 was passed "for the protection of the people of the Indian Territory." It gave the U.S. courts the power to determine the membership of the Five Civilized Tribes. It declared that the Dawes Commission would allot the tribes' lands to individuals as soon as the population rolls were complete. It required residency for anyone to be enrolled. The Curtis Act was the power behind the dirty work of the Dawes Commission, and its author was Senator Charles Curtis (later vice president of the United States), a Kaw Indian.

D.

Dangerous Man

According to oral tradition, the earliest migration of Cherokees took place in 1721, just after the first treaty was signed with the British in the Carolinas. Dangerous Man (Yunwi-usgaseti), believing this treaty to be a portent of things to come, took a portion of the tribe and left, moving west into unknown lands to get beyond the reach of the white man. They managed to keep in touch with the ones they left behind until after they crossed the Mississippi. Then nothing more was heard of them until years later when other Cherokees began to move west. One party found them at the base of the Rocky Mountains, living as they had lived long ago.

Daniels, Victor

Born in 1899 in Muskogee, Cherokee Nation (in what is now Oklahoma), Victor Daniels was a full-blood Cherokee. He studied mining for two years at the University of Arizona, worked on cattle ranches, and was a guide, a boxer, and a rodeo performer before working as a stuntman in films. In 1939, using the professional name Chief Thundercloud, he starred in the title role of the film *Geronimo*. The next year, in *Hi-Yo Silver*, he

Victor Daniels (far right), "Chief Thundercloud," as Tonto, 1940. Ken Jones Collection.

created the role he is best remembered for, that of the Lone Ranger's companion Tonto. He died in Hollywood in 1955.

Davis, Sally Toney

The great-great-granddaughter of Sequoyah, Sally Toney Davis was born in 1895 and died in 1988. She became a widely known and highly respected midwife in and around Texanna, Oklahoma, delivering at least 225 children in her time. She was the grandmother of Cherokee artist Talmadge.

Davis, Talmadge, see "Talmadge"

Dawes Act

In 1887, the U.S. Congress passed the General Allotment Act, popularly called the Dawes Act after the sponsor of the bill, Senator Henry Dawes of Massachusetts. Its intent was clear. Dawes had said, "[T]here was not a family in [the Cherokee] Nation that had not a home of its own. There is not a pauper in that Nation, and the Nation does not owe a dollar. It built its own capitol . . . and built its schools and hospitals. Yet the defect of the system was apparent. They have got as far as they can go, because they hold their land in common . . . there is no selfishness, which is at the bottom of civilization."

So Henry Dawes set about making Indians selfish. The Dawes Act called for the allotment of tribal Indian land to individual landowners, with all "excess" lands to be sold to white people. The Indian-allotted land would be held in trust for the Indian owner by the U.S. government. The Cherokee Nation was at first exempt from the Dawes Act, but on March 3, 1893, the Dawes Commission was set up to deal with the Cherokee Nation and the other tribes of the so-called Five Civilized Tribes.

Dawes Commission

In 1894, the three-member Dawes Commission arrived in the Indian Territory. Their job was to try to convince the members of the Five Civilized Tribes to agree to the individual allotment of tribal lands. In 1895, the commission was increased to five members. Its powers were also increased, and its name was changed to the Commission to the Five Civilized Tribes. Senator Henry Dawes of Massachusetts, the sponsor of

Robert J. Conley

the General Allotment Act, was assigned to the commission. The members began to survey Cherokee lands. In 1896, the power of determining its own membership was taken away from the Cherokee Nation and given to the Dawes Commission. To help it along in its work, the Curtis Act was passed. (See "Curtis Act.")

Dawes Roll

The population roll to determine membership in the Cherokee tribe was finally concluded in 1914 by the Dawes Commission and is referred to as the Dawes Roll. When it was finished, the U.S. Congress declared it to be the Final Cherokee Roll and closed it. No one can be added to the roll, and it is against the law for anyone to make copies of the roll or to sell them. (Bob Blankenship of Cherokee, North Carolina, came up with a clever way of getting around this law, however. In his two-volume work *Cherokee Roots—Eastern Cherokee Rolls* (vol. 1) and *Western Cherokee Rolls* (vol. 2)—he provides an "index" to the 1851 Old Settler Roll, the 1852 Drennan Roll, the 1898–1914 Dawes Roll, and the 1909 Guion Miller Roll. He alphabetizes the names of all individuals on the Dawes and Miller rolls together, so it is not a copy of any one roll, but all the information from each roll is included.) Because Congress closed the roll and declared it final, the Cherokee Nation cannot have an active roll, so it maintains a "Tribal Membership and Voter Registration List." In spite of the highhanded and often shoddy way in which the roll was compiled, the Cherokee Nation bases tribal membership strictly on linear descent from someone listed on the Dawes Roll. The United Keetoowah Band does the same thing, but limits enrollment to those of one-quarter Cherokee blood or more.

Degadoga

Degadoga (alternate spellings: Takatoka, Ticketoke), an old war chief, had gone west just to fight the Osages around 1817 when the U.S. Army told him it wanted to bring an end to the war. He agreed. The only way to do that, though, he said, was to kill all the Osages, who were "a nation of liars." When Bowles left for Texas, Degadoga became the chief of the Western Cherokee Nation. He continued the war against the Osages with a vengeance. His most trusted commander was Captain Dutch, who had been married to an Osage woman. When Dutch's wife was killed by Osages for some reason, Dutch became a thorough-going Osage hater.

Degadoga met the missionary Cephas Washburn at Dwight Mission, established in Arkansas to teach and preach to the Cherokees. They visited often, and Degadoga would ask Washburn how he was coming along in teaching the Indian boys "to wear breeches." He refused to believe the missionary when Washburn told him that the world was round. He figured everybody on the other side would fall off. Finally, Washburn demonstrated centrifugal force by slinging a bucket of water around in a circle without spilling any water. The old chief relented.

Degadoga was a friend of Sequoyah, and when Sequoyah at last convinced the Cherokees of the usefulness of his syllabary, he first taught it in Degadoga's Arkansas village.

In 1818, the Western Cherokees held an election, and Tahlonteskee (John Jolly's brother) was elected chief. Degadoga continued his war against the Osages and his arguments with the U.S. Army. In 1832, the United States at last negotiated a peace between the two tribes. Dutch was not a party to it. Angry, he moved into Texas, settling just south of the Red River. Degadoga joined Dutch in raids against the Osage all the way from the Red River to Clermont's town (now Claremore, Oklahoma). About that time, Degadoga heard of the U.S. government's schemes to move all the Indians to locations west of the Mississippi River. He decided it was a very good idea and that he would go along with it, but, he added, all the white people should move east of the big river. He embarked on a major trip to unite all Indian tribes in this monumental effort, but before he could even get it going, he died en route in Kaskaskia, Illinois, in 1825.

Dick, Cecil

Cecil Dick (Cherokee name, Degadoga) was born in 1915 in Rose Prairie, Oklahoma. He heard the old Cherokee animal stories from his mother. When he was sent off to boarding school, he could speak only Cherokee. He was orphaned at twelve. At seventeen, he went to Santa Fe, New Mexico, to study at Dorothy Dunn's Studio for gifted young Indian artists. With Dick in that first class were Oscar Howe, Harrison Begay, Pablita Velarde, and Allan Houser. Dick said later, "I was the only woodlands painter at the Studio, an individualist that didn't conform to generally accepted styles there, so Dunn left me pretty much alone." Dunn wrote later in her 1968 book *American Indian Painting* that Cecil Dick "is noted for his consistent originality. He has always been an innovator in composition and color while dramatizing experiences and legends of his tribe. Balance and rhythm control the ostensibly carefree action of his pictures, which are always fascinating. Conjured

Robert J. Conley

Cecil Dick, 1985.
Photo by Dan Agent.

colors in combinations and applications reminiscent of Gauguin produce excitement even in the simplest subjects."

When Dick returned to Oklahoma, he found a flourishing art program at Bacone College in Muskogee, headed by Pottawatami artist Woody Crumbo, and he enrolled in the program. Crumbo said of him, "Cecil Dick is one of the main Indian artists who stuck with the traditional ideals in his art. His work has great depth and he is the greatest preserver of the old Cherokee traditions and culture. He deserves a lot more credit than he has gotten." At Bacone, Dick also met Willard Stone, a soon-to-be famous wood sculptor, and they became lifelong friends. Stone said of Dick that he "knows more about Cherokee history, tradition, and background than anyone alive. His style is very authentic, unique and recognizable. He sticks to the true story." Dick taught art at Chilocco Indian School in Oklahoma from 1939 to 1942 and worked as an illustrator in an aircraft plant during World War II. In 1945, he became the first American Indian to win the annual Philbrook Art Show in Tulsa, Oklahoma. The Cherokee Nation awarded him the Sequoyah Medal in 1983, the third in history. The first was given to Sequoyah and the second to Jack Kilpatrick and Anna Kilpatrick. At the Red Earth Art Show in 1990, Dick was named Indian Artist of the Year. He died in Tahlequah, Oklahoma, in 1992.

Doering, Mavis

Mavis Doering was born in Oklahoma. A highly renowned basket maker, she gathers her raw material for baskets and dyes and weaves either traditional Cherokee double-weave baskets or splint baskets. Her works have been exhibited at the Southern Plains Indian Museum, the Coulter Bay Indian Art Museum, the Wheelwright Museum of the American

Indian, the Museum of Fine Art at the University of Oklahoma, the Oklahoma Historical Society, the Kennedy Center in Washington, D.C., and the Smithsonian Folklife Festival. In 1982, she was commissioned by the Oklahoma State Arts Council to create fifty baskets, which were then presented to the governors of the fifty states at the National Governors' Conference, and in 1983 she was commissioned to create the awards for the Governor's Arts Awards. Her baskets are in the private collections of Mikhail Gorbachev and Senator Edward Kennedy.

Doublehead

One of the followers of Dragging Canoe before, during, and after the American Revolution, Doublehead killed the defenders of Cavett's Station after they had surrendered, thus incurring the wrath of Bob Benge, a mixed-blood Indian who was also a follower of Dragging Canoe. Then, in 1807, because Doublehead had signed a treaty selling Cherokee land as a result of a bribe, the Cherokee Nation ordered him executed. The Ridge (later Major Ridge), Alex Saunders, and James Vann were given the assignment. Ridge and Saunders found Doublehead drunk in a tavern (Vann had dropped out somewhere along the way), where Ridge shot Doublehead through the jaw, then he and Saunders fled the scene. They later heard that Doublehead had survived, so they trailed him to the loft of a nearby home. Doublehead rose out of bed to defend himself, but while he was struggling with Ridge, Saunders split his head with an ax.

Downing, Lewis

Lewis Downing (Cherokee name, Lewie Za-wa-na-skie) was born in Tennessee in 1823, the son of Samuel Downing and Susan Daugherty Downing. He was the descendant of a Major Downing, a British officer who had married a Cherokee woman before the American Revolution. Lewis attended Valleytown Mission School. He came west with the wave of Cherokees captained by Jesse Bushyhead in the 1838 removal, settled near Breadtown, and attended the Baptist Mission, becoming an early convert under the influence of Reverend Evan Jones. In the 1840s, he was ordained a minister and upon the death of Reverend Jesse Bushyhead in 1844 became the pastor of Flint Baptist Church.

Downing became involved in politics when he was elected to the Cherokee Senate from the Goingsnake District in 1845. He was a delegate

Lewis Downing, c. 1870.
Public domain. Courtesy of the
Cherokee Honor Society.

to Washington, D.C., in 1851 and
was reelected to the Cherokee
Senate in 1859. During the
Civil War, he joined the Indian
Home Guard as a chaplain. He
was one of those Pin Indians
who were told that they were
serving the Confederacy after
Chief John Ross signed the
Confederate treaty, but he did
not act like a Confederate for long. In the pro-Union Indian Home Guard,
he rose to the rank of lieutenant colonel.

At the end of the Civil War, Downing was serving as deputy principal
chief for the Cherokee Nation, and he opened the negotiations between
the U.S. government and the Cherokee Nation at Fort Smith with a prayer.
He also represented Chief Ross much of the time because Ross was in his
sickbed. On one of Downing's trips to Washington, D.C., he had met a
wealthy woman named Mary Eyre, and although Downing was a married
man (he had been married to Lydia Price and then, following her death,
to Lucinda Griffin), Mary followed him back to Tahlequah, the capital of
the Cherokee Nation in Indian Territory. When Lucinda died a year later,
Downing married Mary Eyre and built her a home he called Eyre's View.

When Chief Ross died, the Cherokee National Council appointed
William Potter Ross to serve out his term. Following Ross's brief term,
Downing was elected principal chief in 1867. According to John Bartlett
Meserve, Downing's "fine judgement accomplished the reuniting of the
discordant Cherokee factions growing out of the Civil War. Chief Lewis
Downing was one of the noblest characters of Cherokee history." But
the U.S. government had created a jurisdictional mess in the Cherokee
Nation and in all of the Five Civilized Tribes with the Treaty of 1866.
The federal court at Van Buren, Arkansas (later at Fort Smith), was given
jurisdiction over Indian Territory. Tribal courts could deal only with
cases involving Indians. Downing served a full term as principal chief
and was reelected in 1871.

In February 1872, Zeke Proctor, a Cherokee, shot and killed Polly Beck Hildebrand, also a Cherokee. The shooting had been an accident, for Zeke had intended to kill a white man, Jim Kesterson, who was living with Polly after having abandoned Zeke's sister and their children. Kesterson escaped and turned himself in to the Cherokee sheriff. The Becks were furious and determined to see Zeke hang. Both the Beck and the Proctor families were influential in the Cherokee Nation, but they had been on opposite sides during the Civil War. The Becks had been Confederates, and the Proctors had been pro-Union Pin Indians.

Afraid that the Cherokee Nation courts would acquit Zeke, the Becks tried delaying tactics, arguing over who would be the judge and other things, hoping that the U.S. court, now located at Fort Smith, would find a reason to arrest Zeke and try him. They located Kesterson and had him file charges against Zeke for attempting to murder a white man. Since Kesterson had married Zeke's sister, the Cherokee Nation considered him a Cherokee citizen by marriage, but the U.S. court considered him a white man and decided that it had jurisdiction. At last, the U.S. court decided on a course of action.

A warrant was issued for the arrest of Zeke Proctor on the charge of assault on a white man, and deputy marshals were sent to the Cherokee Nation with orders to watch the trial of Zeke Proctor. If Zeke were found guilty and sentenced to hang, they could just ride on back to Fort Smith, but if the Cherokee court should let him go, then the deputies were to arrest him on the federal charge and take him to Fort Smith for trial.

On April 15, 1872, the date of the trial, the deputy marshals showed up at the Whitmire School with Kesterson and the Becks. The school-house, which was being used for the trial, was packed, and hundreds of people were gathered outside. White Sut Beck took a double-barreled shotgun and walked to the schoolhouse. He got past the guards and stepped inside, leveling the shotgun at Zeke, who was seated between his attorney and a guard. Zeke's brother, Johnson Proctor, stepped up to grab the shotgun, and Beck killed him instantly. Zeke jumped out a window, receiving a wound in the leg. Then all hell broke loose. When it was all over, nine men had been killed, two more were dying, and an undetermined number had received lesser wounds. The trial was hastily reconvened in a private home the next morning, and Zeke was acquitted.

But there was still the warrant for Zeke's arrest for assault, and the U.S. government issued a new warrant charging everyone it could come up with who could be considered on the Proctor side of the fight, including Johnson Proctor, the first man to be killed. The Pin Indians were said to be helping Zeke Proctor hide out from federal authorities, and the U.S. court appealed to Chief Lewis Downing for assistance in locating and arresting Zeke Proctor. Chief Downing, himself a Pin, considered the matter closed, having been dealt with by the Cherokee Nation courts, so he refused. He wrote a letter to the Cherokee Nation delegation in Washington, D.C., to appeal to the government regarding their treaty rights. In response, President Ulysses Grant authorized the establishment of a federal court within the boundaries of the Cherokee Nation, and authorities at Fort Smith wrote to the army at Fort Sill requesting troops. The Cherokee Nation, amazingly, was suddenly in danger of going to war with the United States again.

The issue was finally resolved in August 1873 by the granting of amnesty for all parties. By then, Lewis Downing had died in office. He had died November 12, 1872, at only forty-nine years old. He was buried on Grand River in Mayes County, Indian Territory, but the exact location of his grave is unknown today.

Downing Party

In 1867, a split in the Ross Party gave rise to a new political party in the Cherokee Nation. It was called the Downing Party, and its platform seems to have been nothing more than opposition to the Rosses. Chief John Ross was dead, but his nephew W. P. Ross was still around and had been appointed principal chief by the Cherokee National Council. The Downing Party's candidate was, of course, Lewis Downing, and it was successful in the election of 1867, in part because refugee Cherokee Confederates in Texas or Arkansas came back to the Cherokee Nation in what is now Oklahoma and allied themselves with it.

Dragging Canoe

Dragging Canoe was born around 1740 in one of the Overhill towns on the Little Tennessee River in Tennessee. His father was Ada-gal'kala. At an early age, Dragging Canoe became war chief of the town of Malaquo, or Big Island Town, on the Little Tennessee River. The story has been told of him that when he was still a child, he wanted to accompany his father and the other men on a raid. He was told that he was too young, but he was insistent. He followed the men to the edge of the river, refusing to obey his father's commands to turn around and go back home. Finally, his father said that he could go with them if he could put his canoe into the water. Thinking that was that, the men heaved up their own huge dugout war canoes and put them into the water, but one of the men looked back and cried out, "Look. He is dragging the canoe."

Dragging Canoe first appears in history in 1775 at Sycamore Shoals in Tennessee, where Cherokees led by the old men Ada-gal'kala and Ogan'sto' were concluding their negotiations with Richard Henderson and Nathaniel Hart of the Transylvania Company to sell Cherokee lands that made up most of Kentucky and middle Tennessee. Dragging Canoe came out in open opposition to the sale. When he saw that he was defeated, he said to the white men, "You have bought a fair land, but you will find its settlement dark and bloody."

John Stuart, British superintendent of southern Indian affairs, was Dragging Canoe's friend and ally, and because the sale was illegal, violating both a Royal Proclamation and an agreement made between the Cherokees and Great Britain, Stuart planned to take care of matters, but then the American Revolution broke out. Dragging Canoe and his followers joined forces with the British and stayed loyal throughout the war, whereas the majority of the Cherokee Nation tried to remain neutral. Dragging Canoe was declared a secessionist, and when the towns where he and his followers lived were burned, they moved south to Chickamauga Creek in Tennessee and built new towns. They became known as the Chickamaugas. Even when the revolution ended and Great Britain abandoned the Chickamaugas, Dragging Canoe continued fighting the Americans, who called him "the Cherokee Dragon" and "the Savage Napoleon." When Dragging Canoe died in 1792, his following slowly broke up.

Drew, John

John Drew participated in the battle of Claremore Mound in 1818. Later he was a business partner of Sam Houston. He was captain of the last group of Cherokees to leave the old country and make the trek over the infamous Trail of Tears to what is now Oklahoma. They started the trip on December 5, 1838, and finished it on March 18, 1839. He was a member of the Cherokee National Council in 1839 and 1843 and a captain of the Lighthorse in 1841. In 1845, he married Charlotte Scales. In 1860, with threats of Civil War, he raised a company of home guards for the protection of Webbers Falls, his hometown in the Cherokee Nation. After Chief John Ross reluctantly signed a treaty with the Confederacy, Drew raised a regiment of Confederate soldiers, but at the battle of Pea Ridge most of his regiment switched sides. Drew afterward enlisted in the Union army. W. Craig Gaines writes, "Drew became a soldier without a command, not trusted by either side. . . . On August 25, 1865, Colonel John Drew died a very poor and a very sad man in a land ravaged by war."

Driver, Myrtle

Myrtle Driver, a member of the Deer Clan, grew up in the traditional community of Big Cove on the Cherokee reservation in North Carolina. She studied musicology at the University of Chicago Field Museum and research methods at the university's Newberry Library. While there, she taught arts and crafts and language at Little Big Horn Indian High School and at Owaya way Indian Way School in Chicago. In 1976, she was involved in First Americans, Inc., a dance group that participated in bicentennial ceremonies from Philadelphia to Florida. She held an internship in Native American history at the Smithsonian Institution. She is currently cultural traditionalist for the Eastern Band of Cherokee Indians as well as clerk and interpreter for the Eastern Band's Tribal Council.

Drywater, Lorene

Lorene Drywater was born in Sequoyah County, Oklahoma, but moved to near Tahlequah more than forty years ago. She has made beadwork, but gave up this craft some years ago. She also makes "tear dresses," but is best known for her unique buffalo grass dolls. She began making these dolls at the age of five, learning from her mother and her grandmother. She begins by harvesting the buffalo grass in May. Lorene is the only person known to make the buffalo grass dolls. She was featured in a 1995 article in *National Geographic* magazine. She has been named a Cherokee National Living Treasure, and in 2000 she received the Cherokee Medal of Honor.

Dugan, Joyce Conseen

Joyce Dugan grew up around Cherokee, North Carolina, and was edu-cated in local schools. She graduated cum laude from Western Carolina University at Cullowhee with bachelor's and master's degrees in educa-tion. Beginning as an aide, she spent twenty-five years with the Cherokee school system, leaving only after she served as director of the Qualla Boundary Education Program. In 1994, she was named North Carolina's Most Distinguished Woman in Education. She was married to Jerry

Dugan, and they had three children. She ran for the office of chief of the Eastern Band of Cherokees on a platform of cleaning house. With 72 percent of eligible voters turning out, she won the election handily. Then with Chief Jonathan L. Taylor already defeated, the Tribal Council impeached him and put him out of office, so Dugan began her term as chief a few days early. She was the first and so far the only female chief of the Eastern Band, serving from 1995 to 1999. She is currently on the management staff of Cherokee Harrah's Casino and continues to serve on various boards.

Dutch, Captain

When the artist George Catlin met the Cherokee named Captain Dutch at Fort Gibson in what is now Oklahoma in 1834, he wrote of him, "I promise you that the life of this man furnishes the best materials for a popular tale, that are now to be procured on the Western frontier." Dutch (or Tahchee) had migrated west as a child to Missouri and then to Arkansas with his mother and uncle, and when he was a young man, he married an Osage woman. In 1817, she was killed by her own people, we do not know why, but thereafter Dutch became a thoroughgoing Osage hater and a leader in the long and bloody war between the Western Cherokees and the Osages in the first thirty years of the nineteenth century. When his ally Degadoga moved down into Texas, Dutch soon followed, establishing towns along the south side of the Red River. He continued raids on the Osages from there. He was declared an outlaw by the Western Cherokees, but when the Cherokee-Osage peace was finally established in 1832, the charge of being an outlaw was dropped, and Dutch was persuaded to move back to the Cherokee Nation. The Removal had already taken place, and the Cherokee Nation was established in its new home, now northeast Oklahoma. Dutch settled near Texanna. The creek by which he built his home was called Dutch's Creek. (Oklahomans don't remember their history too well, so it's now called "Duchess Creek.") In 1834, he served as captain of scouts for the Dodge Expedition, which rode out of Fort Gibson to meet with Comanche and other western Indians. One of his assistant scouts was Jesse Chisholm. When Dutch died in 1848, he was serving as a member of the Cherokee National Council from his district.

E.

Eastern Band of Cherokee Indians

During the forced removal of Cherokees to the West in 1838, a small band of about a thousand Cherokees managed to avoid the roundup by hiding in the mountains of North Carolina. Some had become citizens of North Carolina. In addition, they were living on marginal land not desired by whites. Yonaguska was said to be their leader. Over the years, usually with the help of William Holland Thomas, a white man who was the adopted son of Yonaguska, they gradually purchased the land on which they lived. Yonaguska died in 1839, and Will Thomas was recognized as their leader. Some sources even go so far as to say that Thomas was their chief. In 1848, these postremoval eastern Cherokees were described as being almost wholly ignorant of English, but industrious, moral, sober, and orderly. In 1861, Thomas recruited four companies of Cherokees into the Thomas Legion to fight for the Confederacy. (See "Thomas Legion.") (In contrast, about only thirty Eastern Band Cherokees fought for the Union.) In 1866, Thomas's health began to fail, and in 1868 the Eastern Cherokees met in general council to draw up a constitution, under which the chief was to be elected to serve a term of two years. The new constitution took effect in 1870. In 1875, the chief's term was extended to five years, but later was reduced to four years, at which it remains today.

Tourism has been a major industry for the Eastern Band since the late 1920s, and the opening of Harrah's Cherokee Casino has been a tremendous economic benefit to all the tribe. The chiefs of the Eastern Band to date are:

Yonaguska, 1838–39
Salonita (Flying Squirrel), 1870–75
Lloyd Welch, 1875–80
Nimrod Jarrett Smith, 1880–91
Stillwell Saunooke, 1891–95

Andy Standing Deer, 1895–99
Jesse Reed, 1899–1903
Bird Salonita, 1903–7
John Goins Welch, 1907–11
Joe Saunooke, 1911–15
David Blythe, 1915–19
Joe Saunooke, 1919–23
Sampson Owl, 1923–27
John Tahquette, 1927–31
Jarrett Blythe, 1931–47
Henry Bradley, 1947–51
Osley Bird Saunooke, 1951–55
Jarrett Blythe, 1955–59
Osley Bird Saunooke, 1959–63
Jarrett Blythe, 1963–67
Walter S. Jackson, 1967–71
Noah Powell, 1971–73
John A. Crowe, 1973–83
Robert S. Youngdeer, 1983–87
Jonathan L. Taylor, 1987–95
Joyce Dugan, 1995–99
Leon Jones, 1999–2003
Michell Hicks, 2003–present

For more information on the chiefs, see their individual listings.

Echota

In the earliest days, Echota (Itsodi, also called Chota), a sacred peace town, was considered the capital of the Cherokee Nation. It was located in what is now the state of Tennessee, on the south bank of the Little Tennessee River, a few miles north of the Tellico River. In 1768, at a peace delegation, Ogan'sto' said, "We come from Chotte . . . where the house of peace is erected." In 1780, Echota was destroyed by John Sevier, the self-proclaimed president of the short-lived state of Franklin. It was rebuilt, and in 1786 Chota was a watchword Cherokees used to identify themselves to Americans as Cherokees and not Creeks or other "hostile" Indians. By 1800, white settlers had pushed so far into Cherokee country that the capital was moved to Ustanali. The site of Echota was flooded by the Tennessee Valley Authority's Tellico Dam Project in 1977.

Robert J. Conley

Elliott, J. C.

Jerry Chris Elliott was born in Oklahoma City in 1943 and is a graduate of the University of Oklahoma with a degree in physics. He went to work after graduate school for the Man in Space Program as a flight controller. In 1966, at twenty-three years old, he worked on the Gemini mission and was one of only two American Indians working in the space program. He helped with the first unmanned Apollo flight to the moon, the first human orbit of the moon, and the historic first moon landing in 1969. He was a young NASA retrofire engineer when the *Apollo 13* space module developed problems. Elliott worked four days without sleep to get the flight and crew safely back to earth. For that job, he received the nation's highest honor, the Presidential Medal of Freedom, from President Richard Nixon. Elliott is one of the founders of the American Indian Science and Engineering Society, and he serves as editor of NASA's in-house newsletter *Space Shuttle News*. In addition to all of that, he plays guitar and Indian flute under the name J. C. Higheagle. He has performed with the National Symphony Orchestra in Washington, D.C., and on the *Walker, Texas Ranger* television show. He played himself in the ABC movie *Houston, We've Got a Problem*. He has also received several awards for his poetry. He is recipient of the Daughters of the American Revolution's National Medal of Honor, the Southern California Motion Picture Council's Bronze Halo Award, and the Cherokee Honor Society's Cherokee Medal of Honor.

Etowah

Near the present site of Rome, Georgia, Etowah was an ancient Cherokee town. In 1793, John Sevier burned the town and killed three hundred beeves, leaving their carcasses to rot on the ground. Etowah is today an important archeological site.

Evans, Ernest Edwin

Ernest Evans, three-quarters Cherokee, was born in Pawnee, Oklahoma, in 1908. He graduated from Muskogee High School in 1926 and from the U.S. Naval Academy in 1931. During World War II, he served as commander of the USS *Johnston*, a destroyer. Evans and the *Johnston* played an important part in the battle of Leyte in the Philippines on October 25, 1944. The Japanese were attempting to destroy the U.S. invasion fleet, so the *Johnston* and other destroyers formed a protective barrier around U.S. carriers. Following a three-hour battle in which most of the U.S. carriers were saved, Evans was seriously wounded and his ship badly damaged, so Evans gave the order to abandon ship. He and ninety-one other men disappeared in the waters. He was posthumously awarded the Medal of Honor. His citation reads, "Seriously wounded early in the engagement, Cmdr. Evans, by his indomitable courage and brilliant professional skill, aided materially in turning back the enemy during a critical phase of the action. His valiant fighting spirit throughout this historic battle will venture as an inspiration to all who served with him."

Evans, Max

Max Allen Evans was born in Ropes (Ropesville), Texas, on August 29, 1924, to W. B. Evans and Hazel Swafford Evans. Hazel was part Choctaw, part Osage, and part Cherokee. Her mother, known as both Birdie and Little Bird, was a Cherokee medicine woman and a great influence on Max. It has been Evans's policy, however, never to use his Indian heritage to his advantage professionally because he has not wanted to "be tempted to become a goddamned professional Indian." Evans's early life was spent as a working cowboy on cattle ranches in western Texas and eastern New Mexico. He eventually bought his own ranch, married, and had a daughter. That life was interrupted, though, by service in the U.S. Army during World War II. Evans took part in the Normandy invasion, where he received a severe concussion from a five-hundred-pound shell exploding at close range.

Max Evans (left) with Robert J. Conley, 1993. Photo by Evelyn Conley.

Evans returned from the war to resume his old life as a cattle rancher, but the big ranchers were trying to push the little ones out of business, and Evans, for whatever reasons, had come home with an ambition to paint. He and his wife were not getting along, either. They sold the ranch and moved to Des Moines, New Mexico. Evans painted and tried to sell his paintings, but with no luck. In 1950, he published his first story, "The Killer

on the Carrumpah," in the *Denver Post*. When his wife finally left him, he moved to Taos, New Mexico.

In Taos, Evans met Indian artist Woody Crumbo. He studied painting with Crumbo, and to this day still refers to him as "my mentor." He also met and married Pat James. Evans and Crumbo went into mining together, got rich, and went broke. Then Evans wrote the novella *The Rounders*, which was eventually turned into a motion picture starring Glen Ford and Henry Fonda. After that, he met and worked with director Sam Peckinpah. The two of them tried unsuccessfully to get some of Evans's stories filmed, and Evans worked as a script doctor, fixing up screenplays for money but no credit. He played one small part in a Peckinpah film, *The Ballad of Cable Hogue* (1970).

Although Evans engaged in many other activities over the years, he has been first and foremost a writer since the publication of *The Rounders*. His many works include *The Hi Lo Country*; *The Great Wedding*; *Orange County Cowboys*; *The One-Eyed Sky*; *My Pardner*; *The Mountain of Gold*; *Shadow of Thunder*; *Xavier's Folly*; *Bobby Jack Smith You Dirty Coward*; *The White Shadow*; the monumental *Bluefeather Fellini* and *Bluefeather Fellini in the Sacred Realm*; *Faraway Blue*; and *Madame Millie: Bordellos from Silver City to Ketchikan*.

The Hi Lo Country, a story that Peckinpah had wanted to film, was finally filmed in 1998, starring Woody Harrelson.

Some of Evans's many honors include the 1999 Max Evans Day in the state of New Mexico; the 1998 Golden Chili Award for Lifetime Achievement in Cinema, given by the Taos Talking Pictures Festival; the 1998 Founder Award from the National Cowboy Symposium; the 1995 National Cowboy Hall of Fame Wrangler Award for *Bluefeather Fellini in the Sacred Realm*; the 1993 Cowboy Culture Award for Lifetime Achievement from the National Cowboy Symposium; the 1993 (New Mexico) Governor's Award for Lifetime Achievement in the Arts; the 1990 Saddleman Award for lifetime achievement from Western Writers of America; the 1988 Spur Award from Western Writers of America for *Orange County Cowboys*; and the 1984 National Cowboy Hall of Fame Wrangler Award for "Showdown at Hollywood Park."

Evans is currently writing and living in Albuquerque, New Mexico, with his wife, Pat.

F.

Fields, Richard

Richard Fields was chief of the Texas Cherokees from 1821 until his death in 1827. Assisted by Bowles and others, he spent much time in Mexico City, first with the Spanish government and later with the government of Mexico, trying to acquire a clear title to the Cherokees' land in Texas. The tribe also had to contend with rumors started by white Texans regarding their intended alliances with Comanches, Tawakonis, and other tribes to attack San Antonio.

In 1825, Chief Fields came under the influence of a newly arrived white man, John Dunn Hunter. At first, Hunter convinced Fields to let him travel to Mexico City to try to acquire title for the Cherokee lands. Hunter returned unsuccessful and told Fields that the authorities in Mexico City claimed that they had never heard of Fields. Hunter also told the Cherokees that they were in a dangerous position without title to their land. The Cherokees were ready to go to war, but Hunter asked them to wait while he made a trip to Nacogdoches in eastern Texas to talk with Hayden Edwards. They agreed.

Hayden Edwards and his brother Benjamin were white settlers in Mexico with a number of grievances against the Mexican government. Hunter convinced them to ally themselves with the Indians and go to war against Mexico. Then he returned to the Cherokee towns to report his progress. In the meantime, rumors spread about Hunter and the Cherokees: they were in league with the British, or they were about to attack Stephen Austin and his colonists.

Hayden Edwards then claimed to have a grant from Mexico to settle eight hundred families on land around Nacogdoches. He issued an order for everyone already in residence to appear before him and present their titles to land for his approval. Many of the settlers, including Bowles, were angered by this order. In 1826, the contract for the land was cancelled, and the Edwards brothers were ordered to leave the country. Hayden Edwards, however, believed that he could enlist the Cherokees and the United States to aid him in a rebellion against Mexico. John Dunn Hunter brought Chief Fields to Nacogdoches to see Edwards, and together they signed a compact agreeing to fight a war of independence. Edwards called his proposed new republic Fredonia.

Bowles and Big Mush refused to join the scheme. An army made up of the Mexican army and Austin's colonists marched on Nacogdoches. The Edwards brothers were holed up there while Hunter and Chief Fields were out in the Cherokee settlements trying to get some warriors to join them in the rebellion. Things looked pretty hopeless, and the Edwards brothers fled for Louisiana. The rebellion was over without a shot being fired.

Hunter and Fields had split up, with Hunter heading back toward Nacogdoches, not knowing, of course, that the Edwards brothers had fled from there. Hunter was accompanied by two Indians. When he stopped to water his horse in a stream, he was shot and killed. Fields, discovered in a different location, was also shot and killed. No one ever knew who did the deed, but it was assumed that Bowles at least had ordered it done. The year was 1827.

Five Hole, see "Marbles"

Foreman, James

Although there is no proof that Chief John Ross ever ordered any executions, it is believed by some that James Foreman was his "personal assassin." In 1834, at a meeting of the Cherokee National Council at Red Clay, Tennessee, John Ross gave his reasons for opposing the U.S. government's removal policy. The speech was followed by heated arguments on both sides, with some threats being made. When John Walker Jr., who was in opposition to Ross, left the meeting to go home, he was followed by James Foreman, who shot him in the back along the road. Accounts say that Walker saw Foreman before he died. Following the Removal, Major Ridge, John Ridge, and Elias Boudinot were killed for having signed the Removal Treaty (the Treaty of New Echota) even without the authority to do so. Major Ridge was shot from ambush, much as Walker had been. When Stand Watie saw the body of his brother, Elias Boudinot, he said, "I will give ten thousand dollars for the names of the men who did this."

Watie later met James Foreman at an inn in Arkansas, and a fight followed in which Watie killed Foreman.

Foreman, Stephen

Stephen Foreman was born on October 22, 1807. He attended the Candy Creek Mission School in Tennessee, studied under Reverend Samuel Worcester at New Echota in Georgia, and from there went to the Union Theology Seminary in Virginia. In 1831, he enrolled in Princeton Theological Seminary, completing the course in two years. Back home in Tennessee, he became a licensed minister of the Union Presbytery. He married Sarah Riley in 1834 and built a home near the Candy Creek Mission. For the next few years, he preached and taught at various places around the Cherokee Nation. From 1835 to 1838, Cherokee politics dominated the scene. Foreman's family were mostly followers of Chief John Ross, and E. Raymond Evans claims that James Foreman, one of Stephen's nephews, "was even regarded as being John Ross's principal assassin." In June 1838, Reverend Stephen Foreman was arrested and placed in Camp Hetzel in North Carolina with other Cherokee detainees. While there, he continued his work, doing what he could to help the others. When Chief Ross at last contracted with the U.S. government to allow the Cherokees themselves to conduct the Removal, he placed Reverend Foreman in charge of one of the removal detachments, which began the trek on October 20, 1838, with 983 people. It was one of the detachments that was forced to wait in southern Illinois for the frozen Mississippi to thaw. While trapped there, Mrs. Foreman gave birth to her third child. They finally arrived at their destination on February 27, 1839. Along the way, fifty-seven had died. Reverend Foreman built his house at Park Hill in the new Cherokee Nation (in present-day Oklahoma) near Reverend Worcester, who was already there. He worked with Worcester on translations of the New Testament into Cherokee until Worcester's death in 1859. His wife bore him seven more children. During this time, Foreman also took part in civic affairs. He was court clerk, judge of the Cherokee Supreme Court, and executive councilor and interpreter for the Cherokee National Council. In 1848, he was appointed superintendent of schools for the Cherokee Nation. He lost his oldest son in a hunting accident. His oldest daughter became ill with consumption and was taken to Texas by her mother. Both mother and daughter died in Texas. When the Civil War started, Foreman took his five younger children into Arkansas and later down into Texas. He lost two more children in Texas. Returning to the

Cherokee Nation after the war, he repaired a large frame house, turning it into a church, which he opened and preached at for years after. In 1873, at sixty-five years old, Foreman remarried and had four more children. He died in 1881.

Freedmen, Cherokee

Cherokees became buyers and sellers of black slaves early in the history of Cherokee-white relations. During the time when mixed-blood families were flourishing in Cherokee country and white influence was growing, many Cherokees became plantation owners, and part of that role was owning slaves. By the time of the Removal in 1838, there were hundreds of black slaves in the Cherokee Nation, and they went west over the Trail of Tears with their owners. During the Civil War, the Cherokee National Council voted to free the slaves. After the war, the Treaty of 1866, ignoring what the council had already done, called for the Cherokee Nation to free its slaves. It also called for the former slaves, now called freedmen, to have all the rights of citizenship in the Cherokee Nation. The freedmen never enjoyed those rights and privileges, however. Commissions met to study the problem. Lawyers were hired. Cases went to court. Complaints were made and usually ignored. All this activity seemed to stop with Oklahoma statehood in 1907, but in the revitalization of the Cherokee Nation beginning in 1971 the issue of the freedmen resurfaced. It was intensified in 1983, when Cherokee citizenship was restricted to those with a Cherokee, Shawnee, or Delaware ancestor on the Dawes Roll. The issue was taken to the Cherokee Nation Supreme Court, which ruled that the freedmen had Cherokee citizenship rights. But then in 2007 Cherokee voters amended the Cherokee Constitution to restrict Cherokee citizenship once again to those with Cherokee (or Shawnee or Delaware) blood. The freedmen descendants, with their lawyers, have the case in court again, and the issue is far from resolved.

Frye, Ed M.

Ed M. Frye was a Republican member of the Oklahoma State Senate. He was from Sallisaw and was a longtime unsuccessful candidate for the superintendency of the Five Tribes Agency (Angie Debo refers to him as a "perennial candidate" for that office). In 1921, he was supported in that effort by seventeen of nineteen Republican state senators. An Oklahoma state senator during the incredible period of graft and corruption that stole so much Indian land, Frye authored a bill limiting the amount of a "guardian's" compensation to $50 per month. These so-called guardians had been stealing hundreds and even thousands of dollars per month from minor Indian landowners. The Frye bill also curtailed other illegal and questionable practices of the time in regards to Indian land rights. Frye served as appointed principal chief of the Cherokee Nation for one day, June 23, 1923.

G.

Gatayusti

This game is better known by what James Mooney calls "a corruption of its Creek name," Chunkey. According to the myth of Untsaiyi, or Brass, Brass was the inventor of the game and was passionate about playing it. The game was played over a square piece of ground, cleaned and covered with smooth sand. There are either one player or two players on each side. Each player is armed with a smooth pole about eight feet long and tapered at each end. The players run at the field together, one player hurling a disc-shaped stone so that it rolls. Each player then hurls his pole, guessing about when the stone will stop rolling. The object is to have the end of the pole touching the stone or coming close to it. Players wagered almost everything they had on the outcome of the game. According to Adair, "All the American Indians are much addicted to this game."

Ghigau

Ghigau is the garbled English spelling of the word for a woman in a position of honor and some political power among the Cherokees up until at least the late 1700s. Most probably it should be *giga hyuh* or *giga* (red) and *agehyuh* (woman). It is often translated "War Woman," "Pretty Woman," or "Beloved Woman." This woman had the power to rescue prisoners of war. Beyond that, nothing is known of her specific powers, nor is it clear if War Woman, Red Woman, Pretty Woman, and Beloved Woman are different positions or different translations of the same position. Nancy Ward was the last woman known to be called Ghigau in the late eighteenth and early nineteenth centuries. (See "Ward, Nancy.")

Gist, George, see "Sequoyah"

Glancy, Diane

Diane Glancy is a professor of English at Macalester College in St. Paul, Minnesota, where she teaches Native American literature and creative writing. She received her master of fine arts degree from the University of Iowa. She was the 1998 Edlestein-Keller Minnesota Writer of Distinction at the University of Minnesota. Her novel *Pushing the Bear: A Novel of the Trail of Tears* was published by Harcourt Brace in 1996. Other Glancy books include *The Man Who Heard the Land; The Mask Maker; Designs of the Night Sky; Flutie; The Voice That Was in Travel; Monkey Secret; Firesticks;* and *Trigger Dance.* She has received the Charles Nilon Fiction Award, the 1991 Native American Prose Award, and a 1993 American Book Award.

Glass

Glass was one of the followers of Dragging Canoe in separating from the Cherokee Nation during the American Revolution and fighting on the British side. Later, when Glass went with sixty men to Muscle Shoals, Alabama, in 1791, where a party of whites had illegally set up a blockhouse, he quietly informed them that if they did not leave, he would kill them. The white men packed up and left in their boats, and Glass burned the blockhouse. In 1794, following the death of Dragging Canoe, he joined Bloody Fellow in speaking for peace. In 1816, he was bribed by Andrew Jackson to sign a treaty giving up Cherokee land. After signing another treaty soon after, for which he also accepted bribes, Glass went to Arkansas.

Glass, Bill, Jr.

Bill Glass Jr. lives and works east of Locust Grove, Oklahoma. His interest in ceramics began in 1973 while he was attending Central State University in Edmond, Oklahoma. He thereafter studied sculpture under Allen Houser at the Institute of American Indian Arts in Santa Fe, New Mexico. He worked as arts and crafts director for the Cherokee Nation for three years. He has researched Southeastern Woodland designs for use in his own work. He uses natural clay from Georgia, a potter's wheel, an extruder, and an electric kiln. He has been working as a full-time artist since 1977. Glass has been designated a Master Artist by the Five Civilized Tribes Museum in Muskogee, Oklahoma, and in 1999 he received the Cherokee Medal of Honor. In 2003, he was chosen as the head of "Team Gadugi" (Working Together)—consisting of Glass, his son Demos, Kenneth Foster, Gary Allen, Wade Bennett, and Robby McMurtry—to plan, design, and

Robert J. Conley

create art for Chattanooga's Tennessee Riverpark Master Plan. The Passage is the connecting link between the river and the city. It was dedicated May 13 and 14 with ceremonies that included presentations by the mayor of Chattanooga, the chief of the Cherokee Nation, and the chief of the Eastern Band of Cherokees. Also in attendance was the chief of the United Keetoowah Band of Cherokee Indians. Cherokee actor Wes Studi was on hand to address the crowd. The monumental collection of artwork produced by the team celebrates Cherokee culture and history. It is located at the former site of Ross's Landing on the Tennessee River.

Glory, William

William Glory, a Baptist preacher, was originally appointed by the Keetoowah Council of the United Keetoowah Band of Cherokee Indians in Oklahoma to serve out the remainder of Chief Jim Pickup's term upon the latter's death in 1967. Glory was both fluent and literate in Cherokee and English. An election was then called, and Glory was elected to the office. However, the election results were challenged by the opposing candidate, Reverend Sam Chaudoin. Glory remained chief, but a dissatisfied faction was created.

The factionalism was intensified when Glory, who had been getting along well with the Cherokee Nation's principal chief W. W. Keeler, was suddenly ejected from his office space at the Cherokee Nation headquarters. The situation worsened when the time came for United Keetoowah Band elections, but the elections were not called or held. In 1978, under pressure from the Bureau of Indian Affairs, an election was at last scheduled, and Jim Gordon was elected chief of the United Keetoowah Band.

Goingsnake

Goingsnake fought under General Andrew Jackson during the Creek War in 1813–14. When the U.S. Army first moved Cherokees out on the Trail of Tears, the results were so disastrous, with many deaths occurring, that Goingsnake and others petitioned General Winfield Scott to delay further detachments until the sickly season passed. Scott agreed, and Chief John Ross later contracted with the U.S. government to have Cherokees finish the job for themselves. Goingsnake left with the first detachment to be led by a Cherokee. "I glanced along the line," wrote William Shorey Coodey, "and the form of Goingsnake, an aged and respected chief whose head eighty winters had whitened, mounted on his favorite pony passed before me and led the way in advance, followed by a number of young men on horseback. At this very moment a low sound of distant thunder fell on my ear. In almost an exact western direction a dark spiral cloud was rising above the horizon and sent forth a murmur I almost fancied a voice of divine indignation for the wrongs of my poor and unhappy countrymen, driven by *brutal* power from all they loved and cherished in the land of their fathers, to gratify the cravings of avarice."

As speaker of the Cherokee National Council, Goingsnake signed the Act of Union between the Cherokee Nation and the Western Cherokees on July 12, 1839. When the new Cherokee Nation was divided into eight districts, one of them, Goingsnake District, was named for him. Tahlequah, Oklahoma, also has a Goingsnake Street.

Gold in Cherokee History

There is archeological evidence of Spanish gold mining in Cherokee country in the Southeast in the early days, but there is no historical (written) evidence. The first time gold plays a significant role in Cherokee history is in 1828, when gold was discovered on Cherokee land near Dahlonega and Dalton, Georgia. Whites in Georgia had already been clambering for Cherokee removal, and the newly discovered gold fields simply made the Georgians that much more anxious to achieve this goal. When the infamous Georgia anti-Cherokee laws were passed, one of them forbade Cherokees to dig for gold on their own land.

Around 1849, many Cherokees went to the California gold fields with other forty-niners. Among them were John Rollin Ridge, Dennis Wolf Bushyhead and his brother Ned, Stand Watie's brother David, Sam Mayes (the father of Joel Bryan Mayes and Sam Houston Mayes), and John Ross's business partner Return J. Meigs. Many of these gold seekers returned to the Cherokee Nation (Dennis Bushyhead eventually became chief), but others such as Ridge and Ned Bushyhead remained in California for the rest of their lives. (See "Bushyhead, Ned" and "Ridge, John Rollin.")

Goldsby, Crawford

Better known as Cherokee Bill, Crawford Goldsby was Cherokee, Sioux, Mexican, black, and white. In 1894, when he was eighteen years old, he killed a thirty-five-year-old man following a quarrel and a fistfight. Cherokee Bill fled into the Creek Nation and joined up with Bill and Jim Cook, mixed-blood Cherokee outlaws. They got into a fight at Effie Crittenden's Halfway House with a posse led by Sheriff Ellis Rattlinggourd. Jim Cook was shot seven times, and Sequoyah Houston, one of the posse, was killed. Following numerous robberies and killings, all detailed in S. W. Harman's *Hell on the Border*, Cherokee Bill was betrayed and captured by two of his friends. Incarcerated at Fort Smith, Arkansas, he was tried and sentenced to hang. He somehow obtained a pistol, killed a guard, and was shooting up the prison when Henry Starr, another prisoner, talked him out of the gun. He was hanged on March 26, 1896, at only twenty years of age.

Gordon, James L.

James L. Gordon was the son of a full-blood Cherokee mother and a one-quarter Cherokee father. After finishing high school, he attended American University and took courses in business administration. He thereafter worked as chief auditor for the National Labor Relations Board and the Air Force Defense Department. During World War II, he served in the Pacific. He also served in the Korean War. He was later chief financial manager for the Indian Health Service in the Department of Health, Education, and Welfare in Oklahoma City. He then became chief executive officer and hospital administrative specialist for the department in Oklahoma City. He retired in 1973. Six years later he was elected chief of the United Keetoowah Band of Cherokee Indians in Oklahoma.

Chief Gordon's job was not an easy one. He took over a band that was practically in shambles. Under his leadership, the United Keetoowah Band applied for a grant under the Indian Self-Determination Act. A housing authority was established. The Bureau of Indian Affairs recognized the rights of the Keetoowah Band, but Chief Ross O. Swimmer of the Cherokee Nation filed a lawsuit against the bureau, and it changed its mind. During most of his administration, Chief Gordon was busy reacting to the bureau's position. In the end, he managed to get it to recognize the legitimacy of the Keetoowah Band, but he was unable to secure any funding. The bureau insisted that the Keetoowah roll be totally separated from that of the Cherokee Nation. Because of declining health, Chief Gordon chose not to run for reelection in 1983.

Graves, Thomas

Thomas Graves, a white man who spoke Cherokee as well as English, lived with the Western Cherokees in Arkansas, where he was much involved in their war with the Osages in the early nineteenth century. He was married to a Cherokee woman and had two Cherokee children. He was adopted by the council of the Western Cherokee Nation. In warfare, he was said to be more "savage" than any Indian. When Captain Dutch led the raid on the Osage-friendly Pryor's Post, it was Graves who broke in the heavy front door of the trading post to gain entry. Following a successful Cherokee raid on an Osage camp in which the Cherokees, led by Tom Graves, killed a number of men and took women and children captive, white missionaries told the U.S. Army that Graves had gotten drunk, killed an Osage woman and her child, and thrown the bodies to the hogs. Graves was arrested for murder and held for trial at Little Rock, Arkansas. The federal court found that it had no jurisdiction, and Graves was set free. In 1828, Graves went with a delegation of Western Cherokees that included Sequoyah to Washington, D.C., to protest the organization of Lovely County by the territorial government of Arkansas as an encroachment on their lands. They were told not to give away any land. The Cherokees finally agreed to move out of Arkansas and onto the land known as Lovely's Purchase in exchange for the government's getting the white people out of Lovely's Purchase. When the Cherokee delegates returned home, they found poles in their front yards and were told that the poles were for their heads. They somehow managed to avoid being executed. Tom Graves even received payment from the U.S. government for the time he spent in prison.

Green, Rayna

Rayna Green, of Cherokee descent, was born in Dallas, Texas, and raised in Texas and Oklahoma. She received bachelor's and master's degrees in 1963 and 1966 from Southern Methodist University and a Ph.D. in folklore and American studies from Indiana University in 1973. She is director of the American Indian Program for the National Museum of American History at the Smithsonian Institution in Washington, D.C. She has taught at the University of Arkansas, the University of Massachusetts, the University of Maryland, Yale University, George Washington University, and Dartmouth College. She has published scholarly articles in a number of journals, as well as poetry and fiction in many periodicals. She worked on the scripts of the films *More Than Bows and Arrows* (1996), narrated by N. Scott Momaday, and *We Are Here: 500 Years of Pueblo Resistance* (1992).

Gritts, Levi

Levi Gritts, a bilingual, full-blood Cherokee, was elected chief of the Nighthawk Keetoowahs following the death of Chief W. C. Rogers of the

Robert J. Conley

Cherokee Nation in 1917. The Nighthawks decided that the Cherokees, especially the full-bloods, needed a chief, and since the Cherokee Nation was no longer going to provide one—its chief being appointed by the U.S. government—they must do it. They did not call Gritts the chief of the Nighthawks. They called him chief of the Cherokees.

Grooms, Don

Don Grooms was born in 1930 on the Qualla Boundary (Cherokee reservation) in North Carolina. He taught in the College of Journalism and Communications at the University of Florida for thirty years, retiring in 1996, but it was as a songwriter and singer that he gained fame. For more than twenty-five years, he was a mainstay at the Florida Folk Festival at White Springs. In 1997, he won the Florida Folk Heritage Award. Before turning to folk festivals, Grooms played country music guitar and banjo at nightclubs. Some of his best-known songs are "Whippoorwill," "Tsali Died for Me," and "Walk Proud, My Son." Don Grooms died in 1998, two days before his sixty-eighth birthday.

Don Grooms, 1995. Author's collection.

Guess, George, see "Sequoyah"

Guess, Winnie

Winnie Guess, a Cherokee from Oklahoma, was a twelve-year-old ballet dancer when she saw Jack Anquoe, a Kiowa, and other students from Bacone College in Muskogee, Oklahoma, performing fancy dances. She convinced her mother to contact Anquoe, who responded that Winnie could not do the dances because they were for men only. But Winnie was determined and kept after Anquoe. When he at last relented, she learned the dances and had her own regalia made up, dressing like a man. She danced as a specialty performer at the Indian Exposition at Anadarko. She then danced with Anquoe and the Bacone dancers for tourists at Western Hills Lodge and at halftime at Bacone basketball and football games. Although she received some criticism for doing these dances because she was Cherokee, not from a plains tribe, and a woman, she persisted. She and the other dancers performed on *The Ed Sullivan Show* and the *Today Show* in New York. In 1957, she accompanied Chief W. W. Keeler to Sheridan, Wyoming, to represent the Cherokee Nation at the All Indian Days Festival. She graduated from college in 1958. Although Guess stopped performing the hoop dance and eagle dance at the age of forty-seven, she remains active as a competitive race walker and weight lifter. She has won gold and silver medals in the National Senior Olympic Games, has represented the United States in the World Masters Games in Melbourne, Australia, and in 2004 was honored as Oklahoma's Senior Olympian of the Year. She is married to Ron Perdue and lives in Muskogee.

Guhna-gadoga

Guhna-gadoga's name has suffered perhaps the worst indignities of any Cherokee name of this period. It has been spelled "Connecorte," "Connecote," "Kana Gatoga," "Kanagatoga," "Cunnicatoque," "Cunigatogae," "Canacockte," "Concauchto," "Conogotocke," and "Canackte." Also known as Standing Turkey and Old Hop, he was born around 1690, a brother of Ama-edohi. It is said that he was slightly disabled, the result of an injury suffered while he was a young man "on the warpath," and that his nickname "Old Hop" was given him by the British as a result of his limp. Upon the death of his nephew in 1753, a meeting was held at Charleston, South Carolina, with the influential Ada-gal'kala ("Attacullaculla") presiding for the Cherokees. There were two main items on the agenda: the Cherokees wanted lower trade prices, and they had to have a new "emperor" named. They got their way on both issues. The prices were lowered, and the man they wanted, Old Hop, was named to the post.

At this time, more Cherokees were dying as a result of European diseases than of any other cause. In addition to the horrible suffering and loss of life, this fact also signaled considerable social change. The medicine people were losing faith in themselves, and the people were turning away from them. In addition, because of the growing number of mixed-blood families of English traders, the traditional matrilineal Cherokee family was undergoing slow but significant changes. The white men insisted on being heads of household and giving their children their own surnames. And the situation between the French and English was heating up.

In 1754, the Virginia colony asked the Cherokees to raise a force to help them fight the French. The Cherokees were hesitant to fight the French, so Virginia suggested that they could attack the Shawnees, who were allied with the French. The Cherokees insisted that the English build forts in Cherokee country for the protection of the women and children while the men were off at war. When the Virginians completed their fort across the river from Echota in Tennessee in 1756, Ostenaco and Major Andrew Lewis left with a contingent of Cherokees to attack the Shawnees in Ohio. It was January, not the traditional time for Cherokees to go to war.

Along the way, one of the boats carrying supplies struck ice in the river and overturned. With their supplies lost, Major Lewis took his Englishmen and headed for home. The Cherokees were left on foot far from home and had to get back the best they could. Traveling through Virginia, they killed some stray horses for food. Virginians attacked them from ambush, killing twenty-four and scalping them. In retaliation, the Cherokees attacked settlers in the back country of Virginia and South Carolina. Governor William Lyttleton of South Carolina demanded that the Cherokees turn over to him for punishment a like number of Cherokees for the whites they had killed. A battalion of Highlanders under the command of Colonel Hugh Montgomery left Charleston to invade the Cherokee Lower Towns. They destroyed all the towns, drove the population into the mountains, killed sixty, and took forty prisoner. But when Montgomery attempted to invade the Middle Towns, he marched into a Cherokee ambush. He claimed a victory and retreated to Charleston.

The Cherokees, in the meantime, had laid siege to Fort Loudon, a British fort established near Echota in the Overhill towns in Tennessee. The commander, Captain Raymond Demere, eventually surrendered the fort. The conditions of surrender were that the guns and ammunition would be left for the Cherokees, and Demere and his men would be allowed both safe passage out of Cherokee country and enough guns and ammunition to hunt along the way. The agreement was struck, and the English left the fort. When the Cherokees went into the abandoned fort, they discovered that the English had dumped some weapons into the river and buried others, attempting to hide them from the Cherokees. The Cherokees then overtook the refugees and killed most of them. Old Hop was one of the signers of this agreement and had accompanied the refugees for a ways when they left the fort. Old Hop, at this time about seventy years old, died shortly afterward, leaving the Cherokee Nation in all this turmoil. He was succeeded in his office by his nephew Uka Ulah.

Gulager, Clu

Clu Gulager was born in Muskogee, Oklahoma, in 1928. His name "Clu" is from the Cherokee *tlu-tlu* (or *clu-clu*), the name of the bird known in English as a martin. Clu was born into a rodeo family related to the Will Rogers family. Rodeo announcer Clem McSpadden, a relative, talked about the days when Clu was a youngster, and the family would get together to ride and rope. McSpadden said, "We all thought something was wrong with Clu. He read books." Gulager did a stint in the U.S. Marine Corps and then studied acting at Baylor University under the renowned teacher and director Paul Baker. From there, he went to Paris, where he studied mime under Etienne de Croux, teacher of Marcel Marceau.

Clu Gulager as Billy the Kid in TV's *The Tall Man*, 1960–62. Courtesy of Clu Gulager.

Back in the United States, he returned to Baylor to work with actress Miriam Bird Nethery, who became his wife. In 1955, he went to New York City, where he performed in nearly every classic live TV show of the time: *Omnibus; Playhouse 90; Kraft Theater; U.S. Steel Hour; The Alfred Hitchcock Show; The Untouchables*, and others. He went to Hollywood for an appearance on *Have Gun Will Travel* and then won the costarring role of Billy the Kid on *The Tall Man* (1960–62). He was a regular on *The Virginian* for several years and starred in episodes of *Wagontrain*. He was also in several films: *The Killers* with Lee Marvin and Ronald Reagan; *The Last Picture Show; McQ; Nightmare on Elm Street Part II*; and *The Return of the Living Dead Part II*. For several years, Gulager ran an acting school in Los Angeles with the help of his wife, Miriam. After Miriam's death, he retired from acting. He lives in Los Angeles, where he is directing plays. His son John is a film director, and son Tom is a screenwriter.

Robert J. Conley

H.

Hager, Jean

Jean Hager is a Cherokee writer living in Tulsa, Oklahoma. She is best known for her two mystery series, the Mitch Bushyhead series and the Molly Bearpaw series. Some of her titles are *The Grandfather Medicine; Night Walker; Ghostland; The Fire Carrier; Masked Dancers; Ravenmocker; The Redbird's Cry; Seven Black Stones;* and *The Spirit Caller.* In 2000, she received a Cherokee Medal of Honor.

Hagerstrand, Colonel Martin

Martin Hagerstrand, a white man, served in the U.S. Army from 1934 to 1960. In the early 1940s in New Guinea, he met Marian Brown, a Cherokee Women's Army Corps officer. They were married soon after, and Martin became interested in the culture and history of his wife's people. After his retirement from the army, Martin and Marian moved to Marian's hometown, Tahlequah, Oklahoma. Martin became involved in helping to establish Northeastern State College's Tourism Management Program. Thereafter, he was hired by Chief W. W. Keeler to establish and operate the Cherokee Heritage Center. Martin became its director, producing the Trail of Tears drama and initiating the Trail of Tears Art Show. He was vice president of the Cherokee Historical Society, president of the Oklahoma Historical Society, executive director of the Five Civilized Tribes Museum and Center for Study of Indian Territory, chairman of the Oklahoma State Arts Council, founding president of the Oklahoma Arts Institute, and a member of the Mid-America Arts Alliance. He died in 1999.

Hail, Raven

Raven Hail was born in 1921 near Dewey, Oklahoma. A member of the Cherokee Nation, she attended both Oklahoma State University in Stillwater, Oklahoma, and Southern Methodist University in Dallas, Texas. She is the author of numerous books, including *The Pleiades Stones, The Raven Speaks,* and *Ravensong,* and she is listed in such reference works as *Native American Women, The Reference Encyclopedia of the American Indian, Encyclopedia of North American Indians,* and several others. She died in 2005 in Asheville, North Carolina.

Hair, John

John Hair was born in the Cherokee community of Kenwood in Oklahoma. His parents were divorced when he was young, and his mother raised him in the home of her parents. When he was ten years old, he was taken away from his home and placed in Sequoyah Indian Boarding School in Tahlequah, Oklahoma. He ran away from school several times, but was always caught and returned. He became a Golden Gloves boxer and a football player. At fifteen years old, he lied about his age and joined the National Guard. When the famous 45th Division was called into active service for the Korean War, Hair went with them. He stayed in the army until 1968. When he returned home, he became active with the United Keetoowah Band (UKB), serving on the council as deputy chief, and finally, in 1983, as chief.

As chief, John Hair stayed busy fighting for the full and proper recognition of the UKB, spending time in Washington, D.C., as well as at home. The Cherokee Nation, under the leadership of Chief Ross Swimmer, remained strongly opposed to any recognition of the UKB. The Bureau of Indian Affairs's intention seems to have been that it would serve UKB members only through the Cherokee Nation, but then in 1986 Ross Swimmer went to Washington, D.C., as head of the bureau.

Under Chief Hair, the UKB passed ordinances to establish smoke shops and a bingo operation. In 1990, twenty-two shops were licensed. Two months after they opened for business, they were raided by state officers and closed. When they reopened, they were raided again, this time by the Cherokee Nation. At the same time all this was going on, the UKB acquired land and buildings to establish its bingo operation and set up tribal offices. The bingo operation has continued successfully, but throughout his administration Chief Hair was constantly embroiled in battle with the Cherokee Nation. He chose not to run for reelection in 1990 and was replaced as chief by John Ross in 1991.

Robert J. Conley

Hair, Lucille

Lucille Hair lives in Briggs, Oklahoma, in the same house in which she was born. In 1949, Bill Ames, an instructor at Sequoyah High School just outside of Tahlequah, Oklahoma, gave her the chance to learn to weave textiles. She jumped at it and has been weaving blankets, rugs, and wall hangings ever since. A building that was moved from Camp Gruber to Briggs and renovated by students from Sequoyah High School became the headquarters for the Sequoyah Indian Weavers Association. Ames helped the weavers with marketing their work, and when he was transferred to Montana, Lucille worked hard at keeping the weavers together. Ten years ago it took her thirteen hours to complete one blanket, but now it takes a little longer. She has trained fifteen people as weavers, including her daughter and granddaughter. She has been named a Cherokee National Living Treasure and in 2002 was a recipient of the Cherokee Medal of Honor.

Hanging Maw

In 1793, invited by the U.S. president for a conference, Hanging Maw, a war chief, was with Tassel, the principal chief, and a number of other chiefs friendly to the Americans at Echota, the sacred peace town and capital of the Cherokee Nation in what is now Tennessee, when a party of men led by Captain John Beard attacked them without warning or provocation and killed fifteen Cherokees, including Hanging Maw's wife and Chief Tassel. Hanging Maw was wounded. Beard was later arrested, but the trial was a mockery, and he was released. In 1794, a white man named John Ish was shot and killed while plowing. Hanging Maw sent out a party of Cherokee who captured the killer, a Creek, and turned him over to the Americans, who tried him and hanged him. When a party of one hundred Creeks crossed into Tennessee a few days later, moving against the white settlements there, Hanging Maw sent out fifty-three Cherokees with a few federal troops, and they drove the Creeks back. In 1794, Hanging Maw was at the conference at Tellico Blockhouse in Tennessee with the remaining Chickamaugas and Americans that finally ended the Cherokee wars begun by Dragging Canoe in 1775.

Hard Mush, see "Big Mush"

Harris, Colonel Johnson

Colonel Johnson Harris was born in Georgia on April 19, 1856, one of eleven children. His father, William Harris, was a white man. His mother was Susan Collins, daughter of Nannie Cordrey. William Harris died the same year that C. J. was born. In 1868, C. J. and his mother moved to Indian Territory (present-day Oklahoma) and settled near Warner. He attended the Cherokee Male Seminary and later taught in several of the Cherokee Nation's schools. He married Nannie Fields, daughter of Richard Fields, in 1877. Upon her death, he married Mamie Elizabeth Adair, daughter of William Penn Adair, uncle of Will Rogers. She, too, preceded Harris in death, and he married once more, this time to a widow, Caroline Alice Collins. Harris became a well-established rancher.

Colonel Johnson Harris, c. 1892. Public domain. Courtesy of the Cherokee Honor Society.

In 1881, he was elected senator from Canadian District of the Cherokee Nation. He was president of the Cherokee Senate from 1883 to 1885. In 1889, he was a delegate to Washington, D.C. In August 1891, he was elected treasurer of the Cherokee Nation, but on December 23, following the death of Chief Joel B. Mayes and the brief tenure of Chief Thomas Mitchell Buffington, he was elected principal chief by the Cherokee National Council. By this time, white intruders into the Cherokee Nation far outnumbered the Cherokees. In 1893, President Grover Cleveland appointed the Dawes Commission to hold talks with the Five Civilized Tribes regarding allotment of their lands to individuals and eventual statehood. Much of Harris's time was devoted to these talks and to resisting the allotment process. News of the Dawes Commission's activities and intentions caused Chief Harris to call an international council of Indian tribes at Fort Gibson to outline a plan of action against the commission's propositions. In 1895, Harris chose not to run again for principal chief. He had established residence in Tahlequah, the capital of the Cherokee Nation, and he lived there for the rest of his life. He died at the age of sixty-five in 1921 and was buried in the Tahlequah City Cemetery.

Hart, Gene Leroy

Gene Hart, full-blood Cherokee, was accused of the heinous murder of three Girl Scouts near Locust Grove in 1977. A jail escapee, he was hunted for eleven months in what was then being called the largest manhunt in the history of the state of Oklahoma. He was captured at last and tried for the murders, but was found not guilty. However, he was sent to prison on a charge of jail breaking and died mysteriously while incarcerated.

Hastings, William Wirt

William Wirt Hastings was born in Arkansas on December 31, 1866. His father was Yell Hastings, and he was named for William Wirt, the attorney who had taken the Cherokee removal case to the U.S. Supreme Court before the Trail of Tears (*Cherokee Nation v. Georgia*). When W. W. was three years old, his family moved to the Delaware District of the transplanted Cherokee Nation in the West. He graduated from the Cherokee Male Seminary in 1884, where he had been a tennis champion. From there, he went to Vanderbilt University, graduating in 1889. He formed a law partnership with Elias Cornelius Boudinot and William P. Thompson. When Boudinot died, the Hastings and Thompson partnership continued.

In 1896, Hastings married Lula Starr, and they built a fine home in Tahlequah, the capital of the Cherokee Nation. He became attorney general for the Cherokee Nation and superintendent of education. He also represented the Cherokee Nation before the U.S. Court of Claims and the U.S. Supreme Court in matters concerning the "final rolls" (see "Dawes Rolls"), the allotment of lands, and other cases. He was a delegate to the Sequoyah Convention in 1905.

In 1914, Hastings was elected to the U.S. House of Representatives and served nine terms in all. He was instrumental in having Sequoyah and Will Rogers placed in Statuary Hall to represent Oklahoma, and his daughter, Anawake, unveiled the statue of Sequoyah in the official ceremonies in 1917. He introduced legislation to establish the Indian Hospital in Tahlequah, and it is named after him. He was a member of the U.S. House Indian Affairs Committee and Appropriations Committee. In office during the terrible time of tremendous loss of Indian land to the "grafters" in Oklahoma, Hastings fought hard for the protection of the rights of Indian landowners, particularly the full-bloods. He also fought against the implementation of the Indian Reorganization Act in Oklahoma in 1934, thereby paving the way for the passage of the Oklahoma Indian

General Welfare Act in 1936. He retired in 1934 and served his single day as chief on January 22, 1936. (See "Chief for a Day.") He was also president of the First National Bank in Tahlequah and was a member of its board of directors. He died April 8, 1938, at seventy-two years of age and was buried in Tahlequah.

Heape, Steven R.

Steven R. Heape, a citizen of the Cherokee Nation, was born on Easter Sunday morning, March 25, 1951, in Long Beach, California, the son of Doyle Andrew Heape and Faye Elizabeth Heape. He has one sister. His father retired from the Southern California Edison Company in 1987. Steve attended school in Garden Grove and Fullerton, California; graduated from Fullerton High School in 1969; and studied business administration at Fullerton Junior College. In 1977, he moved to Dallas, Texas.

In 1981, Heape produced *Location to Recovery*, one of the first educational docudramas to be released from sixteen-millimeter film to VHS tape. The film is still being used by several major oil and gas companies in their reference libraries.

In 1999, with business partner Chip Ritchie, Heape incorporated Rich-Heape Films, certified by the Cherokee Nation to preserve the history and culture of American Indians. Rich-Heape Films has become an internationally recognized firm with several award-winning titles to its credit. The American Indian Chamber of Commerce presented Rich-Heape with the American Indian Business of the Year Award in 1999 and 2003.

Heape was a 1993 inaugural inductee into the National Cowboys of Color Hall of Fame in Fort Worth, Texas. He was one of five Native American filmmakers invited to participate in the strategic film and video content planning for the Smithsonian's National Museum of the American Indian in Washington, D.C.

Heape is also president and founding member of the Sovereign Nations Preservation Project, Inc., a nonprofit organization that addresses the high levels of juvenile diabetes in the Native American community, and is involved in capturing and reviving the American Indian languages that are being lost daily.

In March 2006, Rich-Heape Films released the acclaimed documentary, *The Trail of Tears: Cherokee Legacy*. Previous film titles for the company include *Walela Live in Concert*; *Tales of Wonder I*; *Tales of Wonder II*; *Black Indians: An American Story*; *How to Trace Your Native American Heritage*; and *Native American Healing in the 21st Century*.

Robert J. Conley

Rich-Heape Films has been given the National Parenting Publications Award for Children's Resources, the Parents Guide Award of Excellence in Children's Media, the Cine Golden Eagle, the Telly Award (five times), the New York Film Festival Award, and the Heard Museum Film Festival Award.

Henson, Brooks

Brooks Henson, a full-blood Cherokee, is from Locust Grove, Oklahoma. During his childhood, his favorite activity was to hide away with a pencil and plenty of paper. He has been painting professionally since 1988, full-time since 1993. He has received the Special Merit Award from the Trail of Tears Art Show at the Cherokee National Museum and Best of Show at Tallasi Winter Festival.

Henson, Jim

Jim Henson was vice chief of the United Keetoowah Band of Cherokee Indians in 1995 and chief from 1998 until 2001.

Heth, Charlotte

Charlotte Heth was born in 1937 in Muskogee, Oklahoma. She received her bachelor's and master's degrees in music from the University of Tulsa and a Ph.D. in ethnomusicology from the University of California at Los Angeles (UCLA) in 1975. She has been a professor at UCLA since 1974. From 1976 to 1987, she was director of the American Indian Studies Center there. She has taught at Cornell University as a visiting professor; was president of the Society of Ethnomusicology; edited *Selected Reports in Ethnomusicology* in 1980; served as music consultant to the PBS series *Roanoak* in 1987; and was named assistant director of public programming at the Smithsonian Institution's National Museum of the American Indian in Washington, D.C., in 1994. She edited the museum's publication *Native American Dance* in 1992.

Hicks, Charles Renatus

Charles Hicks succeeded Pathkiller as principal chief of the Cherokee Nation in 1827, but he did not live long after that. He was one of the early converts to the Moravian Church and was baptized as "Renatus." From then on, he used that name as his middle name. When Sequoyah was trying to devise his Cherokee syllabary, he went to see Charles Hicks to ask him to write what his name would be in English because he wanted to develop a stamp to use on his silver work. Between them, they came up with the name "Guess," and Sequoyah used that on his stamp. Hicks served as an interpreter, and by 1822 he was second chief and treasurer of the Cherokee Nation.

Hicks, E. D.

E. D. Hicks first encountered a telephone in St. Louis, Missouri, when he was nineteen years old in 1869. Returning home to the Cherokee Nation, he went to see a telegrapher in a nearby town. Because National Council meetings took place in Tahlequah, the capital of the Cherokee Nation, but business was often conducted with the U.S. Indian Agency at Muskogee, and communication was slow between the two, Hicks decided that the Cherokee Nation needed a telephone. He gathered some friends and relatives as investors and went back to St. Louis to buy two telephones. He set up the two telephones in Tahlequah and had two old-timers talk to one another in Cherokee. Then he went to the National Council. The council members reluctant, fearing that the telephone would somehow encourage the railroad and outsiders to move into the Cherokee Nation, but they finally agreed to grant Hicks a permit to operate a business, with the restrictions that the lines had to be strung over rough land between Tahlequah and Muskogee and that no surveying instruments could be used. Hicks strung the wire from a hardware store in Tahlequah to another hardware store in Muskogee. The store owners were his business partners. His company slowly picked up more customers. In 1916, Southwestern Bell arrived, and Hicks sold out to them, becoming Southwestern Bell's manager for eastern Oklahoma. He had been in the telephone business for forty-eight years and had strung the first telephone line west of the Mississippi River.

Hicks, Michell

Michell Hicks is a resident of Painttown, North Carolina, and attends the Rock Springs Baptist Church. He graduated from Cherokee High School in Cherokee, North Carolina, in 1982. He is married to Marsha Ball, and they have three children. Hicks is a certified public accountant with degrees from Southwestern Community College and Western Carolina University. He is a member of the American Institute of CPAs, the Government

Robert J. Conley

Finance Officers Association, and the North Carolina Association of CPAs. He has been the finance officer for the Qualla Housing Authority and the executive director of budget and finance for the Eastern Band of Cherokee Indians, and since 1990 he has been associated with Mohoney Cohen & Company, the twenty-fifth largest accounting firm in the United States. He was elected principal chief of the Eastern Band in 2003.

Hicks, William

William Hicks was the mixed-blood son of Charles Hicks, second chief under Chief Pathkiller. William, like his father, was a Moravian. He was well taught, for the elder Hicks spoke English fluently, served as interpreter on several occasions, and kept his home supplied with good books. And in many ways Second Chief Charles Hicks played a major role in governing the Cherokee Nation while old Pathkiller was just a figurehead for a number of years.

The Cherokee National Council was involved in writing a new constitution when Pathkiller died in 1827. They resolved that a new chief would be elected under the new constitution as soon as it was finally approved. In the meantime, they appointed Charles Hicks, but he died only two weeks after Pathkiller, so they then chose William Hicks, son of their recently departed chief, as principal chief of the Cherokee Nation and young John Ross as second chief. The Whitepath Rebellion, begun while Pathkiller was still chief, died out quietly. (See "Whitepath.") The first election under the new constitution was held in August 1828. Whitepath ran for a council seat and won. William Hicks was principal chief for only a short term, from 1827 to 1828. He favored removal to the West, and when the new council met in October, they ratified the Constitution and elected John Ross as principal chief, George Lowrey as second chief, and Major Ridge and William Hicks as counselors to the chiefs.

In 1834, while Principal Chief John Ross was in Washington, D.C., arguing against removal, a group of disgruntled Cherokees gathered together with the intention of signing a removal treaty and "elected" William Hicks as principal chief. Nothing came of it.

Hitcher, John

Reverend John Hitcher, a full-blood Cherokee and member of the Wolf Clan, could read and write both English and Cherokee. He was elected chief of the United Keetoowah Band in 1939 before the federal recognition process had taken place. As chief, Hitcher worked for the rest of his term until 1946 to get federal recognition of the Band.

Hobson, Geary

Geary Hobson is a writer of Cherokee descent, born in Arkansas in 1941. He served in the U.S. Marine Corps during the Vietnam war. He received his bachelor's and master's degrees in English at Arizona State University and his Ph.D. in American studies at the University of New Mexico. He has taught at Arizona State University, the University of New Mexico, the University of Arkansas, Central Arkansas State University, and the University of Oklahoma, where he is presently in the English Department and is serving as project director of the Native Writers Circle of the Americas. He is also a member of the Wordcraft Circle of Native Writers and associate editor of literature for the *American Indian Quarterly*. Geary has published numerous poems, short stories, critical articles, and book reviews in a wide variety of periodicals, and he was, in fact, one of the first Native literary critics, if not the first. His books include *The Remembered Earth* (editor), *The Last of the Ofos*, and *The Rise of the White Shaman*.

Holland, Evelyn Stone

Evelyn Holland is the daughter of famous Cherokee wood carver Willard Stone and the sister of Jason Stone. Evelyn is known for her distinctive jewelry, Christmas decorations, and small sculptures made of pewter and silver. Much of her work is copies of her famous father's wood carvings. She lives and works just outside of Locust Grove, Oklahoma.

Hood, Robbie

Robbie Hood is a NASA atmospheric scientist and hurricane hunter at the National Space Science and Technology Center in Huntsville, Alabama. She is a descendant of Principal Chief John Ross of the Cherokee Nation. Hood joined NASA's Marshall Space Flight Center in 1987, where she served as lead mission scientist in NASA's Fourth Convection and Moisture Experiment, working toward the goal of improving hurricane predictions. She has an associate's degree in physics from Crowder College in Neosho, Missouri, a bachelor's in atmospheric science from the University of Missouri in Columbia, and a master's in physical meteorology from Florida State University in Tallahassee. In 2002, she was one of twelve women at NASA presented with the Women of Color Government and Technology Awards for contributions made by minority women in traditionally male-dominated fields.

Houston, Sam

Sam Houston, a white man, first lived with the Cherokees on the banks of the Hiwassee River in Tennessee. He lived with and was adopted by the family of John Jolly and learned to speak the Cherokee language. In 1814, he fought with the Cherokees in the battle of Horseshoe Bend under the command of General Andrew Jackson, later known to the Cherokees as "Chicken Snake." He then served as subagent to the Cherokees during the period when John Jolly and other Cherokees moved to Arkansas.

Following an almost meteoric political career culminating in the governorship of Tennessee, Houston resigned after a scandalous, abrupt end to his first marriage. He went back to the home of John Jolly, now with the Western Cherokees in Arkansas, in 1829. Houston was made a Cherokee citizen by an act of the Cherokee National Council, and the Western Cherokees made use of him on more than one occasion, sending him to Washington, D.C., as a delegate. The act reads as follows:

Resolved by the National Committee and Council in General Council Convened, That in consideration of his former acquaintance with and services rendered to the Cherokees and his present disposition to improve their condition and benefit their circumstances, and our confidence in his integrity and honor, if he should remain among us, we do solemnly, firmly and irrevocably grant to Samuel Houston forever all the rights, privileges, and immunities of a citizen of the Cherokee Nation.

Dated October 31, 1831, the act was signed by the National Committee's president and clerk and by the National Council's speaker and clerk, and it was approved by the Western Cherokees' chief John Jolly.

Houston dressed like a Cherokee and spoke Cherokee, even going so far as to speak to white people through an interpreter. He opened a trading post, which he called Wigwam Neosho, and married a Cherokee woman, Dianna Rogers. It has been said that while he was living with the Cherokees, he became known as "the Big Drunk," and one night in 1833, while drunk, he beat his adopted father, John Jolly. Waking up sober in the morning, he was so ashamed of what he had done that he packed up and left for Texas. In Texas, he started over once again, eventually becoming general of the Texas army, president of the Republic of Texas, and then governor of the state of Texas. He died in 1863. An excellent source on the years Houston spent with the Cherokees is *Sam Houston with the Cherokees: 1829–1833* by Jack Gregory and Rennard Strickland.

Houston, Sequoyah

Sequoyah Houston, a full-blood Cherokee, was born in 1862 in the Cherokee Nation in what is now Oklahoma. He lived in Tahlequah. As a lawman, he spent much of his time chasing horse thieves. He was an excellent shot with rifles and pistols and was a good horseman. At social gatherings, he often played the fiddle. When Sheriff Ellis Rattlinggourd led his posse out of Tahlequah in 1894 in an attempt to capture outlaws Bill Cook, Jim Cook, and Cherokee Bill (Crawford Goldsby), Sequoyah Houston was a member of that posse. He was the only member of the posse killed in the fight at the Halfway House on Fourteen Mile Creek. (See "Crittenden, Zeke and Dick"; "Goldsby, Crawford"; and "Rattlinggourd, Ellis.")

Howard, Gregg

Gregg Howard, of Cherokee descent, was born on May 5, 1934, in Central City, Kentucky. After serving in the U.S. Marine Corps from 1953 to 1957, he attended Ohio State University. In the early 1970s, Howard met Sam Hider, a Cherokee who was teaching the Cherokee language in a Tulsa library. He studied with Hider and made some Cherokee-language tapes with him. He later turned the tapes into an "introduction to Cherokee" language program. That was the beginning of Various Indian Peoples Publishing Company, which Howard established with Alfred Houser and Rick Erby in 1988. Since then, working with Native speakers from various tribes, the company has published language programs in Choctaw, Muskogee, Kiowa, Sauk and Fox, Caddo, Delaware, and other languages.

Since 1992, Howard has taught Cherokee-language courses at various colleges and universities in the Dallas, Texas, area. He is a member of the Oklahoma Native Language Association.

Howard was recognized by the Cherokee Nation in 1978 as an Ambassador of Good Will; and he received the International Association of Business Communicators Golden Quill Award in 1984, the Silver Mike Award in 1990, the Wrangler Award from the National Cowboy Hall of Fame in 1996, and the Bronze Telly in 2000.

In addition to all of this recognition, Howard is a much sought after storyteller. He was named Storyteller of the Year by the Wordcraft Circle of Native Writers and Storytellers in 1997. He has been featured in award-winning storytelling videos such as *Tales of Wonder I* and *Tales of Wonder II*, telling traditional Cherokee tales. He currently lives with his wife, Lari, outside Tahlequah, Oklahoma.

Hunt, Charles J.

Charles J. Hunt, a close friend of A. B. Cunningham throughout his life, attended Willie Halsell College in Vinita (in present-day Oklahoma) with Will Rogers. In December 1892 and again in January 1893, he was listed on the Cherokee Roll of Honor. He was appointed principal chief of the Cherokee Nation to serve for one day on December 27, 1928. (See "Chief for a Day.")

1.

Indian Home Guard

The Indian Home Guard was a Cherokee regiment of the Union army during the Civil War, established to fight against Confederate Cherokees. Its members were often called Pin Indians because they wore crossed pins under their coat lapels to identify themselves. It was largely but not totally made up of members of the Keetoowah Society.

Indian Territory

Indian Territory was a formal territory of the United States from just after the Civil War until Oklahoma gained statehood in 1907. It consisted of the eastern part of what is now the state of Oklahoma—mainly the lands of the Cherokee Nation, Creek Nation, Choctaw Nation, Chickasaw Nation, and Seminole Nation. Chief John Ross of the Cherokee Nation battled with U.S. negotiators and managed to get them to agree that Indian Territory would not have the usual presidentially appointed governor. Instead, it was to be governed jointly by the chiefs of the five tribes. They met very informally, and each tribe was allowed to continue governing itself. When it became obvious that the next step was statehood, delegates from the five tribes got together in a convention in 1905 to propose that the Indian Territory be admitted to the union as Sequoyah, an Indian state. The Sequoyah Convention was doomed from the beginning, though, and in 1907 Indian Territory was joined with Oklahoma Territory, its neighbor to the immediate west, to form the state of Oklahoma. (See "Sequoyah Convention.")

Because the U.S. government would not allow the tribal courts jurisdiction over non-Indians, Indian Territory became a haven for outlaws

Robert J. Conley

from all around North America. The United States then used as one of the excuses for Oklahoma statehood that the governments of the Five Civilized Tribes could not maintain law and order within their borders.

Iskagua, see "Bloody Fellow"

J.

Jackson, Walter S.

A member of the Eastern Band of Cherokee Indians, Walter S. Jackson was born May 29, 1923. He was educated in Cherokee schools. He married Sally Sneed, and they had four children. During World War II, he served in the U.S. Navy. In 1951, he was made manager of the Oconaluftee Indian village for the Cherokee Historical Association. He served as chief of the Cherokee Police, head of community services, councilman from Soco for twelve years, and then vice chief for four years. In 1967, at forty years old, he was elected principal chief. He was instrumental in developing the Cherokee Boys Club, improving reservation roads, reopening the tribal rolls, securing a new gymnasium and a new elementary school, and establishing the Public Health Service Hospital. He was a member of the Macedonian Baptist Church, the Veterans of Foreign Wars, and the Steve Youngdeer Post of the American Legion. He died while in office on April 26, 1971, at the age of forty-seven. U.S. congressman Roy Taylor said of him, "He was a warm, friendly individual whom we all looked forward to seeing when he came to Washington. He always seemed to have the welfare of the Cherokee Indians at heart and vigorously pursued those programs which he felt would improve their social and economic conditions. He had the ability to combine his congenial manner with serious purpose."

Jacob, Murv

An artist of Cherokee descent, Murv Jacob was born in 1945 in Glendale, Ohio. His father was a descendant of Kentucky Cherokees. Murv was raised in Topeka, Kansas, where he learned to paint beginning at age ten from his great-grandmother Alice Brooks. He attended San Bernardino

Robert J. Conley

Murv Jacob (left)
with Cecil Dick,
1983. Courtesy of
Murv Jacob.

Valley College in California in 1964, where, he says, he "mostly hung out with Hawaiian surfers and fell in love with California." From 1965 to 1967, he was in San Francisco, making posters for Allen Ginsberg, the Grateful Dead, and beat poet and playwright Michael McClure. Back in Kansas in 1971, he opened the 7 East 7th Gallery in Lawrence with what he describes as a "weird mix of New York pop art and contemporary Kansas artists." There he met Dick West, noted Cheyenne artist and professor of art at Haskell Indian College; Roger Shimomura, Japanese American art professor at the University of Kansas; and Thomas Hart Benton.

In 1979, Murv opened the Smallwood Gallery in Topeka, Kansas, focusing on the Indian artists of Kansas and Oklahoma. He hosted a show of Dick West's work and became friends with Woody Crumbo. In 1982, he organized and curated the Fifty-Year Retrospective Show for Cecil Dick at the Cherokee National Museum in Tahlequah, Oklahoma.

After visiting Tahlequah several times, Murv moved there permanently in 1984 and studied with noted Cherokee artist Cecil Dick. Although overlaid with his own highly decorative and detailed style, Murv's paintings show Dick's influence. His work has won more than fifty awards, including Grand Awards at the 1991 Trail of Tears Art Show in Tahlequah; Grand Awards at the 1992 Cherokee Museum Annual Competition in Cherokee, North Carolina; and the Five Civilized Tribes Museum Competitive Art Show in 1992. He was twice voted Wordcraft Circle of Native Writers' Illustrator of the Year, in 1996 and 2005. Along with his wife, Deborah Duvall, he received an Oklahoma Book Award for his drawings for the children's book series, The Grandmother Stories. He has collaborated with Duvall on eight books. Murv has illustrated books or done cover art for books for Doubleday, Time-Life Books, Harper-Collins, Dial, St. Martin's Press, the Parabola Foundation, University of

New Mexico Press, University of Oklahoma Press, University of Nebraska Press, and others. He has designed a Cherokee National Holiday commemorative shirt each year since 1980. He is a Master Artist of the Five Civilized Tribes Museum and a founding member of the Cherokee Honor Society. Murv says that because he is "of Cherokee descent and not a tribal member," he ran afoul of the Indian Arts and Crafts Act of 1990 and as a result "will be long remembered for the pitched battle he fought with this dubious law's proponents."

Jolly, John

John Jolly was Tahlonteskee's brother. His Cherokee name, Ooloodega (or Ahuludegi), has been translated as "the Man Who Beats His Own Drum," "He Throws Away the Drum," and "He Puts the Drum Away." When Sam Houston first ran away from home and lived with the Cherokees in Tennessee, Jolly was his adopted father. Jolly operated a trading establishment and was a planter at this time. He was also a slave owner and a wealthy man. In 1818, Sam Houston became U.S. subagent for the Cherokees. His job was to talk Cherokees into moving west. It did not take him long to persuade his adopted father. After all, Jolly's brother was already in Arkansas and was in fact chief of the Western Cherokees there. In 1818, John Jolly and 333 other Cherokee people made the move in four keelboats and thirteen flatboats.

John Jolly. Painting by George Catlin, c. 1850. Courtesy of the Oklahoma Historical Society.

He built a new, large, comfortable home in the style of a southern plantation home, where he was attended by twelve servants, and he had at least five hundred head of cattle. He was transported in style in a fancy carriage driven by a black slave.

In 1819, following the death of Tahlonteskee, Jolly was elected chief of the Western Cherokees. Like his brother, he was occupied much of the time with the long-running Cherokee-Osage war and with negotiations

Robert J. Conley

for peace sponsored by the U.S. Army. In 1829, Sam Houston, following his resignation of the governorship of Tennessee, went west to rejoin his adopted father. By then, the Western Cherokees had moved across into what was to become the Cherokee Nation (now northeast Oklahoma). Jolly's home was at Webbers Falls. Six months after Houston's arrival, the former governor of Tennessee was made a full citizen of the Western Cherokee Nation. Jolly was quick to take advantage of his prodigal son's return. He used Houston as a delegate to Washington, D.C., for the Western Cherokee Nation and as a negotiator for peace with the Osages. In 1832, peace was finally concluded, but the Cherokee man named Captain Dutch, the inveterate Osage hater, was living in Texas and still making raids far up into Osage country. The Western Cherokee Nation declared him an outlaw and disavowed any responsibility for his actions, but it was aware that the peace with the Osages would be much more solid with Dutch as a party to it. Jolly sent John Smith, a Cherokee, down to Texas to bring Dutch home. The long and bloody Cherokee-Osage war was at last over. That peace was Chief John Jolly's major accomplishment. He died while still in office in 1838.

Jones, Evan

Born in Wales in 1788, Evan Jones, a white man, was a member of the Church of England and then the Methodist Church. He came to the United States in 1821, stopping in Philadelphia, where he became a Baptist. A month after his arrival there he became a missionary and took over the Baptist Mission at Valley Town in North Carolina that same year. He learned to speak the Cherokee language and attracted Cherokee converts. In 1829, Kaneega, a full-blood Cherokee, was ordained a Baptist minister, and in 1830 Jesse Bushyhead was ordained as well. Lewis Downing and Charles Thompson were also among Jones's converts. During the Removal in 1838, Jones traveled with Jesse Bushyhead's contingent to the new Cherokee Nation in the West. In 1861, Jones is said to have reorganized the ancient Keetoowah Society to fight slavery. Because of their fervent antislavery activity, Jones and his son John were asked by the Baptist Board to leave the Cherokee Nation in 1861. Jones moved to Lawrence, Kansas, where he encountered some Cherokee refugees who told him of Chief John Ross's (reluctantly drawn) treaty with the Confederacy. Jones wrote a letter to U.S. Indian commissioner W. P. Dole defending Ross's action. Jones continued preaching until his death in 1872. He is buried in Tahlequah, Oklahoma.

Jones, Leon

Leon Jones was born in Philadelphia in 1939. He served in the U.S. Air Force in the field of nuclear weapons armament for seventeen years and then spent an additional four years in the Marine Corps in munitions maintenance before his retirement. He moved to the Cherokee reservation in North Carolina after his retirement from the military and owned and operated a real estate appraisal company. He has served as chairman of the Cherokee Children's Home Board, postmaster of the Cherokee Post Office, manager of tribal bingo, member of the Gaming Certification Commission, chairman of the Cherokee School Board, and board member of Friends of the Smokies. He represented Wolfetown Community for one term on the Tribal Council of the Eastern Band of Cherokees and served for twelve years as an appointed magistrate. In 1999, he was elected to the highest office of the Eastern Band and thus became the first chief to have served in all three branches of government. He served as chief until 2003. Chief Jones holds a business degree from Blanton's Business College in Asheville, North Carolina. He is married to Janice Allison of Cherokee.

Junaluska

Tsuhnuhlahuhski, meaning "He Tries but Fails," was first known as Gul'kalaski. At the battle of Horseshoe Bend in 1814, it is said, when Gul'kalaski saw General Andrew Jackson on the ground about to be killed by a Creek, he killed the Creek, saving Jackson's life. Jackson is supposed to have said to Gul'kalaski, "As long as the sun shines and the grass grows, you and me will be friends, and the Cherokees' feet will be pointed east." When Jackson as president was agitating for Cherokee removal to the West, Gul'kalaski went to Washington, D.C., to see him. Jackson would not grant him an audience. At that point, Gul'kalaski said, "Detsinu lahungu," meaning, "I tried, but I failed," and he changed his name to Tsunuhlahuhski, "He Tries but Fails." The latter name has been anglicized to "Junaluska." He was later taken west over the Trail of Tears, but somehow managed to get away and return to North Carolina, where he died in 1858.

Junaluska, Arthur S.

Playwright, director, choreographer, and actor Arthur S. Junaluska, a descendant of both Junaluska and Yonaguska, is a Cherokee from the Eastern Band in North Carolina. He spent three years in the Army

Medical Corps in World War II and returned to the United States to work temporarily for the New York City Department of Health. He then went to the London School of Medicine and worked for the South London Blood Transfusion Department, where he helped to modify a serological test process that is now used by commercial blood banks.

In 1945, he gave up his medical career and began acting with a little theater group, working his way up to the legitimate theater, off-Broadway and Broadway productions, and on to television and motion pictures. He organized the American Indian Dramatic Company and produced, directed, and starred in *The Arrow Maker*. In 1958, he was director of a drama workshop at South Dakota Wesleyan University. He is also the founder of the American Indian Society of Creative Arts and the American Indian Theatre Foundation, Inc., which has the goal of establishing a permanent American Indian theater. Plays he has written include *The Medicine Woman*; *Hell-cat of the Plains*; *Grand Council of Indian Circle*; *The Spirit of Wallowa*; and *Spectre in the Forest*. He is also the author of *Red Hawk's Account of Custer's Last Battle*.

Justice, Dick

Dick Justice was a Western Cherokee who was interviewed by Cephas Washburn sometime around 1835. Washburn says that "Dick" is not short for "Richard," but anglicized from the Cherokee name "Dik-keh." Because Dik-keh was a just man, he was known as "the Just," thus forming the name "Dik-keh the Just," which was then further anglicized into "Dick Justice." When Washburn met him, Justice was said to be 120 years old. Justice, like Ta-ka-e-tuh and Blanket, told Christian tales in a Cherokee way and lamented that his people had become degenerate through the loss of the Sacred Ark many years earlier. (See also "Ta-ka-e-tuh"; "Blanket"; and "Ark.")

Justice, Lillian

Lillian Justice was born October 26, 1914, to Walter (Watt) Justice and Freddie Grant Justice in Green, Oklahoma. She was both fluent and literate in the Cherokee language. Her father was the founder and pastor for forty years of the Cherokee Baptist Church on North Water Street in Tahlequah, Oklahoma, where the services were conducted in the Cherokee language. Lillian attended high school and played basketball in Tahlequah. Her uniform and number were retired and displayed in the high school for many years.

After graduation, Justice attended Tulsa Business College, where she played Association of American Universities (AAU) basketball for the Tulsa Stenos. There were few women's teams, and the Stenos sometimes played against men. The Stenos won the AAU National Finals three years while she was playing with them.

She left school and moved to Galveston, Texas, to work for the American National Insurance Company. The company's basketball team, the Anicos, won the AAU National Championship twice while she played for them. She also played softball for a team in Galveston that won the Texas State Championship twice and for a team that won the Texas State Softball Championship twice. Knee injuries in 1938 cut short her athletic career. She was named AAU National Champion five times and All American six times.

K.

Kaneega

Kaneega (also Kaneeka) was a Cherokee converted to the Baptist faith by Reverend Evan Jones at Springplace, Georgia, in the 1830s. He became a valued teacher and was renamed John Wickliffe. He was associated with Jesse Bushyhead and James Wafford.

Keeler, William Wayne

William Wayne Keeler was a Cherokee born on April 5, 1908, in Dalhart, Texas. He grew up and attended school at Bartlesville, Oklahoma. When Bill was ten years old, his father made a million dollars in the cattle business. Three years later his father died, and the bottom fell out of the cattle business. The Keelers were broke. Bill began working in the summers for Phillips Petroleum Company when he was sixteen years old and soon was attending college at the same time. He married Ruby Hamilton while still in school, and then Phillips pressured him to make up his mind whether he wanted to be a college kid or go to work. He quit school and went to work full-time.

William Wayne Keeler, principal chief from 1949 to 1975. Photo courtesy of the Cherokee Honor Society.

Keeler worked at various jobs for Phillips in Kansas City, Missouri;

Odessa, Texas; and Borger, Texas. Then in 1941, he was made technical assistant for the vice president of the refining department. In 1945, he became head of the department. He was elected vice president of the executive department and a member of the board of directors in 1951; was chairman of the executive committee in 1962; became president and chief executive officer in 1967; and was chairman of the board in 1968. He retired in 1973.

Keeler first showed up in Cherokee politics in 1948, when Chief Bartley Milam was hosting the convention of Cherokees in order to establish an executive committee. Keeler was at the meeting to represent the Texas Cherokees. At this meeting, he pressed for a member of the committee to represent the Texas Cherokees. When the committee members were selected, the representative from Texas was W. W. Keeler. In 1949, he was elected vice chairman of the executive committee, and that same year, following the death of Chief Milam, President Harry S. Truman appointed Keeler principal chief of the Cherokee Nation.

Keeler served as principal chief for more than twenty years, and during his tenure many events significant for the Cherokee Nation occurred. In 1961, the Cherokee Nation received a judgment of $14,789,000 through the Indian Claims Commission when the claim for the real value of the Cherokee Outlet was settled. The money was to be paid out in per capita payments to those Cherokees who had been listed on the Dawes Roll, but while details of the payment were being worked out, the money was drawing interest. The interest was used for a variety of purposes. Projects were established. Employees were hired. In 1962, the land that Milam had selected at Park Hill, Oklahoma, for a museum and archives was purchased. In 1967, under the name of the Cherokee Heritage Center, a re-created "ancient Cherokee village," Tsalagi, was opened to the public on that land. In 1969, an outdoor theater began operations. In 1975, the museum opened its doors. All of this was done under the auspices of a newly created Cherokee National Historical Society, independent from the Cherokee Nation but largely supported by it.

In the 1960s, a group of full-blood Cherokees organized themselves under the name Original Cherokee Communities Organization (OCCO). Headed by George Groundhog, a full-blood, they believed that Keeler was not representing their people properly. They had no money, but they did what they could to help other Cherokee people back in the hills of the southeastern United States. Scholars from the University of Chicago and other institutions became involved with the OCCO, initially to help with language projects, but soon they were delving into other areas as well.

The OCCO put out a newspaper, and a white lawyer, Stuart Trapp, began working with them, primarily on issues of land loss. Keeler's response to these activities was that he supposed the "outside agitators" and "communists" had misled a few Cherokees.

In 1971, President Richard Nixon restored general elections to the Cherokee Nation, and for the first time since 1903 the Cherokee people elected their principal chief. Bill Keeler, after having served for more than twenty years, ran for the office and was elected. He served one full term, but, following adverse publicity regarding illegal campaign contributions to Nixon, decided not to run for reelection in 1975 and instead endorsed Ross Swimmer. Keeler died in Bartlesville, Oklahoma, on August 24, 1987.

Keen, Ralph

In 1967, Chief William Wayne Keeler hired Ralph Keen as general business manager for the Cherokee Nation. Keen resigned in 1969 and ran for principal chief in opposition to Keeler in 1972. He was a Tulsa University law student. During the 1995 race for principal chief of the Cherokee Nation, Keen was sitting on the Cherokee Nation's Judicial Appeals Tribunal. He was one of the three judges who ruled that George Bearpaw was ineligible to run for office and that Chief Wilma Mankiller could not issue Bearpaw a pardon. The tribunal also ruled that Bearpaw's name would stay on the runoff ballot for that year's election, but that no votes for Bearpaw would be counted. The only name left on the ballot was thus that of Joe Byrd, so, in effect, the tribunal declared Joe Byrd chief. Ralph Keen died on November 27, 2002.

Keetoowah

The ancient Cherokee town of Keetoowah, located in what is now North Carolina, is said to be the Cherokees' mother town, or the place where the Cherokees started. All other Cherokee towns grew out of Keetoowah. Cherokees still today often refer to themselves as Ani-Kituwagi, or Keetoowah People. Lost to the Cherokees after the Removal to the West, it was privately owned and farmed for years, its mound worn down by plowing. After two hundred years of having been plowed over, the mound today is 170 feet in diameter and only 5 feet high. The Keetoowah site was reacquired by the Eastern Band of Cherokee Indians in 1996 under the leadership of Chief Joyce Dugan. Today it is kept up and used once again ceremonially.

Keetoowah News

The *Keetoowah News* is the official newspaper of the United Keetoowah Band of Cherokee Indians in Oklahoma.

Keetoowah Society

Some Cherokees say that the Keetoowah Society is an ancient full-blood society, others that it was organized just prior to the Civil War by Reverend Evan Jones, a white missionary and ardent abolitionist. Whatever the truth of the society's origins, it is known that some of its members wore crossed pins under their coat lapels during the war to identify themselves. They thus became known as "Pin Indians" and fought against the Confederate Cherokees throughout the war. Emmet Starr says that from 1859 to 1889 the Keetoowah Society members were Baptist, Methodist, Presbyterian, Quaker, and Cherokee traditionalists and that they existed without dissension. Problems came when white missionaries objected to the "[p]agan form of worship" and called it the "work of the Devil." At that point, the constitution and laws of the Keetoowah Society were amended, making the organization more political. Starr divides the Keetoowahs at this point into Christian Keetoowahs and Ancient Keetoowahs. When the Dawes Commission began its nefarious work in the 1890s, all Keetoowahs were opposed to it, and the Ancient Keetoowahs became known as the Nighthawk Keetoowahs under the leadership of Redbird Smith.

Ketcher, John

John Ketcher was one of the original Sequoyah Weavers. A highly respected full-blood Cherokee, he is bilingual. He served as deputy chief under Chief Wilma Mankiller for ten years, from 1985 to 1995.

Kilpatrick, Anna Gritts

The daughter of Levi Gritts and a descendant of Sequoyah, Anna Gritts Kilpatrick, a full-blood, bilingual Cherokee, married Jack Kilpatrick and worked with him translating Cherokee manuscripts for several books, including *Friends of Thunder; Walk in Your Soul; Run Toward the Nightland; New Echota Letters*; and *The Shadow of Sequoyah*. Anna earned a bachelor's degree from Southern Methodist University. She worked in the Indian Service and later as a teacher in the Dallas, Texas, public schools. In 1959, she and Jack received the Sequoyah Medal from the Cherokee Nation for "[t]heir work in Cherokee linguistics, culture, myth and music." She died around 1977.

Kilpatrick, Jack Frederick

The husband of Anna Gritts Kilpatrick, Jack Kilpatrick was also bilingual in Cherokee and English. Like his wife, he was a native of Stilwell, Oklahoma. He held a bachelor's degree in music from the University of Redlands, a master's in music from Catholic University of America, and a Ph.D. from the University of Redlands. In 1946, he joined the faculty of the School of Music of Southern Methodist University as professor of composition and theory and later became chairman of the Department of Music there. He wrote the musical score for the outdoor Cherokee drama *Unto These Hills*, which is still produced each summer on the Cherokee reservation in North Carolina. He and Anna received the Sequoyah Medal from the Cherokee Nation in 1959. He also composed portions of the musical score for the drama *Trail of Tears*, produced in Tahlequah, Oklahoma, although he died in 1967 before its completion.

Kingfisher, Choogie

Choogie Kingfisher, full-blood Cherokee, was born in Oklahoma. He plays a handmade flute and tells stories, many of which he wrote himself. He travels extensively and has appeared at the Tejas Storytelling Festival in Denton, Texas; the Sandhill Crane Festival in Vonore, Tennessee; and the Giants and Little People Storytelling Conference in Olympia, Washington. He performed with the Painted Horse War Dance Society at the Winter Olympics in Salt Lake City, Utah, and at the Singing River Festival in Florence, Alabama. He is employed by the Cherokee Nation as a culture coordinator, and he sings with his family at community gospel singings. He has performed in the *Trail of Tears* drama at the Cherokee Heritage Center in Tahlequah, Oklahoma. In 2004, he received a Cherokee Medal of Honor, the youngest recipient of one to date.

Knights of the Golden Circle, see "Southern Rights Party"

L.

Lighthorse of the Cherokee Nation

In 1797, the Cherokees took steps toward creating tribal law enforcement officers, who were called "regulating parties." In 1808 at Broom's Town, the first written law of the Cherokee Nation established these officers' pay and delineated some of their duties. With the reorganization of the Cherokee Nation's government from 1817 through 1827, the Lighthorse Police was established, initially to accompany circuit judges (one for each two districts in the Cherokee Nation) on their rounds and to execute their decisions. The Lighthorse officers' main duties came to include chasing horse thieves and running down and capturing runaway slaves. They were reorganized in the West following the Removal in 1838 and eventually disbanded after the disastrous Treaty of 1866 following the Civil War because the treaty forbade military organizations in Indian tribes, and the U.S. government looked upon the Lighthorse as military.

Lighthorse of the United Keetoowah Band

On its lands in Oklahoma, the United Keetoowah Band of Cherokees uses a security force that is called the Lighthorse.

Little Turkey

Little Turkey became principal chief of the Cherokee Nation in 1788 following the brutal murder of Chief Tassel. This cowardly murder accomplished two things. First, it brought back together the two factions of Cherokees—the Chickamaugas in Tennessee and the Cherokees in North Carolina. Many followers of Tassel had moved to the Chickamauga Creek area, and most had prepared for war, ready to follow Dragging Canoe, who

Robert J. Conley

had seceded from the Cherokee Nation. Second, the governor of North Carolina, who had been looking for an excuse anyway, had John Sevier arrested and dissolved the state of Franklin. The Cherokees were summoned to a new treaty council. They met this time at White's Fort on the Holston River near the present site of Knoxville, Tennessee. Twelve hundred Cherokees were present at this meeting. Among them were Dragging Canoe and the Cherokee Nation's new principal chief, Little Turkey. The Treaty of Holston was concluded. Interestingly, neither Dragging Canoe nor Little Turkey signed.

The Chickamaugas nevertheless continued to raid illegal squatters on Cherokee land, and Dragging Canoe went on a trip to visit other Indian tribes in an attempt to form a great alliance of Indians. In 1791, Dragging Canoe died. The Chickamaugas continued fighting for another year, but without Dragging Canoe's leadership their movement soon died out. The Cherokee wars were over. Little Turkey said that his desire for the Cherokees was "to live so that we might have gray hairs on our heads."

In the following years, the Cherokee Nation made great strides in the direction that would lead it to be called one of the "civilized tribes." Women became spinners and weavers. Cherokees raised cotton and cattle to sell. In 1799, Little Turkey advocated that the council permit Moravian missionaries to build a school in the Cherokee Nation. The school was built in 1801 at Springplace, Georgia. When Little Turkey died in 1804, the Cherokee Nation was living well, but at the same time, of course, it was moving farther away from its ancient traditions.

Littlefield, Daniel F.

Dan Littlefield, of Cherokee descent, was born in Salina, Oklahoma. He received his bachelor's degree from Oklahoma State University in 1960, his master's from the University of Arkansas in 1962, and his Ph.D. from Oklahoma State University in 1971. He taught literature at Oklahoma State University from 1961 to 1963; at Bemidji State University from 1963 to 1964; at Oklahoma State University from 1964 to 1967 and 1968 to 1970; and at Southwest Missouri State University from 1967 to 1968; and he has taught at the University of Arkansas at Little Rock from 1977 until the present. In addition, he has been a visiting professor at Colgate University, the University of Alabama, and the University of Arizona. He was an Honorary Fellow at the University of Wisconsin at Madison in the summer of 1984. Since 1983, at the University of Arkansas he has been the director of the American Native Press Archives, which sponsors the annual Sequoyah

Dan Littlefield, 2000.
Courtesy of Dan Littlefield.

Symposium and is the world's largest
repository of Native American newspapers and periodicals.

Littlefield is the author of *Seminole
Burning: A Story of Racial Vengeance*
(1996); *The Life of Okah Tubbee* (1988); *The
Chickasaw Freedmen: A People Without
a Country* (1980); *African and Creeks:
From the Colonial Period to the Civil
War* (1979); and *The Cherokee Freedmen: From Removal to Emancipation*
(1977). He is coauthor or coeditor of numerous other books, along with
Jack Campbell, Lonnie Underhill, Carol Hunter, and James Parins. He has
written numerous journal, anthology, encyclopedia, dictionary, and newspaper articles as well as book reviews. Littlefield is also a poet who has published in *Phoenix, Poet, Poem, Encore*, and other literary magazines. He is
a member of the Cherokee Nation's Great State of Sequoyah Commission,
and in 2001 he was inducted into the Oklahoma Historians Hall of Fame.

Long, Will West

Will West Long (Wili Westi) was born in the conservative community of
Big Cove in North Carolina in 1870. He became a professional interpreter
and translator. In 1887, when James Mooney came to Cherokee from the
Bureau of American Ethnology, Long worked extensively for him. In 1894,
Mooney convinced Long to attend an "experiment in higher education"
at Hampton Institute, and Long spent several years in Massachusetts. He
returned to Cherokee, North Carolina, in 1904 and continued to work with
Mooney until 1920. In addition to his scholarly work, he became famous
for his traditional carved wooden ceremonial masks. He died of a heart
attack at age seventy-seven.

Longhair

Longhair was chief of a group of Chickamaugas who moved across the
Ohio River into the Shawnee country around 1782. When the power of
the confederated northern tribes was broken, these Chickamaugas did

not bother to attend the treaty conference, and in 1795 General "Mad" Anthony Wayne sent them a message to come in. They answered him that they would leave Ohio forever as soon as they gathered their crops.

Looney, John

A nephew of Chief Black Fox of the Cherokee Nation, John Looney served in the army during the Creek War in 1813–14 and moved west in 1826. He was appointed to fill the vacancy left by the death of Chief John Jolly in 1838 until a new election could be held among the Western Cherokees, scheduled for October 1839, but the arrival of the majority of Cherokees over the Trail of Tears and Chief John Ross's insistence that there be but one Cherokee government caused the Western Cherokee Nation to hasten the election. John Rogers was elected, but he was replaced in short time by John Brown. When Brown was deposed, Looney was made chief.

With Looney now chief of the Western Cherokees, or the "Old Settlers," an agreement, the Act of Union, was signed with the Cherokee Nation. The Western Cherokee Nation ceased to exist. In 1846, Looney was with the delegation in Washington, D.C., working on behalf of the "Old Settlers." He died there on May 15, 1846, and was buried in the Congressional Cemetery.

Lowrey, Major George

George Lowrey (Agili, "He is Rising") was born around 1770 in Tuskegee on the Tennessee River in what is now Alabama. He was the son of George Lowrey, a white man, and Nannie, a Cherokee woman, and was a cousin of Sequoyah. He was a captain of the Lighthorse (a tribal law enforcement organization) and attained the rank of major while fighting with Andrew Jackson during the Creek War of 1813–14. He was a member of the first National Committee in 1814 and a member of the committee that drafted the Constitution of 1827 and later that of 1839. As a member of a Cherokee delegation to Washington, D.C., in 1823, Lowrey heard a Georgia congressman present refer to the Cherokees as "savages subsisting upon roots, wild herbs, disgusting reptiles." In the dining room later, he found himself seated across the table from the same Georgian. When a waiter came by with a tray of sweet potatoes, Lowrey took some and said, "We savages are very fond of roots." In 1828, he was elected assistant chief of the Cherokee Nation. He signed the Act of Union between the Cherokee Nation and the Western Cherokees in 1839 as president of the Cherokee National Council. He died in 1852.

M.

Mankiller, Wilma P.

Wilma Pearl Mankiller was Ross Swimmer's deputy chief when he resigned in 1985. She became the first and so far has been the only female principal chief of the Cherokee Nation. Wilma was born November 18, 1945, at W. W. Hastings Indian Hospital in Tahlequah, Oklahoma, the daughter of Charley Mankiller, a full-blood Cherokee, and Claire Irene Sitton Mankiller, a white woman. The sixth of eleven children, she spent her early years at their home, Mankiller Flats, in the Cherokee community of Rocky Mountain, outside Stilwell, Oklahoma. There was a woodstove, no electricity, and no running water.

In 1956, when Wilma was not quite eleven years old, the Mankiller family elected to take part in the U.S. government's "Indian Relocation" scheme and was moved to San Francisco, California. The family boarded a train for San Francisco and upon arrival moved into a hotel room. Two weeks later the Bureau of Indian Affairs found them an apartment. A year later Charley Mankiller and his oldest son Don were able to purchase a small house for the family. As a teenager, Wilma began to hang out at the Indian Center in San Francisco. In 1963, at seventeen years old, she graduated from high school and took a clerical job with a finance company.

That same year she met and married Hector Hugo Olaya de Bardi, an Ecuadoran living in San Francisco. Her first child, a daughter, was born nine months later. Two years later a second daughter followed. In the late 1960s, Mankiller started college classes, first at Skyline Junior College, then at San Francisco State. In 1968, with the assassinations of Martin Luther King Jr. and Robert F. Kennedy, the United States was plunged into a time of deep unrest. In November 1969, a group of Indians from twenty or so different tribes seized Alcatraz Island. Several of Mankiller's siblings took an active part in the protest, and she visited Alcatraz more than once during the seventeen-month occupation.

In 1970, both Mankiller and her father were diagnosed with polycystic kidney disease. In February 1971, Charley Mankiller, fifty-six years old, died. He was taken home to Oklahoma for burial. When Wilma returned to San Francisco after the funeral, she became more active in Indian affairs, as acting director of the Native American Youth Center in East Oakland and as a volunteer for the Pit River Indians in their legal battle with Pacific Gas and Electric. In 1974, she and Hugo Olaya were divorced. Mankiller went to work for the Urban Indian Resource Center. Then Hugo took their youngest daughter, Gina, and kept her for a year in Ecuador. When they returned to San Francisco, Hugo allowed Gina to visit her mother. Gina, nine years old at the time, decided to stay with her mother, so Mankiller packed up her two daughters and made a visit to Oklahoma, where they decided to stay, going back to San Francisco only to retrieve their belongings.

Wilma Mankiller was hired by the Cherokee Nation in 1977 as an economic stimulus coordinator. Ross Swimmer was principal chief at the time. In 1979, Mankiller became a program development specialist. On November 8, 1979, when she was driving on Highway 100 to Tahlequah, Oklahoma, from her home at Mankiller Flats, a car suddenly appeared in front of her in her lane, and they crashed head-on. Mankiller was badly injured. The driver of the other car was her very good friend Sherry Morris. She did not survive.

Mankiller endured six hours of surgery. She was in the hospital for eight weeks and had seventeen more operations. Ten months after the accident, she was diagnosed with systemic myasthenia gravis, a form of muscular dystrophy. She underwent another operation and began taking prescribed drugs. Despite everything, in 1981, she returned to her job at the Cherokee Nation and became director of the new Cherokee Nation Community

Wilma Mankiller, 1980s. Courtesy of Wilma Mankiller.

Development Department. While working in the Cherokee community of Bell, ten miles from Mankiller Flats, she became well acquainted with Charlie Soap, a full-blood Cherokee, whom she had met previously.

In 1983, Ross Swimmer asked Mankiller to run for the office of deputy chief. She agreed. Swimmer was reelected as principal chief, and Wilma Mankiller, following a runoff election with Agnes Cowan, became deputy chief. In 1985, when Swimmer was offered the job of undersecretary of the interior for Indian affairs, he resigned as chief of the Cherokee Nation to accept the appointment, and Mankiller became principal chief, the first and only woman ever to hold that position.

In October 1986, Mankiller married Charlie Soap, and in 1987 she ran for the office of principal chief. John Ketcher, a member of the Cherokee National Council since 1983, was chosen as her running mate. No one received the required 50 percent of the vote, so a runoff was scheduled between Chief Mankiller and Perry Wheeler. Although Chief Mankiller was hospitalized once again with kidney problems, when the final vote was counted, she had won easily.

By 1989, it became clear that kidney failure was imminent. Her older brother, Don, volunteered to serve as a donor. The surgery was performed in 1990 and was successful. The chief was back at work in two months, and in 1991 she ran for another term. She won the election with an incredible 82.7 percent of the vote. She served out the remainder of her term, with Cherokee Nation programs and Cherokee Nation registration continuing to grow. The Cherokee population at this time was already in excess of two hundred thousand. At the end of her tenth year as chief, in 1995, Wilma Mankiller decided that it was time to step aside. She announced that she would not run again. She has written a successful autobiography (with Michael Wallis) and has continued writing as well as speaking around the country.

Marbles

No one knows just when the Cherokees began playing marbles (*diga-dayosdi*), sometimes called "five hole," but the game is not mentioned by either James Mooney or Charles Hudson. Ned Christie is said to have been an excellent marbles player in the latter half of the nineteenth century. The game is played with marbles slightly smaller than billiard balls and shaped from stones. (More recently, some Cherokees have actually been using billiard balls for marbles.) It's an outdoor game, played on a field 105 to 120 feet long, with holes in the ground every 35 to 40 feet. The first four holes are in a straight line, with the fifth one set out at a right angle, so that the entire lineup forms an L.

The game is played by two teams, with the object being for each player to get his marble into each hole. When a player reaches hole five successfully, he turns around and works his way back to hole number one. Players can throw their marbles to knock another player's marble out of the game. Groups of Cherokee players in northeastern Oklahoma are still passionate about the game of Cherokee marbles.

Mathews, Carl Davis

Carl Davis Mathews was born in the Cherokee Nation, Indian Territory, in 1899. Biographical information is sketchy, but by the 1930s he was in Hollywood working in B Western films, mostly as a stunt double or as a heavy. He often used the name Carl "Cherokee" Mathews for his professional name, but he also used Carl Mathews, Karl Mathews, and Duke Mathews. He was a stuntman in at least 127 films and an actor in 176. Most of his work was in Westerns. He doubled for Fred Scott and Crash Corrigan, and he was in many films that starred Eddie Dean, Don Barry, Bob Steele, and Lash LaRue. Some of the many films he appeared in are *Stage to Mesa City; The Return of the Durango Kid; The Cisco Kid Returns; Lightning Raiders; Reap the Wild Wind; Frontier Scout; The Great Adventures of Wild Bill Hickok; The Singing Buckaroo;* and *Law of the Lash.*

Although Mathews was living in California, he did not forget about his Cherokee heritage. In 1947, while working on a film with Lash LaRue, he was involved in the effort to collect $66 million that the United States owed to the Cherokees for reparation, and he had enlisted the aid of other Indian actors in Hollywood. Mathews's grandfather was one of the signers of the Treaty of 1835. Carl Mathews died in Los Angeles in 1959.

Carl Davis Matthews (far right), in *Lawless Plainsmen,* 1942. Ken Jones Collection.

Mayes, Joel Bryan

The son of Samuel Mayes, a white man, and Nancy Adair, daughter of Watt Adair, a Cherokee, Joel B. Mayes was born on October 2, 1833, near Cartersville, Georgia. He was only four years old when his family moved west in 1837. He attended school at Muddy Creek campground in what is now Oklahoma until 1851 and later at the Cherokee Male Seminary, finishing in 1855 with its first graduating class. He taught school at Muddy Creek until 1857. During the Civil War, he served in the Confederate First Indian Regiment, initially as a private, then as paymaster, and finally as quartermaster.

Mayes eventually became clerk of the district and circuit courts in the Cherokee Nation, chief clerk of the National Council, and clerk of the Commission of Citizenship. In 1882, he was elected associate justice of the Cherokee Supreme Court and one year later became chief justice. He resigned his position to run for the office of principal chief on the Downing Party ticket and in 1888 was elected to that high office.

Joel Bryan Mayes, c. 1889. Public domain. Courtesy of the Cherokee Honor Society.

He renegotiated the lease for the Cherokee Strip with the Cherokee Strip Livestock Association, doubling the amount of money the Cherokee Nation had been receiving per year, from $100,000 to $200,000. However, in 1890, President William Harrison issued a proclamation forbidding all grazing in the Cherokee Outlet (the Livestock Association had been improperly named), thereby crippling the Cherokee Nation's budget. It was a move calculated to force the Cherokee Nation to sell the outlet, and it worked. It was also during Mayes's term that the federal court was indeed established in Muskogee, Indian Territory. The U.S. government was making swift moves toward statehood for Oklahoma. Mayes was reelected principal chief in August 1891, but he served only four months of his second term, dying in office on December 14, 1891. He was fifty-eight years old. His wives were Martha J. Candy, who died in 1863; Martha M. McNair, who preceded her husband in death; and Mary Vann. Chief Mayes was a master Mason and a member of the Methodist Church.

Robert J. Conley

Mayes, Samuel Houston

Sam Houston Mayes was the younger brother of Chief Joel Bryan Mayes. One of eleven siblings (ten brothers and one sister), he was born in the Flint District of the Cherokee Nation in what is now Oklahoma on May 11, 1845, shortly after the arrival of his parents and older brother from the East. He was educated at the Muddy Springs School near his home and later at the Cherokee Male Seminary. He enlisted in the Confederate army when he was sixteen years old. Following the Civil War, he attended school in Texas for a time.

In 1881, he was elected the sheriff of Cooweescoowee District. He was elected to the Cherokee Senate in 1885 and re-elected in 1891, then became principal chief in 1895. He served one term and did not run for reelection in 1899. He was a farmer, rancher, and merchant. He was married to Martha Vann until her death, after which he married Minnie Bell. He was a delegate to the unsuccessful Sequoyah Convention. He died at Pryor, Oklahoma, in 1927 at the age of eighty-two. Mayes County, Oklahoma, is named for him.

Samuel Houston Mayes, c. 1895. Public domain. Courtesy of the Cherokee Honor Society.

McAlister, Barbara

Barbara McAlister was born in Muskogee, Oklahoma, in 1941. A descendant of Tassel, she was a barrel racer in rodeos in her youth and aspired to be a country and western singer. However, she found it difficult to fit her voice to country and western music, but easy to mimic the opera singers on her mother's records. Her father studied voice and performed in barbershop quartets and choirs at school and church. He sang German lieder and lullabies to Barbara when she was a toddler. She chose to follow opera.

An acclaimed dramatic mezzo-soprano, McAlister appeared in operas for ten years in Germany, Monte Carlo, France, Spain, Portugal, Hong Kong, and, of course, the United States. Winner of the prestigious Loren Zachary Competition in Los Angeles, she appeared with the operas of Washington, D.C., San Diego, Santa Fe, Tulsa, New England, New York, Florence, and

Barbara McAlister, 2003.
Courtesy of Barbara McAlister.

Arizona. She has been a soloist at
Carnegie Hall, Lincoln Center's Alice
Tully Hall, and the Weill Recital Hall,
and has appeared with the Houston
Symphony Orchestra, the Dusseldorf
Symphony, and the Symphony in
Passau. In 2005, she made her debut
with the Anchorage Opera.

In addition to her operatic ca-
reer, McAlister gives performances of Native American songs in the
Cherokee, Chippewa, and Winnebago languages. She has made appear-
ances over the years on the artist rosters of the Mid-America Arts Alliance
Touring Program and the Oklahoma State Arts Council Touring Program.
In 1995, she created the role of Qualla in the world premiere of *Mountain
Windsong*, a musical play by Robert J. Conley and Linder Chlarson, at the
outdoor theater in Tahlequah, Oklahoma.

In addition to her career as a classical singer, McAlister is well known
as a visual artist. Her paintings have been shown at the Five Civilized Tribes
Museum in Muskogee, Oklahoma, the Jacobson House in Oklahoma City,
the Wharton Art Gallery in Philadelphia, and Bullock's in Los Angeles. Many
of her paintings are in private collections throughout the United States and
Europe. She was a recipient of the Cherokee Medal of Honor in 1999.

Medawar, Mardi Oakley

Mardi Oakley Medawar is a North Carolina Cherokee. She is an author,
lecturer, artist, musician, and American Indian rights activist. She has ten
critically acclaimed novels to her credit. Winner of the Western Writers of
America Spur Award for the Best First Novel and Finalist for the Best Novel
of the West, she was also honored as Writer of the Year by the Wordcraft
Circle of Native Writers and Storytellers. While living on the Red Cliff reservation in northern Wisconsin, she worked for Honoring Our Neighbors'
Origins and Rights (HONOR) and wrote articles for the *HONOR Digest*,
the organization's international publication. She went on to help start up
Team Response: Indians Against Defamation (TRIAD).

As a visual artist, Medawar paints portraits in watercolor and oils that have been displayed in galleries around the United States and that are in demand by private collectors. Former Red Cliff tribal chairperson Rose Gurnoe Soulier, her good friend, taught her the art of beading. Since then, Medawar has been using this ancient craft in her portraits, creating large and intricate designs. In her studio, she also works with stained glass, creating both fitted windows and large hanging panels with American Indian themes. One of her panels hangs in the Red Cliff Tribal Court House.

As a musician, she plays the American Indian flute. She owns a wide range of flutes made for her by the renowned flute master J. P. Gomez. In North Carolina, she is an active member of the Neuse River Flute Circle.

As a lecturer, she has spoken and taught seminars in colleges and universities all across the country. She is currently working on her eleventh novel. She is a member of Wordcraft Circle of Native Writers and Storytellers, Western Writers of America, and Sisters in Crime. Some of her titles are *Murder on Red Cliff Rez*; *The Fort Larned Incident*; *Murder at Medicine Lodge*; *Remembering the Osage Kid*; *The Misty Hills of Home*; *Death at Rainy Mountain*; and *People of the Whistling Waters*.

Medicine

In the Cherokee belief system, there are good medicine people and evil medicine people. The evil medicine people will do things, for a price, to harm individuals. An individual thus harmed must go to a good medicine person, who, if he or she is strong enough, can turn the bad medicine around and make it return to its origins. A bad medicine person is sometimes referred to as a witch, in Cherokee a *tskili* or *sgili*, which means literally "a dusky horned owl." Much of the medicine person's time is spent dealing with this kind of "bad medicine." But the medicine person, or Indian doctor, takes care of other problems, too: injuries, illnesses, and psychological problems. Stories of amazing cures are numerous.

Meredith, Howard

Howard Meredith was born in Galveston, Texas, on May 25, 1938. He was educated in Texas City public schools, the University of Texas at Austin (bachelor's degree, 1961), Stephen F. Austin State University (master's, 1963), and the University of Oklahoma (Ph.D., 1970). His doctorate was in history and American Indian studies. He met his wife, Mary Ellen Milam, at the University of Oklahoma, and they were married in 1967. Meredith taught at Kentucky Wesleyan College from 1967 to 1971; worked for the Executive Council of the Episcopal Church from 1971 to 1974; and worked for the Oklahoma Historical Society from 1975 to 1979, where he established the Historic Preservation Office. He was dean of students at Bacone College in Muskogee, Oklahoma, from 1979 to 1985, when he left to begin teaching at the University of Science and Arts of Oklahoma at Chickasha, where he became head of Indian studies.

Meredith received the Muriel Wright Endowment Award for Excellence in Writing from the Oklahoma Historical Society in 1980, the Best Teaching Award from Bacone College in 1981, the Westerners International Award for Best Book on the West in 1989, the McCasland Award for Excellence in Teaching at the University Level from the Oklahoma Heritage Association in 1994, the Regents Award for Superior Research from the University of Science and Arts of Oklahoma in 1996, and the Regents Award for Superior Teaching from the University of Science and Arts of Oklahoma in 1995 and 1998.

Meredith is the author of ten books, among them *Hasinai: A Traditional History of the Caddo Confederacy* and *Bartley Milam: Principal Chief of the Cherokee Nation*. The latter is not only an excellent biography of Milam, but also probably the only source of information on Cherokee history from Oklahoma statehood in 1907 until Milam's death in 1949.

Meredith is also the author of more than one hundred short pieces: book reviews, articles, and stories that have appeared in countless publications, including *World Literature Today*; *Chronicles of Oklahoma*; *Journal of the West*; *Indian Historian*; *American Indians*; *Journal of American History*; *American Indian Culture and Research Journal*; *Western Historical Quarterly*; and *American Indian Quarterly*.

Howard Meredith died May 8, 2003. The Howard Meredith Indian Humanities Center was subsequently established at the University of Science and Arts of Oklahoma in his honor.

Meredith, Mary Ellen

Mary Ellen Meredith was born Mary Ellen Milam on October 3, 1946, to Mr. and Mrs. W. T. Milam Sr. Her grandfather was a brother of Principal Chief Bartley Milam of the Cherokee Nation. Mary Ellen was educated at Christ the King School in Oklahoma City, Monte Casino High School in Tulsa, Trinity College in Washington, D.C., and the University of Oklahoma in Norman. While at the University of Oklahoma, she met and married Howard Meredith. In 1979, she was the director of the Kirkpatrick Center's Center of the American Indian, but when her husband took a job at Bacone

College in Muskogee, Oklahoma, she moved with him to Muskogee and worked in the Bacone Development Office until 1981. She was administrative vice president of the Inglesrud Corporation from 1982 to 1995. In March 1996, she established her own publishing company, Noksi Press.

Meredith is a member of the Cherokee National Historical Society, where she was president of the board of trustees from 2001 to 2005 and thereafter vice president. She served as interim director of the society from 1999 to 2003. She is also a member of the Cherokee Nation's Government Relations Team.

A member of the Wordcraft Circle of Native Writers and Storytellers, she coedited *Of the Earth* with her husband, Howard Meredith; coauthored *Reflection on Cherokee Literary Expression* and *Cherokee Humanities Course Book*; and authored numerous features, articles, stories, and poetry for organizational publications, newspapers, and anthologies. She currently divides her time between Oklahoma City and Tahlequah.

Milam, Jesse Bartley

Sarah Ellen Couch was a Cherokee, a member of the Long Hair Clan. In 1863, during the Civil War, her mother took her to Texas as a refugee. During the Reconstruction period following the war, both her parents died, leaving her an orphan at twelve years of age to live with relatives in Texas and in the Cherokee Nation in Indian Territory (in what is now Oklahoma). In 1881, William Guinn Milam left his home in Alabama and moved to Texas, where he met and married Sarah. Jesse Bartley Milam, their second child, was born in Texas in 1884. They moved to the Cherokee Nation in 1887. They settled at Sarah's old home and farmed and ranched. Jesse was one of seven children.

In 1893, William and Sarah sold their improvements and moved to the town of Chelsea, Indian Territory, where William opened a hardware store. Jesse Bartley was educated at the Cherokee Male Seminary. In 1901, he went to the Metropolitan Business College in Dallas, Texas. When he returned home to Chelsea, he went to work for the Bank of Chelsea, where his father was vice president. He also went into the oil business, drilling his first well in 1905. He had married Elizabeth Peach McSpadden the previous year. In 1908, Jesse Bartley, his father, and his brother James bought controlling interest in the Bank of Chelsea. Jesse Bartley became president of the bank in 1915.

In the 1920s, dissatisfied with the current Cherokee Nation leadership, Cherokees from four groups—the Eastern Cherokee Council, the Western

Jesse Bartley Milam, c. 1941.
Public domain. Courtesy of
the Cherokee Honor Society.

Cherokee Council, the Tulsa Cherokees, and the Keetoowah Society—began meeting regularly. In 1925, this United Council elected Levi Gritts of the Keetoowah Society their principal chief. The U.S. government, of course, did not recognize this group or its chief. During this time, Bartley Milam was engaged in a great deal of research into Cherokee history and culture as well as into various related legal issues. In 1938, when the United Council met again, they elected Bartley Milam as principal chief. Milam's major activities involved pursuing a variety of claims to the U.S. Court of Claims, but he was involved in cultural, historical, and ceremonial activities as well. He was acting like a chief.

In 1941, because of complications involving the Grand River Dam Authority, the United States found itself in the position of having to appoint a principal chief for the Cherokee Nation once again to get the land it wanted. Its own laws called for such a thing. Bartley Milam was appointed by President Franklin Roosevelt on April 21, 1941, for one year. Milam was the first chief to be appointed for more than one day since A. B. Cunningham in 1919. It was a major step in the direction of reviving the government of the Cherokee Nation.

Milam immediately began to pursue Cherokee Nation claims to the Grand River bed in northeastern Oklahoma. His second major concern was the Cherokee language. He located the original matrices for the Cherokee syllabary and set about getting print type made with a view toward beginning some publishing in the Cherokee language once again. He also pursued the establishment of Cherokee-language classes in schools and universities.

Milam purchased land outside of Tahlequah, the Cherokee Nation's capital, for a museum and archives. It was the site of the original Cherokee Female Seminary, which had burned in 1887. As principal chief, Milam was giving the U.S. government what it wanted, but at the same time he was telling it what he and the Cherokees wanted. He was also trying to get better roads in the Cherokee Nation and working to establish a cattle operation. World War II severely interrupted his efforts. In 1942, the U.S. government demanded the lands of forty-five Cherokee families in Oklahoma for expansion of Camp Gruber. Although all of the families were growing crops, the army moved them out of their lands and into a few old patched houses and Civilian Conservation Corps barracks. They were without food and homes.

Milam took note of this emergency and went to the Cookson Hills. Through his efforts, each family was finally located either on government lands or on relatives' land. He then assisted the families in taking their claims against the United States to court. In 1942, he was reappointed principal chief by President Roosevelt and again in 1943, this time for four years. In 1944, when Indians met in Denver to form the National Congress of American Indians, Bartley Milam was there. He told government officials that he needed a Cherokee council.

In 1947, President Harry S. Truman reappointed Milam as principal chief for another four-year term. Milam's goals were still the restoration of tribal government, preservation of Cherokee heritage, and vigorous pursuit of Cherokee claims. He was president of the Rogers County Bank and active in many civic and community organizations. Milam called another convention of Cherokees in Tahlequah for the purpose of establishing an executive committee to serve as a kind of tribal council. Milam's health had been declining for some time, however, and on May 8, 1949, at sixty-five years old, he died in St. Luke's Hospital in Kansas City, Missouri. His body was returned to the Cherokee Nation in Chelsea for burial. Many of the things that Bartley Milam pursued as principal chief were left unfinished. Some would be picked up by later chiefs, and some even carried to a satisfactory conclusion. He was the right man for the times.

Miller, Mose

Mose Miller is a particularly controversial figure in Cherokee history. He was photographed in the 1890s wearing a Nighthawk Keetoowah sash, which would indicate to some that his so-called outlaw career might very well have been politically motivated, somewhat like that of the better known Ned Christie. At the end of the nineteenth century, many members of the Nighthawks ran afoul of U.S. law when they resisted the allotment of Cherokee lands impelled by the Curtis Act and the Dawes Act. Redbird Smith was jailed in Muskogee, Oklahoma, until he finally agreed to sign up for his allotment.

Stories of Miller, his activities, and even his demise are completely at variance with one another. In a pamphlet called *Experiences of a Deputy U.S. Marshal in Indian Territory*, apparently written by William Frank Jones and published in 1937, Mose Miller is called a "bad outlaw." He is said to have had outlaw headquarters in the Cookson Hills with Will Nale, Little Henry Starr (a cousin of the notorious bank robber), and two white men, Andy Pettit and Greathouse. The story goes that the gang approached an old man named Tom Watson who lived two miles from Lenapah and ordered him to go to town and buy ammunition for them because they planned to rob the new bank at Checotah in the morning. Watson went to Deputy William Jones and told him. Jones told Watson to do what the gang had told him to do.

To avoid possible bloodshed in town, Jones formed a posse and went to the outlaws' rendezvous. The posse surrounded the outlaws, and a gunfight followed. Miller and Greathouse were captured, stood trial, and were sent to the pen. No further information is given.

Other sources have written either that Miller was hanged or that he was shot to death. It is instructive, also, that his alleged crimes are not detailed in any source. It seems likely, then, that Mose Miller was another of those Indian resisters who were seen as troublemakers by the U.S. government and were therefore labeled as outlaws and hunted down as such. His alleged crimes are obscure, like those of Ned Christie and Charlie Wickliffe. The chroniclers seem satisfied simply to call him a "bad outlaw." It would seem that once the government has dealt with one of these men, it then has to come up with a justification for what it has done. The logical conclusion is that Miller, like Ned Christie and others, was not an outlaw at all, but rather a political victim.

Miss Cherokee (Cherokee Nation)

Each year at the Cherokee National Holiday, a Miss Cherokee is selected to represent the tribe as a goodwill ambassador and messenger who promotes the government, history, language, and culture of the Cherokee people. Miss Cherokees to date are: Lindsay Glass (2007); Michelle Lynn Locust (2006); LaShawna Fields (2005); Ashley Downing (2004); Raven Bruner (2003); Kristen Smith-Snell (2002); Amanda Carey (2001); Jamie Standingwater (2000); Janelle Adair (1999); Tonya Still (1998); Christie Sequichie (1997); Lindsey Houston (1996); Julie Deerinwater (1995); Jessica Houston (1994); Walisi Robinson Bowen (1993); Geri Gayle Pierce (1992); Deborah Reed (1991); Tonnette Mouse Hummingbird (1990); Carla Jolyn

Robert J. Conley

Carey Rose (1989); Audra Smoke Connor (1988); Stacy Ziegenfuss (1987); Lisa Trice Turtle (1986); Julie Hill Santomero (1986); Teresa Shoemaker Tackett (1985); Jennie Terrapin (1984); Esther Raper Russell (1983); Regina Christie Bell (1982); Mary Kay Harshaw Henderson (1981); Mary Kay Harshaw Henderson (1980); Lisa Phillips (1979); Brenda Krouse (1978); Nancy Scott (1977); Cynthia Blackfox (1976); Bobbie Scott Smith (1975); Shirley Owl Dawson (1974); Wahleah Baker Turner (1973); Brenda Allen Stone (1972); Deborah Daugherty (1971); Carol Holt McKee (1970); Virginia Stroud (1969); Janice Sue Coon (1968); Carol Chopper Hamby (1967); Judy Satterfield (1966); Jeloria Owens Jensen (1965); Cynthia Ann Orcutt (1964); Mary Ketcher (1963); Ramona Collier Gallagher (1962);

LaShawna Tay Fields, Miss Cherokee, 2005. Courtesy of LaShawna Tay Fields.

Barbara Price Masters (1961); Gloria Mitchell Cooksey (1960); Carol Cochran (1959); Dana Reno Temple (1958); Linda Burrows Priest (1957); Stella Coon (1956); and Phyllis Osage (1955).

Miss Cherokee (Eastern Band of Cherokee Indians)

The Eastern Band of Cherokee Indians also selects its Miss Cherokee annually. The Miss Cherokees of the Eastern Band are: Samantha Crowe (2005); Emra Arkansas (2004); Amy Kalonaheskie (2003); Natalie Hill (2002); Tina George (2001); Brooke Lossiah (2000); Natassia Baldwin (1999); Monica Wildcatt (1998); Molly Hornbuckle (1997); Nakoa Chiltoskie (1996); April Sampson Shuler (1995); Ursula Welch (1994); Sheila Davis Brown (1993); Heather Swimmer Younce (1992); Cynthia Ledford (1991); Keredith Owens (1990); Lori Sanders (1989); Janell Rattler (1988); Becky Wildcatt Crowe (1987); Lavenia West Hicks (1986); Renissa McLaughlin Walker (1985); Mollie Lossiah Grant (1984); Eugenia Thompson (1983); Melvina Swimmer (1982); Gloria West Hyatt (1981); Alice Groenwald (1980); Betty Owle-Moreland (1979); Loretta Ann Hornbuckle (1978); Elista Long (1977); Debbie Conseen (1976); Debbie West (1975); Lawana Cooper Almond (1974); Rowena Teesateskie (1973); Pearl Bradley (1972); Shirley Swayney Cloer

(1971); Loretta Hornbuckle Kirby (1970); Patty Grant (1969); Penny Otter (1967); Faren Sanders Cruz (1966); and Dorothy McCoy Smith (1965).

Missions

In 1801, encouraged by Little Turkey, the Moravians established a school at Springplace in Georgia on land donated by James Vann. In 1804, Reverend Gideon Blackburn started a Presbyterian mission near Tellico, a Cherokee town in Tennessee, and another later at the mouth of Sale Creek. Prior to 1817, many Cherokees who wanted their children educated had sent them away from home to places such as Cornwall, Connecticut, where both Elias Boudinot and John Ridge were educated. John Ross was educated at an academy in Kingsport, Tennessee. In 1817, the American Board of Commissioners for Foreign Missions, headquartered in Boston, Massachusetts, established Brainerd Mission at the site of John McDonald's former home on Chickamauga Creek in Tennessee to teach Presbyterian doctrine, elementary education, mechanical skills (for boys), and household skills (for girls). By 1826, there were eighteen mission schools in the Cherokee Nation, including not only Moravian and Presbyterian, but also Baptist and Methodist. A Cherokee, Catharine Brown, established her own school at Creek Path in what is now Alabama after finishing her education at Brainerd. Many of these schools continued until the Removal in 1838, and several of them accompanied the Cherokees and reestablished themselves in the West.

Mitchell, Anna

Anna Belle Mitchell was born October 16, 1926, at Sycamore, east of Jay, Oklahoma, to Oo-loo-tsa and Houston Sixkiller. A full-blood, bilingual Cherokee, she grew up in a Cherokee world until she attended Seneca Indian School in Wyandotte, Oklahoma, and later Haskell Institute in Lawrence, Kansas. She met and married Robert Mitchell and with him raised four daughters and one son.

She became a potter in 1969 when she and her husband had a pond dug on their property and found good clay there. Bob had always wanted a "Sequoyah pipe," and Anna said, "I'll make you one." She began studying books on Indian culture and working by trial and error. She never bought clay, but used the clay from the open pit they had dug. She experimented with it, adding pulverized sandstone, and she tried firing it in an open pit. After three years of experimentation, she finally got it right.

Robert J. Conley

Anna Mitchell.
Courtesy of
Anna Mitchell.

Mitchell has researched ancient Cherokee pottery in archives at several universities. She uses only old materials and old methods to make her pottery. She was named a Cherokee National Living Treasure in 1988 and a Red Earth Honored One in 1998. Some of her work is housed in the International Peace Museum in Berlin, Germany; the Smithsonian Institution; the Southern Plains Indian Museum; the Heard Museum in Phoenix; the Boston Museum of Fine Arts; the University Museum at Fayetteville, Arkansas; the Five Civilized Tribes Museum in Muskogee, Oklahoma; and the Cherokee Heritage Museum in Tahlequah, Oklahoma.

Anna Mitchell's work has been featured in *Oklahoma Today Magazine* (1974, 1990, and 1998); in *Directory of Oklahoma State Almanac* (1991–92 and 1993–94); *American Indian Pottery* (1984, 2d ed.) by John W. Barry; and *North American Indian Jewelry and Adornment from Pre-History to the Present* (2003) by Lois Sherr Dubin. She is credited with almost single-handedly reviving handmade pottery among the Cherokees in Oklahoma.

Mitchell, Douglas

Earl Douglas Mitchell was born in Owasso, Oklahoma, in 1929, the son of a mother who was one-half Cherokee and a father who was part Cherokee from his mother. The Mitchells were a wealthy family, owning most of the property in and around Owasso, and Douglas's great-grandmother owned land between Oklahoma City and Tulsa. His paternal grandfather was sheriff of Tulsa County. Mitchell recalls watching his grandfather and members of a posse hang a bank robber on a street in Owasso.

When Douglas was fourteen years old, his father moved the family to Houston, Texas, where he worked in the oil fields in Midland and Odessa. Douglas was an intellectual from birth, at one point memorizing the entirety of Shakespeare's *Hamlet*. When the FBI was conducting field tests during World War II for cryptologists, Douglas, though he was only fifteen years old, managed somehow to take the test. He passed it with flying colors, and when the FBI saw the results of his test, they tried to hire him. He told them that he was only fifteen years old, but they tried to hire him anyway, saying that he could finish high school in Washington. He refused, and at last they gave up on him.

Mitchell finished high school in Texas, then went on to Baylor University because of its chemistry department and a linguistics professor who taught Greek and Latin. He has had a lifelong interest in languages and philosophy. He graduated at the top of his class at Baylor and went from there to the University of Oslo in Norway, where he studied Norwegian and Old Icelandic. He returned to Texas to attend the University of Texas at Austin and study philosophy. He stayed there for one year, then made a move to Vienna, Austria. He had by this time determined to add one language a year to his repertoire. He lived in Vienna for ten years, working part-time for the American embassy, translating from German to English and from English to German.

When Mitchell returned once again to the United States, he taught various languages at various universities, including Midwestern University (now Midwestern State University) in Wichita Falls, Texas; Rice University in Houston; the University of Nevada at Reno; the University of St. Thomas in Houston; and the University of Houston. Meanwhile, he added Persian and Sanskrit to his list of languages. Over the years, he has taught French, German, Latin, Greek, Anglo-Saxon, Gothic, Old Icelandic, historical linguistics, history of the English language, and history of linguistics and playwriting. He at last settled down to a adjunct faculty position at Rice, where he continues to teach Sanskrit and playwriting.

Having mastered thirty-two languages, Mitchell decided in 1991 to discontinue the practice of acquiring a new language each year and turn his attention to writing plays. By 2001, he had written 36 one-act plays. His plays have been produced in Houston, New York City, and overseas. Edward Albee directed one of them. They include *The Clearing*; *Inner Space*; *Jocasta, My Love*; *Old Friends*; and *Where Is Thy Sting*.

Montgomery, Jack

Jack Montgomery was born on July 23, 1917, near Long, in Sequoyah County, Oklahoma. Educated in Cushing and at Chilocco Indian School, he graduated from Carnegie High School in 1935. He attended Bacone College in Muskogee, Oklahoma, where he boxed and played football and basketball. While at Bacone, he enlisted in Company I of the 180th Infantry of the 45th Division of the Oklahoma National Guard. He then went on to Redlands University in California on a football scholarship and received a bachelor's degree in physical education in 1940. After the Japanese attack on Pearl Harbor, Montgomery saw action in Sicily and at Anzio Beachhead. He was wounded and returned to the states in 1944, where he was awarded the Congressional Medal of Honor by President Franklin Roosevelt with the following citation:

For conspicuous gallantry and intrepidity at risk of life above and beyond the call of duty on 22 February 1944 near Padiglioni, Italy. Two hours before daybreak a strong force of enemy infantry established themselves in three echelons at 50 yards, 100 yards, and 300 yards respectively in front of the rifle platoon commanded by Lieutenant Montgomery. The closest position consisting of four machine guns and one mortar, threatened the immediate security of the platoon position. Seizing an M-1 rifle and several hand grenades, Lieutenant Montgomery crawled up a ditch within hand grenade range of the enemy. Then climbing boldly onto a little mound, he fired his rifle and threw his hand grenades so accurately that he killed eight of the enemy, and captured the remaining four. Returning to his platoon, he called for artillery fire on a house in and around which he suspected that the majority of the enemy had entrenched themselves. Arming himself with a carbine, he proceeded along the shallow ditch as withering fire from the riflemen and machine gunners in the second position was concentrated on him. He attacked this position with such fury that seven of the enemy surrendered to him, and both machine guns were silenced. Three German dead were found in the vicinity later that morning. Lieutenant Montgomery continued boldly toward the house, 300 yards from his platoon position. It was now daylight and enemy observation was excellent across the flat open terrain which led to Lieutenant Montgomery's objective. When the artillery barrage lifted, Lieutenant Montgomery ran fearlessly toward the strongly defended position. As the enemy started streaming out of the house, Lieutenant Montgomery, unafraid of treacherous snipers, exposed himself daringly to assemble the surrendering enemy and sent them to the rear. His fearless, aggressive and intrepid action that morning accounted for a total of eleven enemy dead, thirty-two prisoners, and an unknown number wounded. That night while aiding an adjacent unit to repulse a counterattack, he was struck by mortar fragments and seriously wounded. The selflessness and courage exhibited by Lieutenant Montgomery in alone attacking three strong enemy positions, inspired his men to a degree beyond estimation.

Montgomery was also awarded the Silver Star, the Combat Infantryman's Badge, the Purple Heart with Cluster, the Military Cross of Valor from the Italian government, and the Oklahoma Distinguished Service Cross. After the war, he worked for the Veterans Administration as a contact representative. During the Korean War, he was an instructor at the Fort Benning Infantry School. He was discharged in 1953 and went back to work for the Veterans Administration. He retired in 1972 and lived near Lake Tenkiller in Oklahoma with his wife, Joyce Magnum.

Mooney, James

A white man, James Mooney was born in 1861 in Richmond, Illinois. Both his parents were from Ireland. He was educated in the public schools of Richmond, where he later taught. He also worked for the *Richmond Paladium*, the local newspaper. Because of a lifelong interest in American Indians, in 1885 he wrote to John Wesley Powell, the founder of the Bureau of American Ethnology, seeking employment. His first assignment was studying the Cherokees, and his work was done primarily in 1887 and 1888. His important work for Cherokees is *The Sacred Formulas of the Cherokees* (Bureau of American Ethnology, Seventh Annual Report, 1885–86); *Myths of the Cherokees* (Bureau of American Ethnology, Nineteenth Annual Report, 1897–98); "Evolution in Cherokee Personal Names," *American Anthropologist*, old series, 2 (1889): 61–62; "The Cherokee Ball Play," *American Anthropologist*, old series, 3 (1890): 105–32; "Improved Cherokee Alphabets," *American Anthropologist*, old series, 5 (1892): 63–64; "The Cherokee River Cult," *Journal of American Folklore* 13 (1900): 1–10; and *The Swimmer Manuscript: Cherokee Sacred Formulas and Medicinal Prescriptions* (Bureau of American Ethnology Bulletin no. 99, 1932). Although unfinished by Mooney at his death in 1921, the latter work was subsequently completed by Frans Olbrechts.

Robert J. Conley

Moore, MariJo

MariJo Moore, of Cherokee descent, was chosen as one of the top five American Indian writers of the new century by *Native Peoples Magazine* in 2000. She received North Carolina's Distinguished Woman of Year in Arts Award in 1998. She serves on the boards of the North Carolina Humanities Council and the Wordcraft Circle of Native Writers and Storytellers. Her works have appeared in numerous magazines, newspapers, journals, and anthologies. Her books include *The Diamond Doorknob; Red Woman with Backward Eyes and Other Stories; Spirit Voices of Bones*; and *Crow Notes*. She lives in the mountains of North Carolina.

"Moytoy," see "Ama-edohi"

N.

Names, Cherokee

By tradition, an older woman of a Cherokee clan gives a child a name at birth. The name is a clan name, passed along within the clan. In earlier times, that name was kept a secret, and the child grew up with a nickname. A boy was often simply called "Boy" or "Choogie," from the word for "boy," *achuja*. Today, many Cherokee males still go by that name. As the boy grew older, he might earn some other nickname, or he might earn a new name. The great Cherokee war chief Dragging Canoe is said to have earned his name when as a boy he was told by his father that he could go to war with the men if he could put his own heavy dugout war canoe into the water by himself. It usually took several men to put one canoe into the water. One of the men looked back and said, "Look. He's dragging the canoe." Men earned war titles, such as "Raven" or "Mankiller," and thereafter would be known by that title. Indeed, some of these titles became surnames—"Mankiller," for instance. Other surnames came about in interesting ways. When John Stuart, the British superintendent of southern Indian affairs, a man with a shock of bushy red hair, came among the Cherokees, he was nicknamed "Bushyhead." He married a Cherokee woman, and when they had children, "Bushyhead" became the family surname. When Buck Watie went north to school in Cornwall, Connecticut, his benefactor was Reverend Elias Boudinot. Watie took Boudinot's name out of honor and respect. He passed that surname on in his family.

Name changes were frequent. It is said that President George Washington changed Bloody Fellow's name to Iskagua, or "Clear Sky," when the man became an advocate of peace. The use of the English language caused changes as well. Gunundalegi, One Who Follows the Ridge (once known as Pathkiller), used the shortened version of the English translation of his Cherokee name, "Ridge." When he served in the U.S. Army under Andrew Jackson, he achieved the rank of major and thereafter was known as Major Ridge.

Gul'kalaski (Junaluska) is said to have saved Jackson's life at Horseshoe Bend, and Jackson pledged perpetual friendship. Later, when Jackson was president and pushing for Cherokee removal, Gul'kalaski went to Washington, D.C., to see him and plead the Cherokee case, but Jackson would not even see him. Gul'kalaski then said, "I tried, but I failed." Thereafter, he was called "Tsunuhlahuhski," "He Tries but Fails." The Cherokee name became anglicized to "Junaluska" and in the next generation became a surname.

National Party

Following the Removal in 1838, the Ross Party became known as the National Party.

New Echota

In 1825, the legislative council of the Cherokee Nation passed a resolution to establish a permanent capital at New Town to be called New Echota. It was estimated that its location, at the confluence of the Coosawattee and Conasauga rivers, was nearly in the center of the Cherokee Nation. A Council House, a Supreme Court Building, and a print shop were erected. Permanent homes for Reverend Samuel Worcester, Elias Boudinot, and Boudinot's printers were also built. New Echota was also within the boundaries claimed by the state of Georgia, however. When Georgia passed its notorious anti-Cherokee laws, it forbade the Cherokee Council to meet, and the Cherokee Nation's government was forced to move. New Echota was used as the meeting place for the signing of the illegal Removal Treaty (Treaty of New Echota). Because of the pressures on the Cherokees in Georgia, the seat of government was moved to Red Clay in Tennessee.

New, Lloyd Kiva

Lloyd Kiva New was born in Oklahoma in 1916. As a young man, he went to Chicago for the World's Fair of 1933, where he was amazed at the artwork he saw. With money from the Bureau of Indian Affairs, he attended the Art Institute of Chicago and received a degree in arts education in 1938. After a stint in the U.S. Navy, New opened a fashion studio in Scottsdale,

Arizona. He became director of the Southwest Indian Arts Project and then helped to establish the Institute of American Indian Arts (IAIA) in Santa Fe, New Mexico, where he became art director and later president. In 1990, he was named president emeritus of IAIA. He died in 1990 at the age of eighty-five.

New Town

New Echota, the capital of the Cherokee Nation, was established in 1825 at New Town, within Georgia. (See "New Echota.")

Nighthawk Keetoowah Society

Sometime between 1898 and 1901, according to Janey B. Hendrix, politics and factionalism reached the Keetoowah Society, a full-blood Cherokee society dedicated to preserving Cherokee culture and traditions and to maintaining Cherokee sovereignty. This change was a result of the Dawes Commission's activities in enrolling Cherokees to receive their individual allotments of land (with anything not allotted to go to white settlers). Redbird Smith and his followers withdrew from the Keetoowah Society and formed their own organization, the Nighthawk Keetoowahs. Redbird Smith urged the members not to vote and not to register. Some of the leaders of the movement, including Smith, were arrested and jailed until they agreed to register. The Nighthawks' first ceremonial ground was built by Smith in 1902. Believing that the Cherokee Nation no longer had a chief, the Nighthawk Keetoowahs changed Redbird Smith's title from chairman to chief in 1906.

Norton, Major John

Major John Norton was born around 1770, the son of a Cherokee father and a Scottish mother. Norton's father had apparently joined the British army and settled in Scotland, where he met his wife. The young Norton was likely educated in Scotland and joined the British army, like his father, at an early age. In 1785, he was stationed in Quebec. While at Niagara, he deserted the army. He taught school at a Six Nations (Iroquois) settlement on the Bay of Quinte in Ontario, where he became familiar with the Mohawk language and culture. He soon left teaching, however, for life as a trader, but it proved to be unsatisfactory as well. In 1791, he was appointed official interpreter for the Indian Department of Lower Canada. During

Robert J. Conley

Major John Norton, c. 1816. Courtesy of the Champlain Society, Toronto, Ontario.

this time, though, he had become acquainted with the Mohawk chief Joseph Brant, and soon he was accepted as an adopted Mohawk and had become an important figure in Mohawk politics.

In 1804, Norton was sent to England to plead for Indian rights on the Grand River in Canada. The trip was unsuccessful politically, but Norton became quite a celebrity in England, spending some time on the lecture circuit. He returned to the Grand River in 1806, then made a trip to Cherokee country in 1809, where he was apparently accepted without question. He stayed for about ten months and returned to the Grand River with a young Cherokee "relative."

During the War of 1812, Norton fought with the Indians and British against the Americans, notably at Queenston Heights, where he led a force of Mohawks, Ojibwa, Mississauga, and Delaware into battle and victory. After the war, he went again to England, this time with a wife and son. While in England, he wrote his now famous *Journal*, but he was unsuccessful in getting it published. He returned to Grand River in 1816. He killed his wife's lover in a duel in 1823 and left the area with his son, traveling to Arkansas, where his Cherokee relatives had removed. While in Arkansas, he became acquainted with Reverend Cephas Washburn, who mentioned Norton in his *Reminiscences of the Indians*. Norton left Arkansas, never to be heard of again. Scholars have assumed that he died around 1831.

It should be mentioned also that some scholars, notably Raymond D. Fogelson, have questioned the generally accepted version of Norton's early life and therefore his claim to Cherokee blood. If they are right, then Norton may have been the first "Indian wannabe."

O.

Oconostota, see "Ogan'sto'"

Ogan'sto'

Ogan'sto,' whose name is usually spelled "Oconostota" and translated as "Groundhog Sausage," was born around 1712. He was badly scarred from one of the epidemics of smallpox that had swept through the Cherokee country, and this disfiguration seems to have been the origin of his hatred of the English. He first appears in history in the year 1736, when the French visited Cherokee Overhill towns in Tennessee and were shunned by Ada-gal'kala. Ogan'sto', however, flew a French flag over his home. Shortly afterward, he achieved the status of war chief of Echota in Tennessee, and he visited the French at Fort Toulouse in the Creek Nation (near present-day Montgomery, Alabama). A British trader quoted him as having said, "What nation or what people am I afraid of? I do not fear all the forces which the great King George can send against me in these mountains." But by 1753, he had reevaluated his position. The French could not supply him with the trade goods he needed, and he began to support the British.

In 1755, Ogan'sto' led five hundred warriors against the Creeks at Talliwa, causing them to vacate northern Georgia. When the so-called French and Indian War broke out between France and England, the British colonies sought the help of the Cherokees, and the Cherokees responded. Fort Loudon was built in the Overhills for the protection of the Cherokee women and children while the men were away fighting. Ogan'sto' led campaigns into Ohio and against Fort Toulouse, but Ada-gal'kala received most of the credit because of his powers of speech. In 1758, Virginia requested that the Cherokees move against the Shawnees, who were allies of the French. Ogan'sto' raised the necessary force, but finally refused to go until the autumn on the advice of the conjurers. When the Cherokees did go, Ogan'sto' did not go with them. This was the disastrous trip through

Robert J. Conley

Virginia that resulted in Cherokees fighting backwoods Virginians and Carolinians, discussed in the entry on Ada-Gal'kala. As result of these fights, Ogan'sto' and fifty-four other Cherokees were captured in Charleston, South Carolina, as retribution.

Governor William Lyttleton of South Carolina then moved the hostages to Fort Prince George, where he had them all imprisoned together in a small room. They were to be exchanged for the Cherokees who were guilty of killing the backwoodsmen. Ada-Gal'kala managed to get Ogan'sto' released. Then both Ada-Gal'kala and Ogan'sto' signed an agreement with Lyttleton that the remaining hostages would be detained until the guilty Cherokees were brought in. Then smallpox broke out in the Cherokee towns and at Fort Prince George, and Lyttleton ran back to Charleston with his army.

In February 1760, Ogan'sto' lured Lieutenant Richard Coytmore, commander of Fort Prince George, outside the front gate. He had a number of warriors hidden, and when he waved a bridle over his head three times, a prearranged signal, the hidden warriors fired, killing Coytmore and wounding two other soldiers. The angry soldiers inside the fort slaughtered the remaining hostages.

Leaving Fort Prince George under siege, Ogan'sto' took some men to lay siege to Fort Loudon. Cherokee women sneaked food in to their husbands and sweethearts, some say at the encouragement of Ada-Gal'kala. Then Ada-Gal'kala fled to the woods with his family. He may have been fleeing from the smallpox, or Ogan'sto' may have driven him off, or both. When the British sent Colonel Hugh Montgomery and his troops into the Cherokee country to rescue the men in Fort Loudon, Ogan'sto' left the siege at Fort Loudon in the hands of Ostenaco and went to meet Montgomery. He ambushed the British troops near Echoe and drove them away. (Montgomery claimed a victory, but the truth is that he had left Fort Loudon under siege.) Ogan'sto' returned to the besieged fort.

When the garrison at last surrendered on August 7, Captain Raymond Demere, in charge, agreed to leave guns and ammunition in the fort to the Cherokees. In exchange, he was allowed to take only enough guns and ammunition to hunt on the way home. Some Cherokees would accompany them part of the way. Ogan'sto' swore to kill the first Indian who harmed a white man. The troops marched out of Fort Loudon, accompanied by a number of Cherokees. Other Cherokees went into the abandoned fort, where they found that the white men had buried the guns and ammunition and thrown a cannon into the river. Outraged, they caught up with the column of fleeing soldiers and attacked them.

Twenty-four were killed. Others were captured, including John Stuart. Ada-gal'kala ransomed Stuart and took him to safety.

Next came a clash of warfare styles. Ogan'sto' was satisfied, having killed enough Englishmen to "cover" the murdered Cherokee hostages, and he went to Governor William Bull of South Carolina to talk peace and lift the siege of Fort Prince George. Governor Bull was inclined to agree, but when word reached Charleston of the fate of the soldiers from Fort Loudon, he changed his tune. In the meantime, Ogan'sto went to New Orleans and signed a treaty with the French there. He returned to the Cherokee country with a commission as a captain in the French army. Even so, he continued to make overtures of peace with the British, but the British had sent Colonel James Grant with a punitive expedition into the Cherokee country.

Grant destroyed fifteen Cherokee towns and fifteen hundred acres of corn, and he claimed to have driven five thousand Cherokees into the mountains to starve. Ogan'sto' continued to send messages to Grant that he was ready to conclude a peace. Grant insisted that Ogan'sto' appear in person, but Ogan'sto' would not do so. Ada-gal'kala took over the process, and, as related in the entry on Ada-gal'kala, the war was finally ended. When Old Hop (Guhna-gadoga) died around 1756, and the mantle of Cherokee "emperor" was passed on to his nephew Uka Ulah, it became obvious that the two real powers were Ada-gal'kala and Ogan'sto'.

The British favored Ada-gal'kala, but Ogan'sto' had more influence with the Cherokees. When Uka Ulah died in 1761, Stuart, who had become the British superintendent for southern Indian affairs, recognized his old friend Ada-gal'kala as the "principal chief." With the French out of the picture, Ogan'sto' had to satisfy himself with cooperating with the British. In 1767, following long and bloody wars with the northern Iroquois tribes, Ogan'sto' accompanied Stuart and Ada-gal'kala to New York to visit Sir William Johnson, Stuart's northern counterpart. In New York, they went to see a production of Shakespeare's *Richard III* and then went on to Johnson Hall, where Sir William helped conclude a peace between the Cherokees and the northern Iroquois.

In 1773, Ogan'sto' was inducted into the Saint Andrew's Society, a fraternal order of Scots. John Stuart was president of that organization.

In 1775, Ogan'sto' joined with Ada-gal'kala in making the sale to the Transylvania Company of much of what is now Tennessee and Kentucky, thereby greatly angering Dragging Canoe and other younger Cherokee men. The old warrior had recently suffered a humiliating defeat at the hands of the Chickasaws, and he maintained that he needed guns and ammunition. He later denied having made the sale, but there is no doubt

Robert J. Conley

that he was closely involved in it. In his old age, though, Ogan'sto' became an advocate of peace. When the American Revolution broke out, he tried to keep the Cherokees neutral, but at a council where Dragging Canoe and other young men spoke out strongly in favor of war against the Americans, Ogan'sto' and Ada-gal'kala sat dejected and let the voices of the young men win the day.

Dragging Canoe led his warriors into battle, and in retaliation the Americans sent Colonel William Christian into the Cherokee country, where he laid waste to the Overhills towns in Tennessee. Dragging Canoe and his followers withdrew into Creek country and built new towns along the Chickamauga Creek, becoming known as the Chickamaugas. Ada-gal'kala and Ogan'sto' called for a peace conference with Christian to try to convince the Americans that Dragging Canoe was not acting for all Cherokees. They agreed to turn over Dragging Canoe and Alexander Cameron, Stuart's assistant, to the Americans. A peace conference followed. Before it was over, the Cherokees had given more land to Virginia, and Ogan'sto' had pledged his undying love to the Americans.

Dragging Canoe continued his war against the Americans, and in 1778 Ada-gal'kala died. Ogan'sto', who many believe to have been the Cherokees' choice anyway, was appointed the principal chief. In 1782, he attempted to resign his position to his son, but the Cherokees would not have it. He died in 1785, at around seventy-three years old, and was buried according to his wishes in his hometown of Echota, but he was not to be left alone. His bones were disinterred in 1976 to make way for the Tennessee Valley Authority's Tellico Dam project. A pair of eyeglasses were found in the casket with the bones.

Old Settlers

After the Act of Union in 1839 between the two main Cherokee factions, those Cherokees who had recently moved from Arkansas to present-day Oklahoma and who had called themselves "Western Cherokees" and their nation the "Western Cherokee Nation" or the "Cherokees West" came to be known as the Old Settlers.

Original Cherokee Communities Organization

Organized in the 1960s, the Original Cherokee Communities Organization (OCCO) was a full-blood Cherokee organization headed by George Groundhog. They had no money, but they did what they could to help other Cherokee people in the Oklahoma hills. They did not believe that the Cherokee Nation under the leadership of Chief W. W. Keeler was representing them properly, if at all. Scholars from the University of Chicago and other institutions became involved with them, initially to help with language projects. The OCCO also put out a newsletter. White lawyer Stuart Trapp worked with them on land issues. Keeler said they had been misled by "outside agitators" and "communists."

Oskison, John Milton

John Milton Oskison was born in 1874 at Pryor Creek in the Cherokee Nation (Indian Territory, in what is now Oklahoma), the son of John Oskison and Rachel Connor Crittenden. He was a lifelong friend of Will Rogers. In 1894, he graduated from Willie Halsell College, and from there he went on to Stanford University, graduating in 1898 with a bachelor's degree. He then did some graduate work in English at Harvard, where one of his classmates was Herbert Hoover. While at Harvard, Oskison entered the short story "Only the Master Shall Praise" in a writing contest sponsored by *Century Magazine.* When he received first prize, he decided that he would make writing his career. He wrote newspaper editorials, magazine articles, essays, short stories, speeches, and novels. He was also editor of the *New York Evening Post* and *Collier's Weekly.* In 1903, he married Florence Ballard Day, a niece of Jay Gould.

In 1917, Oskison joined the U.S. Army and was sent to France, where he worked for and wrote about the relief effort going on there. After the war, he busied himself writing novels about Indian Territory. *Wild Harvest, Black Jack Davy,* and *Brothers Three* are a few of his titles. He chose to live in New York or in Paris and to pay visits to Oklahoma from time to time. In 1920, he and Florence Day were divorced, and later that same year he married Hildegard Hawthorne, a granddaughter of Nathaniel Hawthorne. Oskison died in 1947.

In 2007, Oskison's unpublished manuscript *The Singing Bird* was discovered in a library on the University of Oklahoma campus and was published at last by the University of Oklahoma Press.

Ostenaco

Ostenaco has also been called Austenaco, Ustenach, Judd's Friend, and Mankiller. In 1754, at the urging of Nathaniel Gist, a trader from Virginia, Ostenaco led one hundred Cherokees against the Shawnees, who were

Ostenaco, c. 1762.
Courtesy of the
Smithsonian Institution.

allied with the French. Persuaded by the
British, they left in January, not the traditional time of war for Cherokees. Their
provisions were lost in a frozen river they
were trying to cross. As they attempted to
get back home, they were compelled to kill
their horses for food. Along the way, they
were attacked by colonial Virginians, who couldn't tell one type of Indian
from another or who didn't care. Angered, the Cherokees, led by Ostenaco,
laid siege to Fort Loudon and eventually killed most of the soldiers there. The
Cherokee sense of balance having been restored (a life for a life), Ostenaco
spoke for peace in 1760. Peace was finally negotiated after many complications, thanks largely to the efforts of Ada-gal'kala.

After the Treaty of 1761 between the Cherokees and Virginia, Lieuten-
ant Henry Timberlake went to the Cherokee country from Virginia "to
cultivate their friendship." He stayed at the home of Ostenaco. When
Timberlake returned to Virginia, he was accompanied by Ostenaco,
Pouting Pigeon, and Stalking Turkey. Timberlake showed a picture of
King George III of England to Ostenaco, who is supposed to have said that
now he had seen the dead picture of the king, he wished to see him alive.
Timberlake made arrangements for a trip to England.

The three Cherokees were camped outside of Williamsburg, where
Thomas Jefferson was a student at William and Mary College. Jefferson
stopped by the Cherokee camp one evening. He wrote later, "I knew
much of the great Outassete [Ostenaco], the warrior and orator of the
Cherokees. He was always the guest of my father on his journeys to and
from Williamsburg. I was in his camp when he made his great farewell
oration to his people the evening before he departed for England. The
moon was in full splendour, and to her he seemed to address himself in
his prayers for his own safety on the voyage and that of his people during
his absence. His sounding voice, distinct articulation, animated action,
and the solemn silence of his people at their several fires, filled me with
awe and veneration, although I did not understand a word he uttered."

Timberlake took the three Cherokees to England on the sloop *Epreuve*. It landed at Plymouth on June 16, 1762. Timberlake wrote, "While in the boat that took us ashore, Ostenaco, painted in a very frightful manner, sang a solemn dirge with a very loud voice, to return thanks to God for his safe arrival. The loudness and uncouthness of his singing, and the oddity of his person, drew a vast crowd of boats filled with spectators from all the ships in the harbour." Their interpreter had died at sea, and the only way they could communicate was through signs. The British newspapers called Ostenaco the king of the Cherokees. After a three-week wait, the Cherokees were granted an audience with King George III. They left England on August 25, 1762. Ostenaco was sixty years old at this time. When the American Revolution started, Ostenaco, an old man, lived quietly with his grandson Richard Timberlake, son of Henry Timberlake and one of Ostenaco's daughters. He supported Dragging Canoe's efforts, but he died peacefully around 1780.

Osti, Jane

A Cherokee from Oklahoma, Jane Osti has been making traditional southeastern-inspired pottery since 1991. She graduated from Northeastern State University in Tahlequah, Oklahoma, magna cum laude, in 1989 with a bachelor's in fine arts and in 1992 with a master's in education. In 1989, she met renowned Cherokee potter Anna Mitchell, who introduced her to traditional Cherokee pottery. Since then Osti has exhibited across the country and won many awards. She has been designated a National Living Treasure by the Cherokee Nation. She lives and works in Tahlequah.

Other Cherokee Groups

The Cherokees, more than any other group of American Indians, have large numbers of people who are Cherokees but cannot prove it or who want to be Cherokees or who claim to be Cherokees for whatever reasons. In addition to the three federally recognized Cherokee tribes and the state recognized tribes, Tony Mack McClure, in *Cherokee Proud*, lists more than 250 Cherokee "tribes," some of which charge membership fees and some of which practice strange varieties of "Cherokee culture" and give each other "Cherokee names."

Outacite

Outacite's name is sometimes spelled "Outacity, Outassite, Otacite, Outassatah, Wootasite," and, James Mooney says, "Wrosetasetow." John P.

Robert J. Conley

Brown says that it is literally "Untsi-tee-hee," meaning "Mankiller." Outacite was one of the leaders of the Cherokees who laid siege to Fort Loudon in South Carolina in 1760 and became a follower of Dragging Canoe.

Owen, Narcissa

Narcissa Chisholm Owen was born in Webbers Falls in the Cherokee Nation in 1831, the daughter of Thomas Chisholm and Melinda Chisholm. As a child, she lived with Reverend Jesse Bushyhead and attended his school at Baptist Mission. At twelve years old, she was sent to Evansville, Indiana, to study music at a small college there. She taught school in Greensboro, Tennessee, where she met and married Robert Owen in 1853. Robert died in 1873, his fortune wiped out by the Civil War. With two sons to support, Narcissa went back to teaching school. She taught at Fayetteville, Arkansas, and then at the Cherokee Female Seminary in the Cherokee Nation. Mrs. Owen was also an artist, winning a medal at the St. Louis Exposition for her portrait of the descendants of Thomas Jefferson. She died in Guthrie, Oklahoma, in 1911.

Owen, Robert Latham

Robert Latham Owen was born in Richmond, Virginia, the son of Narcissa Owen and Robert Owen, a white man. He was educated in private schools in Richmond and Baltimore. He graduated with honors from Washington and Lee University in Lexington, Virginia, and moved to the Cherokee Nation in Indian Territory. In 1881, he was secretary to the Cherokee Nation's Board of Education. He was elected a U.S. senator from Oklahoma in 1907 and retired in 1925.

Owl, Sampson

Sampson Owl could hit a six-inch square at one hundred feet with a dart from his blowgun. He was principal chief of the Eastern Band of Cherokees from 1923 to 1927.

Owle, Freeman

Freeman Owle, an Eastern Cherokee, grew up in the Birdtown community in North Carolina. He learned to carve wood at an early age, and while attending school at Cherokee High, he studied wood carving with

Amanda Crowe. He attended college at Gardner Webb College and earned a master's degree in education from Western Carolina University. For fourteen years, he taught sixth grade at Cherokee Elementary School. For more than ten years, Freeman has been a much sought after traditional Cherokee storyteller of Cherokee culture and history. He has told his stories and presented workshops or demonstrations of stone carving and wood carving in North Carolina, Georgia, Kentucky, and Tennessee. He is a member of the board of directors of the Qualla Arts and Crafts Mutual and a coordinator for the Cherokee Heritage Trails Project of the Blue Ridge Heritage Initiative. He is a featured storyteller in the book *Living Stories of the Cherokee* (1998) and appeared in the documentary *Cherokee: The Principal People* (1999) on public television. Freeman is currently an elder-in-residence at Western Carolina University.

P.

Parker, Gerard

Gerard Parker was principal chief of the Eastern Band of Cherokees from September 15, 1995, to October 2, 1995.

Pathkiller

Pathkiller, or Nunna-tihi, served briefly as principal chief of the Cherokee Nation between Black Fox's two terms, from 1808 to 1809, but then a much longer term from 1811 to 1827. He was from the Lower Towns and was a conservative Cherokee. He had sided with Black Fox early on and signed some of the same treaties drawn up in Black Fox's tenure, but sometime around 1808 he changed his position, becoming the leader of the faction opposed to removal to the West. Even so, in 1816, General Andrew Jackson managed to get Pathkiller's signature on a letter claiming to have ratified a treaty selling 2.2 million acres for three cents an acre. Pathkiller had not signed the actual treaty.

It was during Pathkiller's tenure that the Cherokees joined forces with Jackson to fight against the Creek Redsticks. The Cherokee soldiers, including Pathkiller himself, Junaluska, Whitepath, Richard Taylor, Charles Rees, Young Dragging Canoe, John Ross, Major Ridge, Sequoyah, George Lowry, and the "adopted Cherokee" Sam Houston, fought at the decisive battle of Horseshoe Bend that brought an end to the war in 1814.

Pressures for Cherokee removal intensified. It was during this time, too, that Sequoyah presented the Cherokees with his syllabary for reading and writing the Cherokee language, and the so-called Whitepath Rebellion took place. Whitepath was an old and respected Cherokee chief and a member of the National Council. When the council met in 1826 to discuss the writing of a new constitution, Whitepath, apparently because of opposition to the new constitution, was removed from the council and replaced by a young man, a mixed-blood. When the vote to adopt a new constitution passed, Whitepath and other like-minded Cherokees called their own council meeting at Ellijay in Georgia. The "rebellion" was not a violent one. Its sole purpose was the preservation of Cherokee ways. In the midst of all this turmoil, Pathkiller died in January 1827. He had been ably assisted for ten years of his tenure by Second Chief Charles Renatus Hicks, a bilingual Cherokee half-blood and a Moravian convert.

Payne, Andy

Andy Payne was born in 1907 near Chelsea, Oklahoma, the son of Mae Hartley Payne and Andrew J. L. Payne. Andy's father, called Doc, worked for a time for Clem Rogers alongside Clem's son Will on the Rogers Ranch. Doc later bought a farm near Foyil, Oklahoma, and Andy went to school at Foyil. In high school, he participated in track. After graduation, he went to California, hoping to find work. Instead, he found an ad in the newspaper for C. C. Pyle's International Trans-continental Foot Race. Andy and Doc together raised the $125 for the entry fee. Andy won the race from Ascot Park in Los Angeles to Madison Square Garden in New York City, a total of 3,422.3 miles in 573 hours, 4 minutes, and 34 seconds. That's 84 days. The year was 1928. The prize was $25,000. Andy went back to Oklahoma, paid off his family's farm, built them a new home, bought himself some land and a car, and married Vivian Shaddox of Tahlequah, Oklahoma. In 1934, he ran for the office of clerk of the Oklahoma State Supreme Court and won. Except for two years while he was in the army during World War II, he kept that position until his retirement in 1973. During those years, he went to law school at night with a major interest in land. Before his death in 1977, he owned one thousand acres in seventeen counties of Oklahoma, with coal, gas, and oil interests.

Payne, John Howard

Born in New York City in 1792, John Howard Payne, a white man, was an internationally known actor and playwright when he first visited Principal Chief John Ross of the Cherokee Nation in 1832. He had previously not questioned the things he had heard about Cherokees and believed that they would be better off in the West, but for some reason at this time he decided to see for himself what the situation was. He went looking for Chief Ross and wound up being invited to stay, which he did for several weeks. While Payne was staying with Ross in a one-room house that Ross had been forced to flee to when the anti-Cherokee Georgians took over his mansion, he was arrested along with the chief by the Georgia Guard and put in jail for a week.

After the Removal in 1838, Payne was once again a houseguest of John Ross, this time for four months. He attended the first Cherokee National Council meeting in the new Cherokee Nation, wrote a complete account of the trial of Archilla Smith, charged with murdering John McIntosh, and published various stories and articles about the Cherokees. At Ross's home, Payne interviewed Sequoyah, but the interpreter would not interrupt Sequoyah, and when the interview was over, Payne had not gotten in a word. Sequoyah did not return to give Payne a second chance. Payne also wrote a major work on old customs of the Cherokees by interviewing a number of Cherokee old-timers, but other than excerpts here and there, the work has never been published, although it is currently being edited for publication by Bill Anderson at Western Carolina University. Payne was appointed U.S. consul to Tunis in 1842 and lived there until his death in 1852. For all of his accomplishments, Payne is best remembered today as the author of the song "Home Sweet Home."

Pickup, Jim

Reverend Jim Pickup was principal chief of the United Keetoowah Band in 1946, when the Band received federal recognition, and he continued to serve as chief until 1954, when he was replaced by Jeff Tindle. He reemerged to win the 1958 election. There apparently had been a difference of opinion between Pickup and Tindle, probably over Chief W. W. Keeler of the Cherokee Nation. Tindle wanted Keeler removed from the chieftainship of the Cherokee Nation, and Pickup continued to cooperate with Keeler. During Pickup's last term, talks were begun with the Bureau of Indian Affairs for acquiring a piece of land on which to establish business enterprises. The business enterprises failed to come about, however, and soon the land was to be used for office space. Earl Boyd Pierce, who was legal counsel for both the Cherokee Nation and the Keetoowah Band, seems to have manipulated both Chief Keeler and Chief Pickup during this long and involved process. The upshot of it all was that office buildings, a restaurant, and motel were built. One room in the restaurant was designated the "United Keetoowah Room." Chief Pickup died in 1968.

Pigeon, Bill, see "Woyi, Wili"

Pin Indians

The Keetoowah Society was organized shortly before the Civil War in the Cherokee Nation as a secret society for the purpose of promoting a national feeling among the full-bloods. Because of the influence of Reverend Evan Jones and his son John, however, it was also intended to counteract the influence of the Southern Rights Party among Cherokees. Members of the society, or at least some of them, came to be called Pin Indians because of the way in which they wore identifying pins under the lapels of their coats. During the Civil War, the Pins—perhaps three thousand of them—were Union supporters, fought against the Confederate Cherokees, and were distinctly antislavery.

Powell, Noah

Noah Powell was born March 10, 1908, at the Big Cove community on the Cherokee reservation in North Carolina. After he finished high school, he worked on a dairy farm in Pennsylvania for two years before returning to the reservation. He married Emma Washington. For several years, he drove school buses for the Bureau of Indian Affairs and then for the Cherokee Boys Club. He sang with the Soco Valley Quartet, traveling to the surrounding states to perform. In 1971, he was elected principal chief of the Eastern Band of Cherokees, and during his term he was concerned primarily with economic development and had a role in the preliminary work done for a new high school. Chief Noah Powell opposed the Tennessee Valley Authority's construction of the Tellico Dam, requesting intervention from Tennessee governor Winfield Dunn and President Richard Nixon. The Cherokees lost that battle, but they won a settlement of $1,855,254.50 in the Indian Claims Court. It was paid out in per capita payments to 7,200 tribal members. Powell died suddenly in 1973 while still in office. The Cherokee named One Feather called him "a mild-mannered man with deep insight and a kindness which makes you feel comfortable in his presence."

Priber, Christian Gottlieb

In 1736, a white man named Christian Gottlieb Priber, probably a native of Saxony, appeared at Tellico, a Cherokee town in what the colonists called Tennessee, and became friends with Ogan'sto'. He had come to stay. The

British said that he was both a German Jesuit priest and an agent of the French. He cut his hair and dressed like a Cherokee. He told the Cherokees that they had been cheated out of their lands, that they should give up no more land, and that they should trade with British and French alike. The British claimed that he was urging the Cherokees to adopt a government in which all property, including wives, would be common. (It is doubtful that he would have gotten very far among the Cherokees with this last suggestion.) Priber learned to speak Cherokee, and he wrote letters to South Carolina that he signed "Prime Minister." South Carolina sent Colonel Joseph Fox to Tellico to arrest Priber. He did lay hands on Priber, but Priber was defended by Cherokees. In 1741, when Priber and a few Cherokees were on their way to Alabama to talk with some Creeks, they were waylaid by English traders who took Priber to a prison in Georgia. While in prison, Priber is said to have written a Cherokee dictionary and a book describing his proposed government, which he called *Paradise*. Neither manuscript has survived. And neither did poor Priber. Adair says, "Happily for us, he died in confinement." (See also "Ama-edohi.")

Proctor, Dallas

A bilingual Cherokee from Delaware County, Oklahoma, Dallas Proctor was principal chief of the United Keetoowah Band of Cherokee Indians from 2001 to 2005, when he was defeated by George Wickliffe.

Proctor, Zeke

Ezekial Proctor was born in 1831 in Georgia, the son of William Proctor, a white man, and Dicey Downing, a full-blood Cherokee woman. His family was taken west over the Trail of Tears when Zeke was seven years old. When Zeke grew to manhood, he became a prosperous farmer in the Goingsnake District of the Cherokee Nation, near the border with Arkansas. He fought on the Union side during the Civil War. In 1867, he was elected sheriff of Goingsnake District.

Zeke's sister Susan was married to Jim Kesterson, a white man, and they lived near Sallisaw, Indian Territory. When Zeke, no longer sheriff, found out that Kesterson had abandoned Susan and their two children, he went to the rescue, taking his sister and her children home with him. Then Kesterson, adding insult to injury, moved in with another Cherokee woman, Polly Beck, not far from Zeke's home. Zeke went to Beck's Mill, where Kesterson had joined Polly, and there he pulled a gun on Kesterson.

Just as he fired the gun, Polly Beck jumped in the way and was killed. Zeke turned himself in to Cherokee authorities and awaited trial. It was 1872.

Kesterson, however, fled to Fort Smith in Arkansas, where he filed a complaint in the U.S. federal court there, charging Zeke with attempted murder of him, a white man. The federal authorities thus became involved. As Zeke hid out with Nighthawk Keetoowahs, the feds finally decided to let the Cherokee trial proceed. If the Cherokee court found Zeke guilty of murder and sentenced him to hang, all would be well, but if it did not find him guilty, then the deputy marshals were to arrest him and take him to Fort Smith for trial.

When the trial was about to begin, members of the Beck family showed up armed. They were met at the door by Zeke's brother, Johnson, and White Sut Beck fired a shotgun, killing Johnson Proctor. He fired again, and his second shot hit Zeke in the knee. Then both sides started firing. When it was all over, nine men were dead, two were badly wounded and would die later, and many others were wounded. Federal warrants were issued for the arrest of everyone on the Proctor side, including the dead Johnson Proctor. Cherokee Nation warrants were issued for the Becks. Zeke hid out with the Keetoowahs, and the Becks fled to Arkansas. Federal officials tried to enlist the aid of the Cherokee Nation, but Principal Chief Lewis Downing, himself a Keetoowah, refused to cooperate. The U.S. Army was about to be called when someone at Fort Smith suggested an alternative: Why not issue a general amnesty to everyone involved on both sides? That was done, and the whole mess was brought to an end.

In 1877, Zeke was elected to the Cherokee Senate from Goingsnake District. In 1894, he was elected sheriff. He was a deputy U.S. marshal in 1891 and again in 1895. He died at home in 1907 at the age of seventy-six. His story is a dramatic illustration of the problems of jurisdictional confusion in the Indian Territory days. It is also interesting to see how close the Cherokee Nation came to being at war with the United States once again as late as 1872. (For more information, see "Downing, Lewis.")

Robert J. Conley

Q.

Qualla

From 1836 to 1861, William Holland Thomas, using money he had obtained from the U.S. government for the 1,046 refugee Cherokees in North Carolina, purchased a number of contiguous tracts of land for the refugees to live on. The main body of this land, on the Oconaluftee River in the present counties of Swain and Jackson, became known as the Qualla Boundary, taking its name from Thomas's principal trading store. The Cherokee reservation in North Carolina is still formally known by this name. James Mooney says that the name "Kwali," from which "Qualla" derives, is the Cherokee form of "Polly." The store, now a post office, was named for an old woman who lived nearby.

Quatie

Chief John Ross's first wife, Quatie, was a full-blood Cherokee and is often credited with being responsible for Chief Ross's popularity with the full-blood Cherokees. She died in Arkansas during the Removal in 1838 and was buried there.

R.

Rabbit, Bill

Bill Rabbit was born in Casper, Wyoming, in 1946, son of Swimmer Rabbit. He joined the U.S. Army at seventeen and went to Vietnam. After his return home, he worked as a welder and a deputy sheriff before turning to art as a full-time profession. Rabbit won the Grand Award at the Five Civilized Tribes Museum's Annual Competitive Art Show in 1984 and attained the status of Master Artist of the Five Civilized Tribes Museum in 1986. At the Cherokee National Museum's Trail of Tears Art Show, he has won numerous prizes, including first place in both painting and miniatures. He was named the Institute of American Indian Arts's Artist of the Year in 1989, won the Grand Heritage Award at the Five Civilized Tribes Museum Master Show in 2000, and received the Cherokee Medal of Honor in 2004. He lives and works in Pryor, Oklahoma. His daughter, Traci, is also a well-known artist.

Rattlinggourd, Ellis

Ellis Rattlinggourd was sheriff at Tahlequah, Indian Territory, in 1894, when the Cherokee Strip money was being paid out per capita in Tahlequah to Cherokee citizens. Outlaws Bill Cook, Jim Cook, and Cherokee Bill (Crawford Goldsby) were hiding out at Effie Crittenden's Halfway House on Fourteen Mile Creek, fourteen miles from Tahlequah. They wanted to receive their share of the money but did not care to be seen in Tahlequah, so they gave Effie Crittenden notes, or orders, for their shares. She took the notes to Tahlequah, presented them, and received the money, but she was followed by Sheriff Rattlinggourd, who had spotted the notes, and a posse of seven men. As the posse approached the Halfway House, Cherokee Bill had just stepped out the door, so he saw them, and shots were fired. It is not known which side fired first. One member of the posse, Sequoyah Houston, was killed. Jim Cook was shot seven times and was captured, but the others escaped. (See "Cook, Bill" and "Goldsby, Crawford.")

Reconstruction in the Cherokee Nation

The treaty between the Cherokee Nation and the United States of July 19, 1866, was a Reconstruction treaty following the Civil War. It, of course, abolished slavery and forced the Cherokee Nation to make all freed slaves full citizens of the Cherokee Nation, but it also established Indian Territory with a territorial government; abolished Cherokee courts and established U.S. courts in the Cherokee Nation; took the Cherokee Neutral Lands and called for the establishment of U.S. military posts within the Cherokee Nation; and authorized the granting of railroad rights-of-way through the Cherokee Nation.

Chief John Ross, having died shortly after the signing of the treaty, was replaced as chief by his nephew William Potter Ross. The Ross Party soon split into two factions known as the Downing Party and the Ross Party, and the Southern Cherokees joined with the Downing Party because of their hatred for John Ross and any of his kinsmen. Southern Cherokees who had fled the Cherokee Nation during the Civil War returned and settled near Webbers Falls.

After the war, one-third of the women in the Cherokee Nation were widows and one-fourth of the children orphans. Money was scarce. Homes had been destroyed during the war, and livestock had been killed or had run off. When the Cherokee Nation was paid for its Neutral Lands, it reopened its schools and established an orphanage. Chief W. P. Ross invited Congregationalists, Presbyterians, Methodists, Baptists, and Moravians to return to the nation. A national jail and an asylum for deaf, mute, blind, mentally disabled, and indigent Cherokees were also established. Cherokees fought hard to reestablish the Cherokee Nation and all of its institutions, but all to no avail, as Oklahoma statehood was snapping hard on their heels.

Red Clay, Tennessee

General Winfield Scott established headquarters at New Echota, the capital of the Cherokee Nation , in 1838. When the Cherokee National Council met again in 1832, however, the meeting was held at Red Clay, Tennessee, instead of at New Echota, which was situated within the boundaries claimed by the state of Georgia, in order to avoid persecution by Georgians and the U.S. Army.

Reed, Jesse

The 1899 election for chief of the Eastern Band of Cherokees at Cherokee, North Carolina, was hotly disputed, and the council finally declared Jesse Reed (Tsesi Skatsi, or "Scotch Jesse"), a mixed-blood, the victor over Sampson Owl. Reed served until 1903.

Religion, see "Worldview"

Removal

The Removal of all Indians east of the Mississippi River was first called for by President Thomas Jefferson in 1803, but it was left to President Andrew Jackson to put it into effect. Georgia began agitating for the removal of the Cherokees and became insistent with the discovery of gold in Cherokee country there. A series of laws called the anti-Cherokee laws were passed by the Georgia legislature: a Cherokee could not testify in court against a white man; no white man could live in the Cherokee country without swearing an oath of loyalty to the government of Georgia and obtaining a permit from Georgia; Cherokees could not dig for gold on Cherokee land; and the Cherokee Council was forbidden to meet. In response to these laws, the Cherokee Nation moved its seat of government from New Echota in Georgia to Red Clay in Tennessee. Reverend Samuel Worcester and others were arrested for refusing to swear the oath of loyalty and to obtain permits to live among the Cherokees.

In 1830, Andrew Jackson pushed his removal bill through Congress and had it passed into law. In response, the Cherokee Nation challenged the law in the U.S. Supreme Court twice and won the second case, *Worcester v. Georgia.* For a time, they were elated, but then they heard of Jackson's alleged response to the Court decision: "John Marshal has made his decision. Now let him enforce it." With that, it seemed to some that removal was inevitable. Certain members of the Cherokee Nation, but not representing the Cherokees—including Major Ridge, his son John, and Elias Boudinot—began meeting with U.S. government officials and on December 29, 1835, signed the Treaty of New Echota, known as the Removal Treaty, agreeing to move the entire Cherokee population to a new home west of the Mississippi River and to sell all Cherokee lands in the East to the United States. None of the treaty signers were Cherokee Nation governmental officials, so the treaty was illegal. Nevertheless, it was ratified by the U.S. Senate and acted upon as a legally binding treaty.

The signers, now known as the Treaty Party, packed up and moved as ordered, but the majority of Cherokees, under the leadership of Principal Chief John Ross, held out. In 1838, the U.S. Army began rounding them up and held them in stockade prisons for removal. Many sickened and died in prison. One man, Tsali, and his family resisted, killing some soldiers. He was eventually captured (or he actually surrendered), and he and all but his youngest son were shot and killed by firing squad. (See "Tsali.") A number of Cherokees in the mountains of North Carolina managed to avoid being rounded up. (See "Eastern Band of Cherokee Indians.") The first detachment of what came to be called the Trail of Tears left on August 23, 1838. The thirteenth and final detachment left on December 5, 1838, and arrived the area now known as Oklahoma on March 18, 1839. Around four thousand Cherokees died along the way.

Removal Treaty

The Treaty of New Echota, also known as the Removal Treaty, was negotiated at New Echota in Georgia and signed on December 29, 1835, between U.S. government negotiators and members but not elected officials of the Cherokee Nation. The Cherokees who were at New Echota and signed the treaty became known as the Treaty Party. Their leaders were Major Ridge, his son John, and Elias Boudinot, a cousin of John Ridge. The treaty called for the sale of all Cherokee lands east of the Mississippi River and the removal of all Cherokees to new homes west of the Mississippi. Though clearly illegal, it was ratified by the U.S. Senate, and the Cherokee Nation was held to it. Chief John Ross and others protested the treaty, but to no avail, and it led directly to the infamous Removal in 1838, known as the Trail of Tears.

Ridge, John

John Ridge was the son of Major Ridge and Susie Wicket Ridge. He attended school first at the Springplace Mission in Georgia and then at Brainerd Mission in Tennessee. He was sent to the Foreign Mission School in Cornwall, Connecticut, in 1819, where he met the white daughter of the steward of the school, Sarah Bird Northrup. When he married her in

John Ridge, c. 1826.
McKenney-Hall Portrait
Gallery, Smithsonian
Institution.

1824, the town of Cornwall
rose up in arms, hanging
John in effigy, so John and
his bride had to flee. The
school was closed in 1827 as
a result of the citizens' rage
over the mixed marriage.
In 1824, John went with his
father and Chief John Ross
to Washington, D.C., to pro-
test the imminent removal of the Cherokees from all lands east of the
Mississippi River. Following President Andrew Jackson's refusal to enforce
the Supreme Court ruling in favor of the Cherokees in 1832 (*Worcester v.
Georgia*), Ridge changed his position. Feeling that the Cherokees had
no other course, he began to speak in favor of negotiating a removal
treaty with the United States. Along with his father and his cousin Elias
Boudinot, he signed the Treaty of New Echota (Removal Treaty) in 1835
and moved with his family to the area now known as Oklahoma in 1837.
On July 22, 1839, following the Trail of Tears, he was dragged from his bed
and stabbed to death in front of his wife and child, apparently as punishment for signing the treaty.

Ridge, John Rollin

John Rollin Ridge (Tsisqua Dahlonega, or Yellow Bird), son of John Ridge
and Sarah Bird Northrup, was born in Georgia in 1827. He came to the
new Cherokee country in the West (in present-day Oklahoma) with his
family in 1837 at the age of ten. He was twelve years old when he witnessed
the brutal killing of his father one night for signing the Removal Treaty.
His mother then moved with her children to Fayetteville, Arkansas, to get
away from the violence that was raging in the Cherokee Nation. She sent
John Rollin to the Great Barrington School in Massachusetts to finish his
education. In 1844, he wrote a letter to his uncle Stand Watie expressing

Robert J. Conley

his delight at the news that Watie had executed James Foreman, one of the killers of his grandfather, Major Ridge, who was also a signer of the treaty. He returned home because of ill health and was tutored by Reverend Cephas Washburn at Mount Comfort, near Fayetteville. By 1846, Ridge was studying law at Fayetteville. In 1849, however, he shot and killed a man named David Kell in an argument over a horse. Kell was a pro–John Ross man and may have been encouraged to provoke the fight. Ridge then fled to Springfield, Missouri. He wrote to Stand Watie, "There is a deep-seated principle of revenge in me which will never be satisfied until it reaches its object." Its object was, of course, Principal Chief John Ross, whom Ridge blamed for the killings of his father, grandfather, and uncle, Elias Boudinot. In 1849, Ridge returned to Arkansas, near present-day Bentonville. By 1850, he had signed on to travel to the California gold-fields, and he left in April of that year, intending to return "as soon as I can get back conveniently." In California, he mined for gold for a brief time, but soon turned to a literary career, rapidly becoming one of California's leading poets. He became editor of several newspapers. In 1854, his novel *The Life and Adventures of Joaquin Murieta* was published. The book apparently sold well, but Ridge claimed that the publisher did not pay him. In 1866, he was one of the delegates from the Southern (Confederate) Cherokees to Washington, D.C. He died in 1867 in Grass Valley, California. In 1868, his first volume of poetry was published by his wife. He wrote under his Cherokee name, Yellow Bird.

Ridge, Major

In 1771, the Ridge (Gunundalegi, One Who Follows the Ridge) was born into the Deer Clan, a brother of Uweti (the father of Stand Watie and Elias Boudinot). He participated in the war against the Creeks under the command of Andrew Jackson in 1813 and was promoted to the rank of major. Thereafter, he was known as Major Ridge. After the war, he was head of the Cherokee Nation's Lighthorse police. He went to Washington, D.C., with John Ross and Charles Hicks to protest the removal of the Cherokees from their homelands. While there, they were the guests of Secretary of War John C. Calhoun. Ridge was elected speaker of the Cherokee National Council in 1825. He evicted sixty whites from Cherokee land and burned their homes. He introduced legislation that called for the death penalty for selling Cherokee land. When Doublehead was convicted of selling Cherokee land and sentenced to be executed, Ridge was appointed one of the executioners.

Major Ridge, c. 1826.
McKenney-Hall Portrait Gallery,
Smithsonian Institution.

Ridge married Susie Wicket, and
they soon had a son named John.
While John was in school at Cornwall,
Connecticut, Major Ridge and his
wife went to visit him, arriving "in
the most splendid carriage that had
ever entered town, [with Major Ridge]
wearing white top boots and a coat
trimmed in gold lace, attended by [a] waiter of great style."
    Up until President Jackson's refusal to uphold the decision of the
Supreme Court in the *Worcester v. Georgia* case, Ridge had been a strong
voice against removal. But upon hearing this news, he, his son John, and
his nephew Elias Boudinot decided that removal was the only choice
left for them and that if the Cherokees cooperated with the U.S. government, the move would be easier on them. They and others signed the
Removal Treaty in 1835 and made the move in 1837. After the removal of
the majority of Cherokees, Ridge was shot from ambush on the morning
of June 22, 1839, as he was traveling a road near present-day Stilwell,
Oklahoma, probably by James Foreman. His son John and Elias Boudinot
were killed the same day for violating the same law for which Ridge had
earlier executed Doublehead—selling Cherokee lands.

Ridge Party

Major Ridge, John Ridge, Elias Boudinot, and other Cherokees who illegally signed the Treaty of New Echota (Removal Treaty) in 1835 were
known variously as the Ridge Party and the Treaty Party.

Riggs, Lynn

Born Rollie Lynn Riggs in 1899 near Claremore, Indian Territory, Lynn
Riggs was educated in local public schools and at Eastern University
Preparatory School in Claremore. He attended the University of Oklahoma,
then clerked for a time at Adams Express Company in Chicago before
moving to New York City, where he worked as a reporter for the *Wall Street*

Journal. He subsequently went to Hollywood for a time, looking for work as a film extra, then returned to the University of Oklahoma in 1920. His first book of poetry, *Fandango,* was published in 1922. He taught English at the university for a time. Following a nervous breakdown, he went to Santa Fe, New Mexico, to recuperate and to write poems and plays. His major play *Green Grow the Lilacs* was produced in New York City in 1931 by the Theater Guild and was a success. In 1933, he wrote *The Cherokee Night* and worked with Rogers and Hammerstein to turn *Green Grow the Lilacs* into a full-blown musical. It was produced in 1943 as *Oklahoma!* Riggs died in New York City in 1954 and was returned to Claremore, Oklahoma, for burial.

Robbins, W. Lee O'Daniel

W. Lee O'Daniel Robbins—known as Dan, W. Lee, or Mr. W—was born in Tahlequah, Oklahoma, on January 11, 1941. His father, Price Robbins, was a preacher and a country singer. A fan of W. Lee "Pappy" O'Daniel and his Light Crust Dough Boys, he named his son after Pappy. Mr. W went to school in Tahlequah, although he did not finish high school. He married at seventeen and joined the U.S. Army, serving for two years, from 1958 to 1960. After his return home, he took his family, now a wife and child, to Los Angeles, California, on the Relocation Program. He worked at various jobs before being picked up by the Los Angeles Angels as a pitcher in 1961. While playing for the Angels, owned by Gene Autry, Mr. W became personally acquainted with Gene and through him with many other B Western movie stars,

W. Lee O'Daniel Robbins with the Los Angeles Angels, 1961. Courtesy of Jennie Robbins.

including Roy Rogers and Lash LaRue. He had two active seasons with the Angels and sat out one season. When he left the Angels, Mr. W played and sang with a country and western band for a while, before returning to Tahlequah to attend Northeastern State University. He sped through the curriculum and completed a degree in geology in record time. Thereafter employed by the federal government as a geologist, he worked for a time in

W. Lee O'Daniel Robbins having just reviewed Larry Mcmurtry's *Zeke and Ned* with a shotgun, 1997. Author's collection.

South America and checked oil wells on Indian reservations in the United States. He eventually retired from this his third profession and settled down in Tahlequah with his wife, Jennie, and their three boys, Shannon, W. Lee Jr., and Chris. He died in Tahlequah in 2002.

Rogers, Clement Vann

Clem Rogers was the father of the famous Will Rogers. He was born at Breadtown, or the Baptist Mission, in the Goingsnake District of the Cherokee Nation (in what is now Oklahoma) in 1839. He attended Baptist Mission and the Cherokee Male Seminary. He left school without graduating in 1855 and drove a herd of cattle for Joel Bryan to Kansas City, Missouri. When he returned, he opened a store, which prospered until the Civil War disrupted life in the Cherokee Nation. Clem enlisted in Stand Watie's Confederate Cherokee regiment and rose to the rank of captain. Returning to the Cherokee Nation at the war's end, he and his wife, Mary America Schrimsher, found their house burned. Clem worked hauling freight for five years. Then he started ranching in the Cooweescoowee District and soon became one of the richest men in the district. He was elected to the Cherokee Senate in 1879, 1881, 1883, and 1901 and was judge of Cooweescoowee District in 1877. After Mary America died in 1890, Clem remarried. He became a principal stockholder in a bank in Claremore, Oklahoma, and died in 1911.

Rogers, Dianna

Dianna Rogers (her first name is often misrepresented as "Diana," "Tiana," "Talhina," "Talahina," "Hina," "Titania," "Tyania," or "Tenia") was the daughter of Jennie Due Rogers and John Rogers, a white trader known as Hell Fire Jack. Dianna married David Gentry, who was killed in battle with the Osages and left her a widow. When Sam Houston returned to the Cherokees in 1829, they were married. When Houston left her and went to Texas, she married Samuel McGrady. She died in 1839. Her grave marker in the Fort Gibson National Cemetery in Oklahoma reads "Talahina Rogers."

Rogers, John

A white trader to the Cherokees, John Rogers, known as Hell Fire Jack, had been a Tory captain in the American Revolution and then a veteran of the battle of Horseshoe Bend in 1814 under the command of Andrew Jackson. He had been living with the Cherokees since before the Revolution and moved west in 1817 to join them on the White River in Arkansas. He was married to Elizabeth Due, and their two sons were John and James. When Elizabeth died, he married her daughter (by a previous marriage), Jennie Due, thus making his sons' half-sister their stepmother. John and Jennie had two daughters, Dianna, who married Sam Houston, and Martha, who would become the mother of Jesse Chisholm. Descendants of John Rogers include not only his son John, but also Chief W. C. Rogers and the world famous Will Rogers.

Rogers, John (Captain Jack)

John Rogers was the son of the white trader John Rogers (Hell Fire Jack) and Elizabeth Due. He was half-brother to Dianna Rogers, Sam Houston's Cherokee wife. Born in Burke County, Georgia, he was sometimes called Nolichucky Jack. He obtained the rank of captain during the Creek War in 1813–14. He moved to Arkansas in 1821 and then across the border into what is now Oklahoma in 1829. He was a member of the Cherokee delegation to Washington, D.C., in 1828 and again in 1831. For a time, he operated a trading post at Fort Gibson, but his last home was near Claremore, both in what is now Oklahoma. His wife was Elizabeth Coody, and they became the parents of Charles Coody Rogers, who married Elizabeth McCorkle. The latter were the parents of W. C. Rogers, the last elected principal chief of the Cherokee Nation before Oklahoma statehood in 1907.

John Rogers became chief of the Western Cherokees when his uncle Chief John Jolly died in 1838. In 1846, he was in Washington, D.C., pleading for the rights of the Old Settlers (Western Cherokees) when he died at the age of sixty-seven. He is buried in the Fort Gibson National Cemetery in Oklahoma.

Rogers, William Charles

William Charles Rogers was born on a farm near Pryor Creek in the Cherokee Nation on December 13, 1849. His mother was Elizabeth McCorkle, his father Charles Coody Rogers, and his grandfather Captain John Rogers, the last chief of the Western Cherokees and the brother of Dianna (Tiana) Rogers, Sam Houston's sometime wife. As a young man, W. C. farmed and operated a store near present-day Skiatook, Oklahoma. He was only thirteen years old when he enlisted in the Confederate army in 1861.

He served as deputy sheriff of Cooweescoowee District in the Cherokee Nation and was elected to the lower house of the Cherokee National Council from Cooweescoowee District in 1881 and 1883. He then was elected to the Senate in 1889 and reelected in 1895. On August 3, 1903, he was elected

William C. Rogers, c. 1903. Public domain. Courtesy of the Cherokee Honor Society.

principal chief, defeating E. L. Cookson. The Cherokee Nation's bones were already being picked by the federal government. Rogers's defenders credit him with helping make the entire process of allotment and the dismantling of the Cherokee Nation go smoothly. In his own words, he expressed that kind of feeling: "A crisis in our affairs is at hand. The government which our forefathers cherished and loved and labored so hard to perfect has been sentenced to die. The scepter must soon pass to other hands. Still we must force back the resentment we feel and accept the conditions as they are."

The Cherokee National Council did not feel so reconciled to the situation and in 1905 impeached him and put him out of office, replacing him with Frank J. Boudinot. But the Curtis Act called for federal approval of all National Council actions, and the feds did not approve of this action. They instead reinstated Rogers, and he remained chief until his death in 1917 at the age of seventy. Thus, W. C. Rogers was the last regularly elected chief before Oklahoma statehood in 1907 and the first of a string of federally appointed chiefs.

Robert J. Conley

Rogers, Will

Colonel William Penn Adair Rogers was born November 4, 1879, the son of Clement Vann Rogers and Mary America Schrimsher Rogers, near Oologah, Indian Territory. In later life, Will told people that he was born in Claremore because "no one but an Indian can pronounce Oologah." He was named for his uncle Colonel William Penn Adair. He attended Drumgoole School near Chelsea, Indian Territory, the Cherokee Female Seminary as the only boy, and Harrell International Institute. He spent four years at Willie Halsell College and a brief time at Kemper Military Institute. He was an incorrigible student and finally left to become a cowboy. He worked for a time at the Ewing Ranch near Higgins, Texas, where he helped drive a herd of cattle to Medicine Lodge, Kansas. He went home and tried several times to run the ranch for his father, but he proved to be too lazy and too full of the spirit of adventure. He went to South America with a friend, John Parris, but Parris grew homesick and returned to Oklahoma, so Will went on to Africa. Broke in South Africa, he teamed up with a traveling Wild West show and earned his way as a trick roper. At the St. Louis World's Fair in 1904, he joined up with Colonel Zack Mulhall's Wild West Show and was billed as the Cherokee Kid. He was doing rope tricks at Madison Square Garden when he started wisecracking on stage.

In 1908, Will married Betty Blake after an eight-year courtship. He joined the Ziegfield Follies in 1916 and became a star of the show. He was a popular movie star of the 1920s and 1930s and for a time was a top box office attraction. In 1922, he began writing a newspaper column in which he poked fun at any and all celebrities, and he had a radio show. He traveled all over the world, meeting major politicians in almost every country and raising

Will Rogers, 1906. Courtesy of the Will Rogers Memorial Museum, Claremore, Oklahoma.

money for worthy causes. In 1935, he was killed with Wiley Post when their small plane crashed at Point Barrow, Alaska. He was mourned worldwide.

Some of Will's better known films are *Judge Priest*; *A Connecticut Yankee in King Arthur's Court*; *Steamboat Round the Bend*; *Laughing Bill Hyde*; and *Cupid, the Cowpuncher*. Perhaps, though, he is best remembered today for his many "quotable quotes." Surely the best known is, "I never met a man I didn't like." There were some things, though, that he did not like much. For example, "We spoiled the best territory in the world to make a state."

Rogers, Will, Jr.

Will Rogers Jr. was born October 20, 1911, in New York City while his father, Will Rogers, was working in the Ziegfield Follies. He graduated from Stanford University in 1935 and was Democratic U.S. Congressman from California's Sixteenth District from 1942 to 1944, when he joined the U.S. Army as a tank commander. He was wounded at the Battle of the Bulge and decorated for bravery. In 1952, he starred as his father in the motion picture *The Story of Will Rogers* and thereafter made a number of films. Among them are *The Boy from Oklahoma*; *Wild Heritage*; *The Golden Age of Comedy*; *Will Rogers: Look Back in Laughter*; *Stories of American Indian Culture*; and *Ghost Town Hunters*. He served as a special assistant to the U.S. commissioner of Indian affairs from 1967 to 1969. In 1993, at the age of eighty-one, plagued by strokes, heart problems, and a recent hip implant, he drove from his Arizona home out into the desert and committed suicide by shooting himself.

Ross, Andrew

Born in 1798, youngest brother of Principal Chief John Ross, Andrew joined with the Treaty Party in 1832 at the council at Red Clay, Tennessee. He was also at New Echota, Georgia, on December 29, 1835, with the Treaty Party and U.S. negotiators to conclude the Treaty of New Echota, otherwise known as the Removal Treaty. He was a judge in the Saline District of the Cherokee Nation in 1859.

Ross, Gayle

Gayle Ross, renowned Cherokee storyteller, is a member of the Cherokee Nation and a direct descendant of Principal Chief John Ross. Her interest in

Robert J. Conley

storytelling was sparked by her grand-mother. She has appeared at almost every major storytelling festival and folk festival in the United States and Canada, and in theaters and performance halls throughout the United States and Europe. She is in great demand as a lecture artist on college campuses and as a keynote speaker at education and humanities conferences. She tells stories to children at schools and libraries across the country. The National Council of Traditional Arts has included her in two of its touring shows, the Master Storyteller's Tour and From the Plains to the Pueblos. In 2004, she was featured on Peter Buffet's stage performance, *500 Nations*, based on Kevin Costner's CBS miniseries.

Gayle Ross, 1990s.
Courtesy of Gayle Ross.

Ross was invited by Vice President Al Gore to a gala at his residence entitled "A Taste of Tennessee" and was selected by the Clinton White House as the only Native American speaker at the "Millennium on the Mall" celebration in Washington, D.C. First Lady Laura Bush selected her to perform at the National Book Festival's opening gala, along with Bob Shieffer and Julie Andrews.

In addition, Ross is the author of five critically acclaimed children's books and has been a featured speaker at events sponsored by the American Library Association, the International Reading Association, and the International Board of Books for Young People. She was featured in the award-winning documentary *How the West Was Lost* (1993) on the Discovery Channel, and her stories are often heard on National Public Radio's *Living on the Earth* and *Mountain Stages*. Ross currently lives with her family in Fredericksburg, Texas.

Ross, John

John Ross, whose Cherokee name was Cooweescoowee, was born October 3, 1790. His father was Daniel Ross, a Scot, who established a trading firm with John McDonald, another Scot, who had settled among the Chicka-maugas, a pro-British Cherokee faction that had broken off from the

John Ross, c. 1846. From a painting by John Neagle. Courtesy of the Oklahoma Museum of History, Oklahoma Historical Society.

Cherokee Nation just prior to the American Revolution. McDonald married Anne Shorey, the one-half Cherokee daughter of an interpreter. Their daughter Mollie married Daniel Ross. Daniel and Mollie had nine children, John being the third. John was born at Turkey Town (Kanagatugi, probably Guhna-gadogi) on the Coosa River in Alabama. He was only one-eighth Cherokee, but he was born into a clan because his mother was Cherokee. From Turkey Town, the family moved to Willstown, Chickamauga, and then a location near Lookout Mountain at present-day Chattanooga, Tennessee.

John's grandfather, John McDonald, was assistant to the British superintendent of southern Indian affairs until the end of the American Revolution. As such, he was closely associated with the Chickamaugas and Dragging Canoe. McDonald remained with the Chickamaugas after the war. Young John, known as Tsan Usdi, or Little John, was initially educated at home with private tutors. He later attended Gideon Blackburn's mission school and an academy at South West Point, Tennessee. Upon finishing school, he clerked for William Neilson of Neilson, King, and Smith.

In 1811, the agent to the Cherokees, Return J. Meigs, commissioned John Ross to make a trip to Arkansas to visit the Cherokees who were already settled there. Nothing seems to have come of the trip, but when Ross returned home in April 1813, he found the Cherokees ready to go to war against the Red Stick Creeks. He joined Captain Sekekee's company of mounted Cherokees as an adjutant with the rank of second lieutenant. Colonel Gideon Morgan was in command. Pathkiller, Sequoyah, George Lowrey, and the Ridge, who would become Major Ridge, were other Cherokees who enlisted. Their involvement in the war was minimal until the battle of Horseshoe Bend in 1814, where the Cherokees, led by General Andrew Jackson, soundly defeated the Red Sticks. Ross left the service

Robert J. Conley

shortly afterward. In the midst of his military service, most likely while he was on furlough in 1813, he became a partner of Timothy Meigs, son of Agent Return Meigs, in Meigs and Ross. The firm did a thriving business during the Creek War with government contracts. He also found the time to marry Elizabeth Brown Henley, known as Quatie (a better spelling would probably be "Gwedi").

In 1815, Meigs died, and Ross went into business with his brother Lewis, establishing a trading post on the south bank of the Tennessee River. The location became known as Ross's Landing. Late that same year Agent Return Meigs accompanied a delegation of Cherokees to Washington, D.C., made up of John Ross, John Lowrey, John Walker, Major Ridge, Richard Taylor, and "Cheuncunsenee." The latter may have been Tsiyu Gan'sini, the son of the late Dragging Canoe. The delegation signed two treaties while in Washington, one ceding a tract of land to North Carolina, and the other dealing with boundaries, payment to individual Cherokees for damages done to their property during the Creek War, and other things. On his return home, Ross occupied himself with business affairs, continuing to obtain valuable government contracts.

In June 1817, General Andrew Jackson showed up at the agency on the Hiwassee River with a group of U.S. delegates for a new treaty negotiation. They astonished the Cherokees by proposing that the entire nation move west, exchanging their homeland for Arkansas land. Jackson, of course, did not achieve this goal at that time, but he did manage to acquire a sizeable tract of land, and the treaty included a clause stating that the United States would aid any Cherokee desiring to move to Arkansas. In the summer of 1818, many Cherokees, perhaps thirty-five hundred, did make the move.

The Cherokee National Council met in November 1818, with John Ross serving as president of the National Committee (one arm of the National Council). Principal Chief Pathkiller was seventy-three years old at the time. Governor Joseph McMinn of Tennessee was there and offered the Cherokees $200,000 to move west. He was refused. John Ross wrote a protest and had it published in the *Raleigh Register*. It emphasized the Cherokee determination to remain in their ancestral homeland.

It is interesting to note that the big split in the Cherokee Nation had begun with the Chickamauga alliance with Great Britain during the American Revolution. The Lower Town Cherokees, mostly full-blood and conservative, tried to remain neutral. The Chickamaugas, from the Upper Towns, though led by full-blood Dragging Canoe, were a group of full-bloods, mixed-bloods, whites, and British Tories. John

Ross's grandfather, John McDonald, was one of them. But when the war was finally over, the former Chickamaugas joined forces with the United States in calling for Cherokee removal. At that point, John Ross departed from their ranks to associate himself with the conservative Lower Towns.

In 1819, Ross was one of a delegation of Cherokees who went to Washington, D.C., in an attempt to clarify ambiguities in the Treaty of 1817. They wound up signing a new treaty. This new treaty called for "life reservations": individuals would live on them the way white people did and be citizens of the United States and of the states in which they resided. Ross was assigned a reservation, but he never lived on it and maintained that he never considered U.S. citizenship.

That same year Ross was assigned the task of rescuing a child who had been captured during the Cherokee-Osage war in the west. The child had been transported east and was about to be sold into slavery in Mobile, Alabama, when Ross effected the rescue. He was also given the chore of leading a company of Lighthorse (Cherokee police) to remove intruders from Cherokee lands. By the middle of 1820, however, he was relieved of those duties and assigned to Chief Pathkiller as his clerk. In 1822, the Cherokee National Council resolved to make no new land cessions to the United States. Fifty-nine members of the Cherokee legislature, including John Ross, signed this document. Agent Meigs was shocked at this bold statement. At least he pretended to be. For the next several years, the business of the Cherokee Nation was primarily to formalize its government in order to stave off more effectively the U.S. government's constant demand for more land and to try to obtain from the United States the annuities promised in previous treaties. A new Cherokee capital was established at New Echota within the boundaries claimed by the state of Georgia.

In 1827, Ross moved to Coosa, about thirty miles from the capital. He built a two-story house and several outbuildings, including slave quarters for his twenty slaves. He controlled about 170 acres, which included orchards of fruit trees and planted fields. It was in this year that the Cherokee Nation adopted a new constitution, and the Georgia legislature refused to recognize it, referring back to the 1802 Compact with the United States and demanding that the U.S. government fulfill it. When Chief Pathkiller died in 1827, William Hicks was elected principal chief by the council, and John Ross was elected as second chief.

Sequoyah had presented the Cherokee people with his amazing syllabary in 1821, and 1828 was the year in which the *Cherokee Phoenix* began publication with Elias Boudinot as editor. Hicks and Ross took

Robert J. Conley

full advantage of the bilingual newspaper in getting their message out to the people. Around this time, Georgia passed a series of laws that have become known as the anti-Cherokee laws and began an all-out campaign to drive Cherokees out of the state.

The new constitution called for a council vote in 1828 to elect the principal chief and second chief. Such an election was to be held every four years thereafter. When the council met, they elected John Ross as principal chief and George Lowrey as second chief. Ross recommended Richard Taylor, Edward Gunter, and William Shorey Coodey as delegates to Washington. The council approved the recommendations and requested that Ross accompany the delegation. Ross agreed, and the delegation left for Washington in January 1829.

Ross and the delegates complained to Secretary of War John Eaton about the behavior of their agent Hugh Montgomery and about the way in which Georgia had extended its laws over the Cherokees. Eaton told them that their only remedy was removal to the West. They next appealed to Congress, but the short session did not allow time for consideration of the Cherokees' appeal. After four months in Washington, Ross and the delegates went home having accomplished nothing.

Andrew Jackson had been elected president of the United States within a month of John Ross's election as principal chief of the Cherokee Nation in 1828. Jackson immediately set to work trying to get the Cherokees and other Indians removed from their homelands. When Georgians accelerated their brutal efforts to drive out the Cherokees, the Cherokee Nation appealed to the United States for help. Jackson refused. Ross sent Major Ridge with a party of Lighthorse to remove intruders. They did so, but were set upon by a gang of Georgians who beat them and left one badly beaten Cherokee to die. In July 1829, gold was discovered on Cherokee land in Georgia, and floods of white gold seekers poured in. Ross complained again to the U.S. government, but to no avail. In May 1830, Congress passed Jackson's removal bill.

In response, Chief Ross hired a lawyer for the Cherokee Nation, William Wirt, former U.S. attorney general. Wirt took *Cherokee Nation v. Georgia* to the Supreme Court, but the Court ruled that it had no jurisdiction. It referred to Indian tribes as "domestic, dependent nations." Ross and the majority of Cherokees continued to maintain their right to remain on their own lands. Then in March 1831, the Georgia Guard arrested two missionaries, Elizur Butler and Samuel Worcester, for being on Cherokee lands without having signed an oath of allegiance to Georgia and thus breaking one of its anti-Cherokee laws.

Wirt once again went to the Supreme Court with the case *Worcester v. Georgia*. On March 3, 1832, the Court delivered its opinion: it demanded the release of Worcester and Butler, declared all of Georgia's anti-Cherokee laws unconstitutional, and determined that the Cherokee Nation had never yielded its sovereignty. Georgia and President Jackson ignored the ruling, and Georgia passed a new law forbidding the Cherokee National Council to meet, with the penalty for breaking this law being four years at hard labor. The Cherokee capital was moved across the line to Red Clay, Tennessee.

Georgia laws forbade Cherokee elections, so in 1832 the National Council voted to retain the same people in office as a provisional government until such time as elections could be held peaceably. Andrew Jackson was reelected president of the United States. Ross led another delegation to Washington to impress upon the U.S. government that the Cherokees had no intention of moving. They also requested the annuities that had been withheld from them now for three years. They received no satisfaction on either point.

In that same year, Major Ridge; his son, John Ridge; and Elias Boudinot, John's cousin, gave in to the pressures. The Supreme Court decision had been in the Cherokees' favor, but they felt it had not changed anything. They decided that it would be better for everyone if they went along with the U.S. government and made the move. Boudinot resigned as editor of the *Phoenix*. John Ross called them traitors at a council meeting and expressed the idea that in a democracy the minority was required to go along with the majority. In spite of the fact that this group of Cherokee men was at odds with their legitimate government, they met with U.S. negotiators at New Echota on December 19, 1835, and on December 29 they signed a treaty of total removal.

Ross was in Washington at the time. His fine home in Georgia had been confiscated by the Georgia Guard, and he was living in a two-room log cabin in Tennessee. He had been living there when the world-famous playwright and actor John Howard Payne stopped in for a visit and stayed. While Payne was a guest in the humble Ross home, the Georgia Guard burst in and arrested both men. When Payne protested, one of the guards slapped him across the face. They were kept in prison slightly more than a week and then released.

After the Treaty of New Echota was signed, Ross immediately began protesting that it was illegal because it had not been signed by any elected official of the Cherokee Nation. In spite of his protests, the treaty was ratified by the U.S. Senate. The U.S. government's position was that the treaty

Robert J. Conley

represented the will of the Cherokee people, that John Ross was a dictator, and that he was "stubborn and perverse." Furthermore, the United States did recognize Ross as the leader of the Cherokees.

On May 3, 1836, President Jackson signed the treaty, and the Cherokees were given two years in which to move. According to the treaty provisions, a committee was established to appraise Cherokee property. Ross's property was valued at $23,665.75. John Ross, his brother Lewis Ross, and Major Ridge were three of the five richest men in the Cherokee Nation. John Ross made a trip to Arkansas to meet with the Western Cherokee Nation, and at his urging they passed a resolution condemning the fraudulent treaty. They then formed a delegation to travel to Washington with Ross and the delegation from the Cherokee Nation to protest the treaty.

Along the way, the group stopped in the old Cherokee country to visit their former homes, and Ross stopped at his log cabin. He was warned by his brother Lewis, however, to get out in a hurry or he would be arrested. When Ross and the other delegates went on to Washington, they were all but ignored. In 1837, Ross made a tour of the East hoping to sway public opinion in favor of the Cherokees. At last, the federal government grew weary of Ross's protests and set a deadline for Cherokee removal: May 23, 1838. In April 1838, General Winfield Scott was sent into Cherokee country to enforce removal.

Around 2,000 Cherokees had already moved west to join the Western Cherokee Nation in what is now Oklahoma during the years 1836–38, leaving 15,000 refusing to abandon their homeland. Much has been written about the Trail of Tears, so the topic will not be belabored here. General Scott began the roundup of Cherokee families, tearing people from their homes and marching them to stockade prisons for holding until time for the move. Many people sickened and died in these prisons. The first group of about 800 started to the West on June 6, 1838. On June 15, a second party was started, and later in the month a third party of 1,071 left. The people in these three groups were treated badly by the soldiers, and many of them became sick and died along the way.

Chief Ross was in Washington at this time, but Second Chief Lowrey requested, in Ross's name, that the rest of the Removal be postponed until the sickly season was over. General Scott granted the request. When Ross returned to the Cherokee Nation, saw the conditions, and heard the reports regarding the first contingents who had been removed, he asked General Scott to allow the Cherokees to remove themselves. Scott agreed. Around 13,000 Cherokees still remained to be removed. Ross presented Scott an estimate of the cost, and Scott approved it.

Ross then divided the Cherokees into thirteen groups, or waves, of about a thousand each, and appointed a Cherokee captain for each group. The first group, under Hair Conrad, left on August 28, 1838. The last wave, under John Drew, arrived in the West on March 18, 1839. The entire removal had taken nine months to complete, not counting those who had moved on their own earlier. The cost to the United States was more than half a million dollars. The cost in Cherokee lives has been estimated at one-quarter of the population, or nearly 4,000 people, mostly the old and the very young. John Ross's wife, Quatie, was one of those who died. She is said to have given her only blanket to a sick child.

Almost immediately after the Trail of Tears, violence erupted between the main group of Cherokees and the members of what had become known as the Treaty Party, the followers of the Ridges, Boudinot, and Stand Watie, Boudinot's brother. John Ross busied himself with trying to effect the reunion of the Western Cherokees and the Cherokee Nation, but he was meeting with resistance from both the Western Cherokees and the Treaty Party. On June 22, 1839, members of the Ross faction killed three of the major leaders of the Treaty Party. Major Ridge was ambushed and shot from his horse's back. John Ridge was dragged from a sickbed, stabbed numerous times, flung outside, and then trampled by horses in front of his wife and child. Elias Boudinot was lured down a country lane and then hacked to death.

Stand Watie barely escaped a similar fate. A rider came to his house, giving him the news and a warning. Watie fled for his life and set about raising a small army for the purpose of killing John Ross. Killings on both sides became common after that. Two hundred Cherokees gathered around the home of John Ross to protect him. Although Ross has been accused of killing the two Ridges and Boudinot, there is no evidence to back up the accusations. He did not actively pursue the killers, however.

Ross called a meeting in July 1839 at Illinois Camp Ground. It was attended by 2,000 Cherokees, including some members of the Western Cherokee Nation. A new constitution was drafted at this meeting. Ross invited the chiefs of the Western Cherokee Nation to the meeting, but they refused to attend, instead calling their own meeting elsewhere. The Western Cherokees who were present at Ross's meeting, including Sequoyah, met, deposed their chiefs, and signed the Act of Union with the Cherokee Nation, effectively dissolving the Western Cherokee Nation. The new constitution called for the principal chief, deputy principal chief, and members of the council to be elected directly by the people. An election was held at Tahlequah, the location for the new Cherokee Nation capital, and John Ross was elected principal chief.

Trouble continued. There were now three factions of Cherokees: the Ross Party, by far the largest; the Western Cherokees, now being called the Old Settlers; and the Treaty Party. Any discussions with the U.S. government, whether in Washington or at Fort Gibson (in present-day Oklahoma), were hampered by representatives from all three groups giving their own points of view.

In February 1841, Ross led a Cherokee delegation to Washington. William Henry Harrison was president and John Tyler vice president. The purpose of the trip was to secure money owed to the Cherokee Nation and to get a new treaty that would guarantee the security of Cherokee lands. The delegates remained in Washington until August; during their stay Harrison died, and Tyler became president. The long stay proved worthwhile, though, for Ross went home with everything he wanted.

In 1843, the Cherokee Nation, under John Ross, sponsored a large Indian gathering that was attended by members of at least eighteen different tribes. The meeting lasted for several weeks, and the members drew up an agreement in which they pledged perpetual peace and friendship and never to sell any of their land. Shortly after this convention concluded, the next scheduled Cherokee election took place. John Ross won again handsomely. Because the *Cherokee Phoenix* had ceased publication before the Removal, the National Council authorized the establishment of a new newspaper to be called the *Cherokee Advocate*. John Ross's nephew William Potter Ross was named editor.

In 1844, Ross was back in Washington with a Cherokee delegation. Some of the Old Settlers and the Treaty Party had been there ahead of him, each group petitioning the president to set aside land for their exclusive use and to award it one-third of the monies being given to the Cherokee Nation. Ross's trip was unsuccessful, but when the delegates went home, Ross instead went to Wilmington, Delaware, the home of Mary Bryan Stapler. He proposed marriage, was accepted, and the wedding took place September 2, 1844, in Philadelphia. Ross was fifty-four years old; his bride was nineteen.

Following a honeymoon in New York, Ross took his new bride and her sister Sarah home to the Cherokee Nation. By this time, he had a new house built, calling it Rose Cottage, but it was much more than a cottage. A two-story house with guest rooms, family rooms, a library, and a parlor, Rose Cottage had a front porch all the way across the front with large pillars. A long driveway lined with rose bushes led up to the porch.

The years 1845 and 1846 were especially bad for the Cherokee Nation as the violence between the Ross Party and Treaty Party factions reached terrible levels. In addition to the domestic strife, members of the Treaty Party and disaffected members of the Western Cherokee Nation sent delegates to Washington to plead for the splitting of the Cherokee Nation into two separate divisions, claiming that there was no way they could live safely under the Ross government. Ross spent much of his time in Washington arguing for the continued unity of the Cherokee Nation. Stand Watie kept his own armed guard around his home, and around two hundred armed Cherokees continued to guard John Ross's home. At last, in July 1846 an agreement was reached, and a treaty was signed between the two factions in Washington. Ross and Watie shook hands. Peace and tranquility seemed to be in the Cherokee Nation's future.

In 1849, Ross's son-in-law, Return J. Meigs, joined in on the California gold rush, and Ross took over his store in Tahlequah. John Ross and Company was run by Ross's two nephews, William P. and Daniel H. Ross. When the firm closed, to be reopened later by the nephews, Ross went into business with his brother-in-law, John Stapler. Most of Ross's wealth, however, was in land improvements and property he owned in Delaware. The government of the Cherokee Nation was in constant financial difficulty throughout the 1850s, and even though Ross was able in 1851 to build and open two seminaries there, one for men and one for women, they were closed in 1856 due to lack of funds.

At the same time, whites from Kansas began squatting on Cherokee lands, and when Ross complained to Washington, little was done about the problem. The situation remained relatively calm, though, and Ross was handily reelected when the time came.

But the Cherokee Nation also found itself caught up in the growing controversy regarding slaves, and in 1859 two factions had again arisen. Among the conservative full-bloods, a secret society known as the Keetoowah Society—its members called "Pin Indians" because of the identifying crossed pins they wore under their coat lapels—was developed to preserve Cherokee culture and ancient Cherokee ways. The Baptist missionaries Evan Jones and his son John seem to have been influential in this group and added the abolitionist cause to its agenda. At the same time, Stand Watie and his followers organized the Knights of the Golden Circle, a proslavery group. As secessionist talk grew all around the South, Ross did all he could to keep the Cherokee Nation neutral, reminding Cherokees and others of the many treaties signed between the Cherokee Nation and the United States. Ross was seventy years old at this time.

In 1861, Chief Ross was approached by agents of the Confederacy. He received them amicably but refused to sign their treaty, even though they offered generous terms. In addition, they threatened to approach the mixed-bloods who were already sympathetic to the Confederate cause. Although this treaty was never concluded, the Confederacy secured treaties with the other four of the so-called Five Civilized Tribes and some plains tribes, and Stand Watie raised a small army to join the Confederacy. By August 1861, the Union had lost the battle of Bull Run in Virginia and the battle of Wilson's Creek in Missouri. Stand Watie was becoming a Confederate hero. Evidence indicated that Watie was prepared to take over the Cherokee government. Ross felt hemmed in.

On October 7, 1861, the Confederate treaty was concluded at Tahlequah, and the Pin Indians suddenly found themselves on the other side of the war. Many of them continued to fight against Stand Watie's troops anyway. Reverend Evan Jones wrote a letter to U.S. Indian commissioner W. P. Dole explaining the circumstances that surrounded Ross's signing of the treaty and stating that he believed Ross still to be as loyal to the Union as ever. Nevertheless, on July 15, 1862, a federal detachment under the command of Captain H. S. Greeno moved into the Cherokee Nation and arrested Ross, taking him and all the Cherokee Nation records to Kansas. From there, Ross was taken to Washington, where he was paroled, and then to Philadelphia, where he established a residence. He remained there throughout the war, spending much of his time in Washington. President Abraham Lincoln assured Ross that his treaty with the Confederacy would never be held against the Cherokee Nation.

In Ross's absence, Stand Watie had himself proclaimed principal chief of the Cherokee Nation. He burned Ross's home at Park Hill and his store in Tahlequah. In February 1863, Ross's National Council met. They officially abrogated the Confederate treaty and protested Watie's claim to the chieftainship. They abolished slavery and deposed all Cherokee officials who were disloyal to the United States. William Potter Ross, with a company of one hundred men, was busy supplying the needs of destitute Cherokees.

When the war at last came to an end on April 9, 1865, Stand Watie continued to hold out. He surrendered finally on June 23, 1865, the last Confederate to do so. John Ross was in Philadelphia. His wife died July 20. His oldest son had died in a Confederate prison camp. The Cherokee Nation was in shambles. Ross was grief stricken and in poor health, but he traveled from Philadelphia to Fort Smith, Arkansas, to take part in the treaty negotiations that followed the war. He made it to the home of relatives in Park Hill, the Murrell Home, the only antebellum-style home in the Cherokee Nation that had survived the war.

By this time, Ross was near collapse and unable to attend the opening day of the negotiations in Fort Smith. Second Chief Lewis Downing went in his place. The U.S. commissioners showed up at Fort Smith ready to destroy the Indian nations in the area that would become Oklahoma. Stand Watie and the Southern Cherokees did not show up on the first day. Even so, the commissioners opened up the session by saying that all of the tribes were traitors to the Union cause and accusing them of "crimes of secession." Because of that, they said, the tribes would have to give up their tribal lands and tribal annuities. Abraham Lincoln was dead, replaced by Andrew Johnson, and Lincoln's promise to Ross meant nothing. The commissioners refused to recognize John Ross as chief of the Cherokee Nation and recommended to the Cherokee delegates there that they depose him. Ross showed up at the negotiations late, as did the delegation of Southern Cherokees, headed by E. C. Boudinot, son of Elias and nephew of Stand Watie. Astonishingly, the U.S. commissioners favored the Southern delegation. A treaty was eventually signed, but it, of course, had to go to Washington to be ratified by the Senate. Chief Ross also went to Washington with a delegation from the Cherokee Nation, and the Southern Cherokees sent their own delegation as well.

In Washington, Ross met with the president to present his case. He spent most of his time in bed at his hotel, though. He directed the Cherokee delegation from there, and the treaty was modified. A compromise treaty was not what Ross wanted, but it was much better than what had preceded it. It set up U.S. courts in the Cherokee Nation, made the freed slaves citizens of the Cherokee Nation, and created Indian Territory out of the lands of the Five Civilized Tribes. Ross also prevented the appointment of a white territorial governor. The chiefs of the five tribes were to meet on a regular basis and act in lieu of a governor. The treaty was signed July 19, 1866.

When visited in his sickbed by commissioners from the U.S. government, Ross said, "I am an old man and have served my people and the government of the United States for a long time, over fifty years. My people have kept me in the harness, not of my own seeking, but of their own choice. I have never deceived them; and now I look back, not one act of my public life rises up to upbraid me. I have done the best I could, and today upon this bed of sickness, my heart approves all I have done. And still I am John Ross, the same John Ross of former years. Unchanged! No cause to change!" John Ross died in Washington on August 1, 1866. He was seventy-five years old and had served as principal chief of the Cherokee Nation for thirty-eight of those years, the longest run ever for a principal chief.

Robert J. Conley

Ross, John, Jr.

John Ross Jr., born in 1954, is a full-blood Cherokee, the eldest of six children. His father is a medicine man. When John went to the first grade, he could speak no English. He attended Greasy Public School in Stilwell, Oklahoma, and graduated from Cave Springs High School in Bunch. He then went to Claremore Junior College in Oklahoma and graduated. From there, he went to the University of Arkansas on a baseball scholarship. Following an accident that prevented him from playing ball any longer, he left the school. He later went back to school, along with his wife, a white woman, and finished at Northeastern State University in Tahlequah, Oklahoma. John and his wife have two sons.

Ross became involved with the Keetoowah Band of Cherokee Indians in Oklahoma as a member of the membership committee. In 1986, he ran for the position of treasurer and won. Then in 1990, he ran for chief unopposed. He took office in 1991. He was thirty-six years old, the youngest person ever elected to that office. The cold war continued between the United Keetoowah Band and the Cherokee Nation, the latter with the Bureau of Indian Affairs on its side. Much of Chief Ross's energy was expended in fighting this battle. In 1994, he won a second election, serving until 1998.

Ross Party

When the Cherokee Nation divided over the issue of removal in the 1830s, and the signers of the Removal Treaty (Treaty of New Echota) and their followers became known as the Treaty Party, the majority, followers of Chief John Ross, became known as the Ross Party.

Ross, Quatie, see "Quatie"

Ross, William Potter

William Potter Ross was the oldest son of Elizabeth Ross and John Golden Ross, a white man who had settled in Tennessee and met and married Chief John Ross's sister Eliza. That the couple shared a last name was a coincidence; the families were not related. Their son, William Potter, was born in Tennessee, near Lookout Mountain, on August 28, 1820. His education began at the Presbyterian Mission School in Will's Valley, Alabama, run by the man for whom he had been named, William Potter. From

William Potter Ross, c. 1866.
Public domain. Courtesy of the
Cherokee Honor Society.

there, he went to Greenville, Tennessee, and then, at the age of seventeen, to a preparatory school
in Lawrenceville, New Jersey.
Finally, he entered Princeton. He
was nineteen years old during the
Removal, but he did not move west
over the Trail of Tears with his
family along with the Cherokees
under Chief John Ross. He was in
school at Princeton during that
time, and upon his graduation
with high honors in 1842 he joined the Cherokees in their new home.

Chief John Ross had taken a special interest in his nephew and had
helped him financially through school. The chief's efforts were rewarded
when W. P. graduated at the top of his Princeton class of forty-four students. In the school year 1842–43, W. P. Ross taught school at Fourteen
Mile Creek in the new Cherokee Nation. He attended the large convention of Indian tribes in Tahlequah, the nation's new capital, in 1843. He
was elected clerk of the Cherokee Senate and was named first editor of the
Cherokee Advocate in 1843. He became a merchant for a time, practiced
law, and was elected from Tahlequah District to the Cherokee Senate in
1849, 1851, 1853, 1855, and 1857. After Chief John Ross signed the treaty with
the Confederacy, W. P. joined the First Cherokee Regiment of Mounted
Rifles and became a lieutenant colonel. After the chief repudiated the
treaty, W. P. switched sides. Upon the death of his uncle, W. P. was named
by the Cherokee National Council to fill out the rest of the old chief's term,
and he served as principal chief from 1866 until the next scheduled election in 1867, when he was defeated by Lewis Downing. In 1869, he became
secretary to his uncle Lewis Ross, who was then serving as the Cherokee
Nation treasurer.

Upon the death of Chief Downing in 1872, the council once again
appointed W. P. Ross to fill out the unexpired term, and he served until
1875. Although twice principal chief of the Cherokee Nation, he was never
elected to that office. Much of his time and effort during his second term

Robert J. Conley

were spent fighting against the railroads. Taking full advantage of the Treaty of 1866, the railroads made an all-out assault on Indian Territory, including the Cherokee Nation. Ross protested vigorously, but to no avail. His uncle, John Ross, had been strongly opposed to the railroads, and W. P. had picked up his banner. In 1874, Congress created the position of commissioner to the Five Civilized Tribes at Union Agency in Muskogee, Indian Territory. Discouraged, Ross predicted the allotment of Indian lands in severalty and the ultimate absorption of the Cherokee population into the general population.

Ross was also editor of the *Muskogee Indian Journal*, the *Vinita Indian Chieftain*, and the *Tahlequah Indian Arrow*. A strong supporter of education, he was a trustee of the Cherokee Nation's seminaries and had served on the nation's Board of Education. He was also mayor of Fort Gibson for a time. He died on July 20, 1891, at the age of seventy-one. His widow wrote a biography of him titled *The Life and Times of Hon. William P. Ross*.

S.

Salonita

Salonita, or Flying Squirrel, was the leader of a group of Cherokees who went out to hunt for Tsali for the U.S. Army. When Tsali and his family had been rounded up for removal from their southeastern homelands, Tsali or one of his sons had killed some soldiers. Tsali finally surrendered and was brought in, but he and all except his youngest sons were shot. Legend has it that he agreed to surrender so that the remaining Cherokees hiding in the mountains of North Carolina would be left alone. The leader of these mountain refugees was Yonaguska. Upon the death of Yonaguska, Salonita claimed to have assumed the position of chief and was certainly chief of Painttown. He was very suspicious of whites who claimed to speak for the Cherokees, especially William Holland Thomas, a white man who was said to be the chief of this group of refugees and may even have been the reason why Salonita claimed the chieftainship. Salonita did become the first chief elected under the new Cherokee constitution in 1870, and he served until 1875. His Cherokee names are given variously as "Saunooke (Sawnook, Sawanugi)," "Salonita," and "Kalahu" (All-bones). While he was in office, a new constitution was adopted, and the term of the chief was changed to four years.

Salonita, Bird

Bird Salonita, also known as Young Squirrel, was chief of the Eastern Band of Cherokee Indians from 1903 to 1907.

Saunooke, Joe

Joe Saunooke was principal chief of the Eastern Band of Cherokees from 1911 to 1915 and again from 1919 to 1923. During his administration, the first

Robert J. Conley

Cherokee Fair was organized in 1914 to display and sell Cherokee wares. It was so successful that it has continued on an annual basis. Tourism increased dramatically during Chief Saunooke's second term owing to the dramatic increase in automobile ownership.

Saunooke, Osley Bird

Principal chief of the Eastern Band of Cherokees from 1951 to 1955 and again from 1959 to 1963, Osley Bird Saunooke was born in 1906 in the Yellow Hill section of the Cherokee reservation in North Carolina. He attended Cherokee Indian School in North Carolina and then Haskell Institute in Kansas. At six feet, six inches tall and 369 pounds, he became a professional wrestler and in 1937 became the Super Heavyweight Wrestling Champion of the World, a title he held for fourteen years. Before his retirement in 1951, he wrestled in 5,217 matches and in every state of the nation. He married Bertha Smith in 1934, and they had five children.

As chief, Saunooke managed to keep the U.S. government from shutting down the Indian hospital at Cherokee, North Carolina, and the state government from levying taxes on the reservation. At the same time, he was able to have the tribal government levy its own taxes and thereby assume more responsibility for police and fire protection and for sanitation. In 1955, when termination of the Eastern Band of Cherokees was proposed, Chief Saunooke opposed it.

At the nineteenth annual convention of the Congress of American Indians, Chief Saunooke was elected vice president of that organization. He had good relationships with people in all walks of life, from presidents of the United States to any Indian on the reservation to giants in the sports world. He died on April 15, 1965, from complications owing to diabetes. He was fifty-eight years old. His widow, Bertha, was elected to the Eastern Band Tribal Council in 1969.

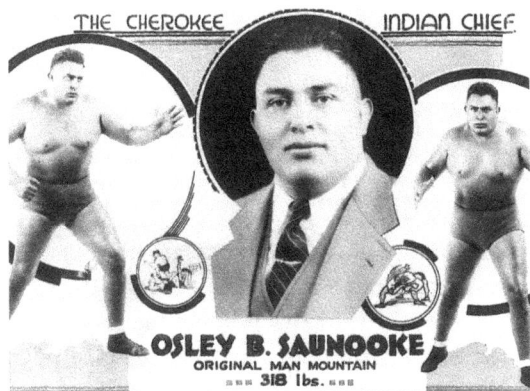

Osley Byrd Saunooke, 1937 to 1956. Courtesy of the Saunooke family.

Saunooke, Stilwell

Stilwell Saunooke (Saunooka) was chief of the Eastern Band of Cherokees from 1891 to 1895. During his term, many of the Eastern Cherokee land claims cases were at last resolved, giving them title to almost all of the land they claimed.

Seabourn, Bert

Bert Seabourn was born at Red Barn, Texas, in 1931. He completed junior and senior high school in Purcell, Oklahoma. He married Bonnie Jo Tompkins in 1950, when he was nineteen and she was sixteen. When the Korean War started, Seabourn joined the navy. At Hickam Air Force Base in Honolulu, Hawaii, he became a full-time artist. Before he got out of the navy, his mother, his wife, and his daughter had moved to Wyoming, so Bert went to Wyoming, too. He then bought a 1950 Ford and headed with his family to Oklahoma City, where he found employment as a draftsman for the Oklahoma Gas and Electric Company (OG&E) in 1955. He enrolled in night classes in art at Oklahoma City University. In 1962, he became company artist for OG&E and stayed with them until 1978. During the late 1960s, he began painting the style of Indian art that captured a great deal of attention and for which he is known today. He paints not only Cherokees, but Indians of many different tribes. *Key Magazine* of Phoenix and Scottsdale, Arizona, said in 1976 that Bert Seabourn is "one of the country's most prominent Indian artists."

Seabourn, Connie

Connie Seabourn is the daughter of Bert Seabourn. A gifted watercolorist, she followed in her famous father's footsteps and began working full-time as an artist in 1980. She has a bachelor's degree from the University of Oklahoma. Her work is displayed in the Museum of the American Indian in New York City and in the Heard Museum in Phoenix.

Sequoyah (George Gist, George Guess)

The date of Sequoyah's birth is unknown. Various scholars have placed it anywhere from 1760 to 1780. Biographer Stan Hoig speculates the year was 1778, which seems reasonable. Sequoyah's hometown, Taskigi in Tennessee, was twice burned in his childhood, once by troops under the command of Colonel William Christian and then again by the

Sequoyah, 1828. McKenney-
Hall Portrait Gallery,
Smithsonian Institution.

Indian-hating John Sevier.
Sequoyah joined the Cherokees
fighting with General Andrew
Jackson in attacking the Red Stick Creeks in 1813. At Dwight Mission
in Arkansas in 1821, he first revealed to the Cherokees the remarkable
Cherokee-language syllabary he had perfected. Having convinced the
Western Cherokees in Arkansas of its usefulness, he taught many of
them to write in the Cherokee language. Then he had them write letters
to friends and family still in the old Cherokee country, and he made a
trip back there to deliver the letters. The syllabary was quickly adopted
by nearly all Cherokees. When the Cherokee Nation started to publish
its own newspaper, the *Cherokee Phoenix*, in 1828, it was printed in both
English and Cherokee, the Cherokee being presented in the syllabary.
Sequoyah became a major celebrity. In Washington, he was wined and
dined, interviewed, and painted. The Cherokee Nation presented him
with a medal. Back in Arkansas, Sequoyah planned a trip to Mexico and
left in the company of his son Teesee, a young Cherokee man named
Ujiya, and four other Cherokee men. The four other men returned home
after a short while, but Sequoyah, Teesee, and Ujiya made the rest of the
trip. Sequoyah died in Mexico, but his burial spot is unknown.

Sequoyah Convention

In July 1905, four of the so-called Five Civilized Tribes met in convention (the Chickasaws held out) and drew up a constitution for the state
of Sequoyah. It was a last-ditch effort to keep Indian Territory from being
combined with Oklahoma Territory into one state. Sequoyah would have
been an Indian state. The measure was presented to the U.S. Congress, but
it received little attention.

Sequoyah High School

Sequoyah High School was originally established as the Cherokee Orphan Asylum by an act of the Cherokee National Council in 1871 to care for the many Cherokee children orphaned as a result of the Civil War. The first structure at its present location was built in 1875. In 1914, Chief W. C. Rogers was authorized to sell the building to the federal government. He did so, and the Bureau of Indian Affairs operated it as a boarding school until 1985, when the Cherokee Nation contracted to run the school. It continues to do so. One of the graduates of Sequoyah High School was Houston Teehee.

Sequoyah Indian Weavers Association

The Sequoyah Indian Weavers Association was begun at Sequoyah Indian School in 1938 under a Bureau of Indian Affairs program to promote the production and sale of American Indian arts and crafts. The bureau sent William Ames from New York to Tahlequah, Oklahoma, to teach loom weaving to Cherokees. Ames designed the looms, and boys in the shop constructed them. In 1940, the Sequoyah Indian Weavers Association was officially formed, with Ames setting up classes in several Cherokee communities. The association became a profitable enterprise. In 1953, it included fifty members, with seven full-time workers at the main center in Briggs, Oklahoma. The year 1954 marked the end of federal funding for the program, though, and shortly after that a burglary at the center hurt the association badly. In 1967, Ames returned to Tahlequah to revive it, but with limited success. Most of the weavers dropped out. Today, only a few weavers work at the center in Briggs, and the center itself is badly in need of repair.

Shade, Hastings

Hastings Shade is well known as a traditionalist among Oklahoma Cherokees. He is bilingual and is known for his craftsmanship in making gigs and Cherokee marbles, among other things. He was deputy chief of the Cherokee Nation during the first administration of Chief Chad Smith, from 1999 to 2003, and during that time he spent much of his time attending and teaching at Cherokee Cultural Camps, not just locally but also around the country. He lives in Lost City, outside Hulbert, Oklahoma.

Robert J. Conley

Sixkiller, Sam

Sam Sixkiller was born in the Goingsnake District of the Cherokee Nation in what is now Oklahoma around 1842, the son of Redbird Sixkiller and Pamela Whaley Sixkiller. He was educated at Baptist Mission. He was nineteen years old when the Civil War broke out. His father went north with some other Cherokees to join up, leaving Sam to work the farm, but Sam ran off with friends and joined the Confederacy. He later deserted and went to Fort Gibson (also in present-day Oklahoma), where he found his father in charge of an artillery company. He enlisted and stayed with the company until the end of the war. At the war's end, Sixkiller married Fannie Foreman and moved with her to Tahlequah, the capital of the Cherokee Nation. In 1876, he was appointed high sheriff of the Cherokee Nation and warden of the Cherokee National Prison. His father, Redbird, was appointed to the Cherokee Nation's Supreme Court. In June 1877, when Sixkiller was chasing some rowdies out of Tahlequah, they turned and fired shots. He fired back and killed one, Jeter Lester. Sixkiller was charged with murder and tried, but the trial resulted in a hung jury. The case was turned over to the National Council. The council found that there was no implication of guilt, so Sixkiller was released from custody, but thereafter, feeling that his reputation had been smirched, he moved with his wife and six children to Muskogee in the Creek Nation.

In 1880, the agent for the Five Civilized Tribes in Muskogee was authorized to raise a force of thirty Indian police. He named Sam Sixkiller captain. Sam also held a commission as a deputy U.S. marshal. In one case, he waylaid a bootlegger named Coppell and ordered him to surrender. Coppell was on a wagon seat, and Sixkiller was standing in the road. Coppell reached for a shotgun, but Sixkiller drew his pistol and shot first, killing Coppell. In another case in 1885, Sixkiller and a posse ran down and killed the notorious Dick Glass and three of his gang. In 1886, Sixkiller wounded Black Hoyt in a gun battle in Muskogee and locked him in jail. Hoyt's companion, Nicholson, was also wounded but escaped. The next day Hoyt's father showed up and was abusive to the lawmen, so Sixkiller locked him up, too. He then sent a policeman out to arrest Nicholson, but Nicholson was staying with a man named Dick Vann, who drove the policeman off at gunpoint, so a warrant was issued for the arrest of Vann. Nicholson died from his wound. Vann was arrested and jailed. Hoyt's father was released. On Christmas Eve 1886, Vann, having been released from jail, was in town with his brother-in-law Alf Cunningham, who had stolen a shotgun at a hardware store and had used it to get a pistol away from a policeman. Unaware of these events, Sam Sixkiller, off duty and unarmed, was walking down the street when the two stepped into his path. As Cunningham fired the shotgun, Sixkiller sprang forward and knocked it aside, but Vann fired three shots from the pistol, killing Sixkiller.

Sixkiller, Sonny

Alex (Sonny) Sixkiller was born in 1959 in Oklahoma, but his family moved to the Rogue Valley in southern Oregon when Sonny was one year old. Following a promising high school record as a football player, Sonny went to the University of Washington, where he became the quarterback for the Huskies in his sophomore year in 1970. That year he led the nation in passing, averaging 18.6 completions per game. He appeared on the cover of *Sports Illustrated* in October 1971. By the end of his senior year, he held fifteen passing records. He was inducted into the Huskies Hall of Fame in 1985. He acted in the Bert Reynolds film *The Longest Yard* and is the subject of the song "The Ballad of Sonny Sixkiller." He played professional football briefly in 1974 for Toronto of the Canadian Football League and then for both Philadelphia and Hawaii in the World Football League. He has since been a color analyst for Fox Sports Network Northwest on Washington games, an analyst for the Fox Sports Network, and an official spokesman for the 7 Cedars Casino in Sequim, Washington, fifty-two miles west of Seattle, owned by the Jamestown S'Klallam Tribe. He has also written a book, *Tales from the Huskies' Sidelines*. Sonny and his wife, Denise, live in Seattle.

Smith, Archilla

Archilla Smith was one of the signers of the Treaty of New Echota in 1835. He moved west in 1837 and was arrested for the murder of John McIntosh in 1839. The trial began on December 15, 1840. Isaac Bushyhead was counsel for the Cherokee Nation, and Stand Watie was counsel for the defendant. The foreman of the jury was Stephen Foreman. The trial lasted for nine days, and Smith was judged guilty and sentenced to hang. It was the first murder trial conducted by the Cherokee Nation and was followed by the first hanging for the nation. John Howard Payne was present and did an admirable job of recording the proceedings. His articles were later published as *Indian Justice: A Cherokee Murder Trial at Tahlequah in 1840*, which was reissued by the University of Oklahoma Press in 2002.

Smith, Betty Jo

Betty Jo Smith is a full-blood, bilingual Cherokee who is known for her basketry, pottery, beadwork, and traditional Cherokee cooking. During the Wilma Mankiller administration, 1985–95, Betty was named a Cherokee National Living Treasure. She was elected to the Cherokee National Council in 1979, and she worked at the Cherokee Heritage Center in Tahlequah, Oklahoma, from its inception, reenacting the life of a seventeenth-century villager, creating costumes for the entire village, managing the village, directing the gift shop from 1979 to 1992, and performing a role in the annual Trail of Tears drama. Betty and her late husband, Columbus, had eleven children, and she now has twenty-four grandchildren and sixteen great-grandchildren. In 2004, she received the Cherokee Medal of Honor.

Smith, Chadwick

Born December 17, 1950, in Pontiac, Michigan, Chad Smith (Ugisata or Corntassel) is a great-grandson of the famous traditional Cherokee leader Redbird Smith. He is the son of Nelson Smith, a full-blood Cherokee, and Pauline Smith, a white woman. Chad holds a bachelor's degree in education from the University of Georgia (1973), a master's in public administration from the University of Wisconsin (1975), and a juris doctorate from the University of Tulsa (1980). In the 1970s, he was planner for the Cherokee Nation. After finishing law school at the University of Tulsa, he served as Creek County prosecutor, then as prosecutor for the Cherokee Nation in the Wilma Mankiller administration (1985–95), and had his own private law practice in Tulsa. He originally ran for the office of principal chief of the Cherokee Nation in 1995. He came in third to George Bearpaw and Joe Byrd, but a runoff had to be held because neither of the two top candidates had won a majority of the votes. When George Bearpaw had to withdraw, Smith was in the running again, and many people believe he would have been elected that year had

Chad Smith. Photo by and courtesy of D. L. Birchfield.

the Judicial Appeals Tribunal allowed new ballots to be printed with his name on them instead of Bearpaw's. New ballots were not printed, so, of course, Joe Byrd won. In 1999, however, Smith ran again, defeating Byrd. Chief Smith established the first independent Cherokee press and continued the development of tribal programs. In 2003, he ran for reelection. His only serious opponent was former chief Joe Byrd, whom he defeated without the need for a runoff.

In 2007, Smith won his third term of office. During his eight years as principal chief, he has led the Cherokee Nation into expanding casino gaming and challenging the U.S. government regarding Cherokee Nation sovereignty.

Smith, Janet L.

Janet Smith (Nuh Tse, or One Who Walks About as in Spirit) is a highly respected Cherokee artist. She studied under Ruth Blalock Jones and Dick West at Bacone College in Muskogee, Oklahoma, was encouraged by Acee Blue Eagle, and went on to earn a degree in fine arts from Northeastern State University in Tahlequah, Oklahoma, and a degree in art therapy from Emporia State University in Kansas. She taught at various colleges and universities across the country for thirteen years before establishing the first art therapy program for the Cherokee Nation's Jack Brown Center in 1991. She was named director of the center in 1995. She is a member of the Cherokee Nation's Cultural Committee, the Cherokee Artists Association, the American Art Therapy Association, and One Sky, a center for the treatment of substance abuse. In 2004, she received the Cherokee Medal of Honor.

Smith, Nimrod Jarrett

Born January 3, 1837, on Valley Road near Murphy, North Carolina, Nimrod Smith Jarrett (Tsaladihi) was the son of a full-blood Cherokee mother and Henry Smith, a half-blood Cherokee. When full-grown, he was six feet, four inches tall. He could speak both Cherokee and English. When he was twenty-five years old, he enlisted in the Thomas Confederate Legion and served throughout the Civil War, achieving the rank of first sergeant. A disciple of Lloyd Welch, he was clerk of the Eastern Band of Cherokees's Tribal Council when it drew up a constitution in 1868. Welch, elected principal chief of the Eastern Band in 1875, died in 1880, and Smith was chosen to fill his unexpired term. The Eastern Band had filed suit against the Cherokee

Robert J. Conley

Nimrod Jarrett Smith,
c. 1886. Courtesy of
the Smithsonian Institution.

Nation for its share of the money paid
by the United States for the eastern
Cherokee lands, and Chief Smith
spent much of his time in Washington,
D.C., securing the title to the Eastern
Cherokees' land. The federal boarding
school at Cherokee, North Carolina,
was opened in 1884 during Smith's
term. Without asking for the Bureau of Indian Affairs's approval, Chief
Smith negotiated outside contracts for cutting timber to raise tribal rev-
enues. The Constitution called for a salary of $500 per year for the chief,
but Chief Smith was never paid. He was partly reimbursed for expenses
incurred during his travels to Washington. He married a white woman,
Miss Mary Guthrie. He continued to serve as chief until 1891, when he lost
the election due to a falling out with the council based on accusations of
bad conduct, including drunkenness, brawling, and adultery. When Smith
died on August 2, 1893, at the age of fifty-seven, he was still a poor man.

Smith, Redbird

Redbird Smith was born July 19, 1850, near Fort Smith, Arkansas. Pig Redbird
and his wife, Lizzie Hildebrand, were on their way to the new Cherokee
Nation in the West when their son Redbird was born. Emmet Starr says that
the name "Smith" was added by people in Arkansas because Pig Redbird
was a blacksmith and an "old and ardent adherent of the ancient rituals."
Redbird Smith, the son, was dedicated at an early age by his father "to the
services and causes of the Cherokee people in accordance with ancient
customs." In 1859, the elder Smith, Bud Gritts, and James Vann decided to
reorganize the Keetoowah Society, dedicated to preserving Cherokee customs, and Gritts drew up a constitution. During the Civil War, almost all
the Keetoowahs went with the North. In 1889, the Keetoowah constitution
and laws were amended, making the organization more political. A split in
the Keetoowahs ensued, and Redbird Smith and his followers, opposed to
involvement in politics, became known as the Nighthawk Keetoowahs. In
1895, with the U.S. government agitating for allotment of Cherokee lands,

A Cherokee Encyclopedia | 219

the Keetoowahs were united in their resistance. Redbird Smith urged his followers not to participate in the deliberations concerning allotment. He felt that the Treaty of New Echota with the United States was sacred, and they would surely abide by it. Following the passage of the Curtis Act, by which the United States simply took over and began the allotment process without Cherokee approval, Redbird advised his followers to avoid enrollment. He was arrested and jailed. After a night in jail, he registered. He was later arrested again because of the illegal activities of Charlie Wickliffe and his brothers. (See "Wickliffe, Charlie.") They were known to be Keetoowahs, so the authorities thought that Redbird should be able to tell something about them. A mob gathered outside the jail, threatening to lynch Redbird, and authorities had to sneak him out the back door and spirit him away. He was released after being questioned by U.S. marshals.

By 1905, most of the Cherokee ceremonial grounds had been established in the West, and Redbird spent his time traveling between the twenty-two fires and teaching. Janey B. Hendrix says that after Oklahoma statehood in 1907, "the fullbloods were forgotten." By 1910, when Redbird realized that the United States was not going to live up to its treaty obligations, he delivered the following speech to the Nighthawk Keetoowah Council:

> After my selection as chief, I awakened to the grave and great responsibilities of the leader of men. I looked about and saw that I had led my people down a long and steep mountainside, now it was my duty to turn and lead them back upward to save them. The unfortunate thing in the mistakes and errors of leaders or of governments is the penalty the innocent and loyal followers have to pay. My greatest ambition has always been to think right and do right. It is my belief this is the fulfilling of the law of the Great Creator. In the upbuilding of my people it is my purpose that we shall be spiritually right and industriously strong.
>
> I have always believed that the Great Creator had a great design for my people, the Cherokees. I have been taught that from my childhood up and now in my mature manhood I recognize it as a great truth. Our forces have been dissipated by the external forces, perhaps it has been just a training, but we must now get together as a race and render our contribution to mankind.
>
> We are endowed with intelligence, we are industrious, we are loyal, and we are spiritual but we are overlooking the particular Cherokee mission on earth, for no man nor race is endowed with these qualifications without a designed purpose.

Robert J. Conley

Work and right training is the solution of my following. We as a group are still groping in darkness in many things, but this we know, we must work. A kindly man cannot help his neighbor in need unless he have a surplus, and he cannot have a surplus unless he works. It is so simple, and yet we have to continually remind our people of this.

Our mixed-bloods should not be overlooked in this program of a racial awakening. Our pride in our ancestral heritage is our great incentive for handing something worthwhile to our posterity. It is this pride in ancestry that makes men strong and loyal for their principle in life. It is this same pride that makes men give up their all for their Government.

When World War I started, Redbird urged all young men to register for the draft. Special ceremonies were held for their protection, and they all returned home safely. Redbird Smith died in 1918.

Southern Rights Party

After the Removal and the killing of Major Ridge, John Ridge, and Elias Boudinot, Stand Watie moved to Arkansas with a number of fighting men around him for his protection from the Ross Party. They were supported by the secret secessionist organization called the Knights of the Golden Circle. It was made up mostly of the old Ridge Party, or Treaty Party— those who had signed the Treaty of New Echota in 1835 for removal to the West against the wishes of the majority of Cherokees at the time. They also called themselves the Blue Circle and finally the Southern Rights Party. They formed the nucleus of the Cherokee Confederacy.

Springfrog

Springfrog (Tooan Tuh, Too an tuh, Dustu, Toostoo, Yoosto, Du nas du, Dewi Gwedu) was born in 1754 in a place that is now encompassed by Chattanooga, Tennessee. He fought in the Creek War of 1813–14 under Andrew Jackson. By 1817, he had migrated to Arkansas and was one of the Cherokees at the battle of Claremore Mound in 1818. He is said to have been a guide for John James Audubon, after which he himself became known as a naturalist and sportsman. He accompanied Degadoga in 1824 on the old war chief's final journey. When the Arkansas Cherokees were moved across the Arkansas River into what is now Oklahoma, Springfrog settled

Springfrog, c. 1826.
McKenney-Hall Portrait Gallery,
Smithsonian Institution.

at Briartown, where, according to a 1836 McKenney-Hall Portrait Gallery description, he "had a small log cabin, a faithful old wife, some ponies, dogs, a patch of beans and pumpkins, and a fireplace where he could drink some whiskey and talk with the old men about the days of their youth." He died there in 1859 at 105 years old. A wildlife sanctuary has been established on the site of his birthplace in Chattanooga.

Stalking Turkey

Stalking Turkey (Cunne Shote) made the trip to England with Englishman Henry Timberlake and fellow Cherokees Ostenaco and Pouting Pigeon in 1762. While there, the three Cherokees were painted in a group portrait by Sir Joshua Reynolds, and Stalking Turkey was painted in an individual portrait by Francis Parsons.

Standing Deer, Andy

During the administration of Chief Andy Standing Deer of the Eastern Band of Cherokees (1895–99), an epidemic of grippe swept through the Cherokee country, and by 1897 the Band's population had been reduced to 1,312 people.

Starr, Emmet

Emmet Starr was born in the Goingsnake District of the Cherokee Nation in Indian Territory on December 12, 1870. He was the oldest son of Walter Adair Starr. He was educated in Cherokee public schools, graduated from the Cherokee Male Seminary in 1888, and then received a degree from Barnes Medical College in St. Louis in 1891. He started practicing medicine that same year, but he was also already gathering material for his *History of the Cherokee Indians*. In 1896, he quit the practice of medicine to devote himself full-time to his work with Cherokee history. He served one term on the Cherokee National Council as a representative from Cooweescoowee District, and he was a delegate to the unsuccessful Sequoyah Convention, whose purpose was to establish an Indian state. Following Oklahoma statehood, Starr continued work on his histories. He published *Cherokees West* in 1910, *Encyclopedia of Oklahoma* in 1912, *Early History of the Cherokees* in 1917, and his most important work, *History of the Cherokee Indians*, in 1922. Notes for a part of his history, "Old Families and Their Genealogy," were used by members of the Dawes Commission in establishing eligibility for enrollment, and they are still used today by Cherokees searching for their "roots." Starr dreamed of becoming the "Herodotus of the Cherokees," but he died in St. Louis in 1930, disappointed and convinced that he had failed his people.

Starr, Frank, see "Boudinot, Frank"

Starr, Henry

Henry Starr was born in 1873 near Fort Gibson, Indian Territory. He was the son of George (Hop) Starr and Mary Scott. His grandfather was Tom Starr, and one of his uncles was Sam Starr. Henry's father died in 1886, and his mother married a white man named C. N. Walker. Henry and C. N. did not get along. In 1888, the family moved to a location in the northern Cherokee Nation about twenty miles south of Coffeeville, Kansas. Henry, fifteen years old at the time, got a job working on a ranch. He lost the job when he fought with another cowboy over a horse. Jobs on other ranches followed. In 1891, Henry was accused of stealing two horses from a man named Eaton. He was arrested and thrown in jail at Fort Smith, Arkansas. At the trial, Eaton admitted that Henry had not stolen the horses, and Henry was acquitted. The incident, however, left a sour taste for the law in Henry's mouth. In July 1892, he and another man robbed the railroad depot at Nowata, Indian Territory. Henry was found out, arrested again, and taken to Fort Smith once more. He was released on bond but did not show up for the trial. Instead, he began robbing country stores. While on the road, Henry met a man named Floyd Wilson, who suddenly fired five shots at him. Henry returned fire and killed Wilson. It was learned later that the railroad had hired Wilson as a detective to run Henry down, but Henry swore that the man never identified himself and had just started shooting. Finally, Henry settled down to robbing banks. He was captured in Colorado in 1895 and returned to Fort Smith, where he was tried for the murder of Floyd Wilson and found guilty. While he was waiting to be hanged, Cherokee Bill (Crawford Goldsby), also awaiting his death sentence, got hold of a gun somehow and killed a prison guard. He was shooting up the prison when Henry made his way to Bill's cell and talked him out of the gun. Because of that act and because of persistent efforts by his mother, Henry Starr received a pardon from President Theodore Roosevelt. He married Olive Griffin, a Cherokee, in 1903, and when they had a son, Henry named him Theodore Roosevelt Starr. Henry served three prison terms over the years, but each time he was released, he went back to his favorite profession. While he was in prison on one occasion, he wrote his life story, *Thrilling Events: Life of Henry Starr*. It was published in 1914. On another occasion, he starred in a movie, *A Debtor to the Law*, in which he reenacted one of his own bank robberies. He said that the filmmakers robbed him so badly that he had to go back to robbing banks. In February 1921, Henry Starr and his latest gang drove a car into Harrisonville, Arkansas, and held up the People's National Bank. The bank president shot Henry, and Henry fell to the floor. When one of the other outlaws aimed a gun at the bank officer, Henry said, "Don't shoot him. Just get out of here." Henry's gang scattered. On his deathbed, Henry Starr said, "I've robbed more banks than anyone in history."

Starr, James

When delegates from the Western Cherokee Nation made a trip to Washington, D.C., in 1832, they stopped in the old Cherokee Nation in the Southeast along the way. While there, they persuaded James Starr and John Walker to accompany them. Then at the Red Clay Council later that year, following the U.S. Supreme Court's decision in *Worcester v. Georgia*, favorable to the Cherokees, and President Andrew Jackson's notorious remark, "John Marshal has rendered his decision. Now let him enforce it," Starr was noticeably more familiar with U.S. commissioners. He added his name to a list of pro-removal treaty advocates. When the Treaty of New Echota was signed in 1835, his signature was among the names appended. He moved west with other Treaty Party members in 1836. Following the killings of other signers—specifically Major Ridge, John Ridge, and Elias Boudinot—in 1839, Starr fled to Fort Gibson for protection. In 1843, his sons Tom, Ellis, and Bean were said to have been harassing voters at the polls and were accused of murdering a white family in their home. In 1845, Starr made an exploratory trip into Texas with other Cherokees looking for a place where they might settle safely. He was back in the Cherokee Nation on the night of November 9 that same year when a band of thirty-two men rode up to his house and shot him and his twelve-year-old son Buck to death.

Starr, Pony

Pony Starr was a major participant in the Porum County Range War, said easily to rival the famous Lincoln County Range War in New Mexico in which Billy the Kid was involved. In the 1880s, a family named Davis moved from Alabama to Porum, twenty miles south of Muskogee, Indian Territory. A big rancher, Judge Hester, resented their intrusion. For the next few years, accusations of rustling were thrown at the Davises, but there was no evidence. Pony Starr, a cousin of Cherokee outlaw Henry Starr, became associated with the Davis family. Old Man Davis had five sons. On September 11, 1906, Cicero Davis, the oldest, was shot to death from ambush. A man named Mack Alfred was accused and arrested. About that same time, an old man named Spivey was murdered in his home, and the house was burned down around him. Alfred said at his trial that he had been with a party of four who killed Spivey, but that all he did was hold the horses. He said that Bob Davis had been the killer. Davis and two other men were arrested, and just before their trial, Alfred was ambushed in the same place and in the same manner as had been Cicero. Davis and the others were acquitted at their trial. Then, in 1911, Bob and Amon Davis were accused of the murder of a U.S. deputy marshal in Porum. They fled to Colorado but were arrested there and returned to Muskogee, Oklahoma, and held without bond. While they were in jail, Judge Hester accused Pony Starr and Joe Davis of stealing some of his cattle. Starr and Davis countered with a writ served on Judge Hester. When three deputies went to the judge's house with the writ, they were surrounded by armed men, and Hester threatened their lives. Some of Hester's men held the deputies captive, while others rode for the Starr ranch. Pony Starr, his wife, and Joe Davis were sitting at the table drinking coffee when they were suddenly attacked. They drove off the attackers, killing five of them and wounding two. There were eleven dead horses in the yard. When the wounded and killed attackers were unmasked, they all were found to be Hester men. One of them was his son Cliff. Armed gangs of men organized in Porum and went looking for Joe Davis and Pony Starr. Mrs. Starr went to the sheriff in Muskogee and told him that Pony and Joe Davis would give themselves up to him if he could promise them protection. He agreed. In the meantime, an old man who had once worked for the Davises was attacked and beaten in Porum by a gang of thugs. Then the citizens of Porum, who had not been involved, suddenly armed themselves. They went to the Davis home, where Joe Davis and Pony Starr had arranged to meet the sheriff, and stood guard. Starr and Davis were cleared of any wrongdoing because their part in the fight had been self-defense. Bob and Amon Davis were tried for the earlier killing of the deputy marshal, but they were acquitted. Then when Starr and Davis were tried for rustling, they, too, were acquitted. Bob Davis moved to Arizona. Sam Davis moved to Tahlequah, Oklahoma. He later became frail, and Bob returned from Arizona to take care of him. They died in Tahlequah. Amon Davis moved to Wagoner, Oklahoma, where he died in 1924. Pony Starr moved to southeastern Oklahoma and ranched for a few years. When he became too old to keep up the ranch work, he sold out and moved to Fort Worth, Texas, where he died in 1947.

Starr, Sam

Sam Starr was a son of the notorious Tom Starr. Sam married Myra Belle Shirley when he was thirty-two and she was twenty-eight. They settled on the Canadian River near Briartown, Indian Territory, and engaged in horse stealing for a living. In 1885, Sam disappeared for a time, and Belle took up with a murderer from Texas named John Middleton. Some thought that Middleton had killed Sam, but when Middleton himself was killed, Sam reappeared. In 1886, a reward of $10,000 was posted by the U.S. government for the apprehension of Sam and Belle Starr, dead or alive, for "robbery, murder, treason, and other acts against the peace and dignity of the U.S." They were arrested and taken to Fort Smith, Arkansas, but the charges were dismissed for lack of evidence. Later that same year Sam Starr and a deputy marshal shot and killed one another in a gunfight.

Starr, Tom

Tom Starr was born in Tennessee in 1813, the son of James Starr and Susie Maugh Starr. When the Treaty of New Echota, the Removal Treaty, was signed in 1835, James Starr was one of the signers. In 1837, the Starr family moved to the Flint District of the new Cherokee Nation in the West. Following the Trail of Tears and the killings of Major Ridge, John Ridge, and Elias Boudinot, who were also signers of the Removal Treaty, Tom Starr killed David Buffington, a follower of Chief John Ross, who had opposed the Treaty Party, during an argument at a footrace.

In 1845, thirty-two armed men rode up to the James Starr home. Without warning, one of the men shot James dead as he sat on the porch. His son Buck, twelve years old and disabled, was also shot and killed. Hearing of these murders, Tom Starr vowed revenge. He was aided in his efforts by his brothers Ellis, James, and Bean. When the brothers were killed by Cherokee Nation Lighthorse police, Tom continued alone. In later years, he claimed to have killed all the men in the party that had killed his father and young brother except for a few who died before he could get to them. After Lewis Downing became principal chief of the Cherokee Nation following Ross's death, the Cherokee Nation made peace with Tom Starr.

Tom's wife was Catharine Reese. Their son Sam married a white woman named Myra Belle Shirley, who became famous (or infamous) as Belle Starr. Tom died in 1890 at the age of seventy-seven.

State-Recognized Cherokee Tribes

In addition to the three federally recognized Cherokee tribes, there are six state-recognized Cherokee tribes, five in the United States, and one in Mexico. In the United States, there are the Cherokees of Georgia Tribal Council, the Cherokee Tribe of Northeast Alabama, the Northern Cherokee Nation of Missouri, the Northern Cherokee Nation of the Old Louisiana Territory, and the Northern Cherokees of Missouri and Arkansas. The Cherokee Nation of Mexico has been recognized by the Mexican state of Coahuilla.

Stickball, Cherokee

The ballplay, or *anetsa* (little brother of war), according to James Mooney, "is the great athletic game of the Cherokee." The national game of Canada, lacrosse, is a development from stickball. The game is played on a field similar to a football field, with a goal at each end. There is no out of bounds. The object is to get the ball between the goals, or upright posts, at each end of the field. Players carry a set of ballsticks, one in each hand, and the ball is caught and thrown with these sticks. The sticks are about a yard long with a small webbed racquet at the end. The ball is about the size of a golf ball, hard and made of animal skins.

In the old days, it is said, players were sometimes killed because the game was so rough. The game was also used as a metaphor for war, as in "some land was won in a ballgame," meaning in an actual battle.

Nowadays, about the worst damage a player can expect is a black eye, bloody nose, or broken bones.

Stone, Jason

Jason Stone, a Cherokee descendant of the Wolf Clan, is an award-winning sculptor and the son of famous wood sculptor Willard Stone. He learned from his father and has continued to work in the same tradition. Stone was named Master Artist by the Five Civilized Tribes Museum in Muskogee, Oklahoma, in 1981. He lives and works at the Stone Family Studio on Highway 412 near Locust Grove, Oklahoma. In 2002, he received a Cherokee Medal of Honor from the Cherokee Honor Society.

Stone, Willard

Willard Stone, of Cherokee descent, was born in 1916 and lived just east of Locust Grove, Oklahoma. When he was thirteen years old, an accidental explosion of a dynamite cap cost him parts of his thumb and two fingers on his right hand. Despite this disability, in 1936 he entered Bacone College in Muskogee, Oklahoma, and began developing his own style of woodcarving, for which he was to become world famous. In the 1940s, he received a three-year grant as artist-in-residence at the Gilcrease Institute of American History and Art. Stone died in 1985.

Strickland, Rennard

Rennard Strickland, Cherokee and part Osage was born in St. Louis, Missouri. He graduated from Northeastern State University in Tahlequah, Oklahoma, and then went to the University of Virginia for his law degrees. He has been a professor of law at the University of Tulsa, the University of Oklahoma, Oklahoma City University, and the University of Oregon. In addition, he is the author of *Fire and the Spirits: Cherokee Law from Clan to Court; Tonto's Revenge*; and many other books and articles. A well-known art collector and historian, Strickland currently lives in Norman, Oklahoma.

Stroud, Virginia

Virginia Stroud is Cherokee, but was raised by a Kiowa family. In 1969, she was crowned Miss Cherokee, and she won the title of Miss Indian America

Robert J. Conley

in 1970. Today she is one of the most prolific and well-known Cherokee artists. In 1981, the Indian Arts and Crafts Association named her Artist of the Year. In 1987, she was named Master Artist by the Five Civilized Tribes Museum. She was presented with a Cherokee Medal of Honor in 2000.

Studi, Wes

Wes Studi, full-blood bilingual Cherokee, was born in 1947, in Nofire Hollow, Cherokee County, Oklahoma. As a teenager, he attended Chilocco Indian School and graduated in 1964. He served in the U.S. Army in Vietnam. In 1972, he was one of the American Indian Movement occupiers of the Bureau of Indian Affairs building in Washington, D.C., and in 1973 one of the protesters at Wounded Knee, South Dakota. Back in Oklahoma, he trained horses, translated for the Cherokee Bilingual Program, and was a reporter for the Cherokee Nation's newspaper. In the 1980s, he enrolled in acting classes in Tulsa, Oklahoma, and worked with the Tulsa American Indian Theater Company. After he went to Los Angeles, he appeared in the television movie *Longarm* and the film *Powwow Highway* (1989). His big break came in *Dances with Wolves* in 1990, which was followed by *The Last of the Mohicans* (1992) and *Geronimo: An American Legend* (1993). In 1999, Wes received the Cherokee Medal of Honor. He currently lives in Santa Fe with his wife, Maura.

Wes Studi, 2001.
Courtesy of photographer
David G. Fitzgerald.

Sullivan, Dorothy

Dorothy Sullivan is the daughter of Harold Tidwell. A native of Oklahoma, she holds a bachelor's degree in art and history. She is a member of the Indian Arts and Crafts Association, the Cherokee National Historical Society, and the National Association of Pen Women. She has received awards at the Cherokee Trail of Tears Art Show, the Five Civilized Tribes

Museum, the National Indian Arts Expo, the Chisholm Trail Art Show, the University of Oklahoma Heritage Art Contest, the American Indian Heritage Center Art Show, and the Museum of the Cherokee. Sullivan's artwork draws on Cherokee history, legends, and culture. She lives in Norman, Oklahoma.

Sunday, Jesse

In 1897, Jesse Sunday, a forty-four-year-old full-blood Cherokee, was the sheriff of Saline District of the Cherokee Nation, Indian Territory, and just about to complete his term of office. Dave Ridge, Jesse's half-brother, was the newly elected sheriff. Ridge went to town to buy something for his wife, but he ran into some cronies and got drunk instead. By the time he started home, the store had already closed. He banged on the door and called out to the store owner, Baggett, who opened an upstairs window and told Ridge that he was closed. Someone fired a shot from the darkness and killed Baggett. A crowd soon gathered, and many of them thought that Ridge had done the shooting, but he managed to get away and head for home. On the way, he met Sampson Rogers and William Towery. Rogers accused Ridge of having killed Baggett, and Ridge accused Rogers. Rogers hit Ridge over the head. Andy Sunday, the sheriff's nineteen-year-old son, had been watching from the woods. He stepped out to confront Rogers, who threatened to kill him. Ridge died during the night. Someone found Sheriff Sunday at Ulm Prairie, where he was guarding some prisoners at a private home for the night, and told him of the events at Saline. Sunday deputized someone to guard the prisoners and headed for Saline. Back at Saline, Sunday, accompanied by Cooie Bolin, stopped at the home of Martin Rowe and found Rowe and John Colvord sitting on the porch. He questioned them and was about to leave when shots sounded in the night. Sunday fell to the ground. Martin Rowe started to run through the woods, and Bolin fired at him. Jesse Sunday died the following night. Martin Rowe was arrested, tried, convicted, and sentenced to hang, but the sentence was commuted to ten years in prison by Principal Chief Sam Mayes.

Swimmer, see "Ayunini"

Swimmer, Ross O.

Ross O. Swimmer was born October 26, 1943, in Oklahoma City, the son of lawyer Robert Swimmer. He attended college at the University of Oklahoma, graduating in 1965 and receiving his law degree in 1967. He went into practice in Oklahoma City, concentrating in real estate and civil law. Robert Swimmer had worked with the Cherokee Nation from time to time and was well acquainted with Chief W. W. Keeler. When the Cherokee Nation began its housing program, Ross Swimmer was hired as its legal counsel, and when Earl Boyd Pierce resigned as tribal counsel, Swimmer took over his duties. In 1974, he also became president of the First National Bank in Tahlequah, Oklahoma. When Chief Keeler decided not to run for reelection in 1975, he chose Swimmer to be his successor. In order to accomplish his purpose, Keeler twice postponed the election, and then, because Swimmer was too young to run for the office, waived the age requirement. When Swimmer had not filed for office by the deadline, Keeler waived the deadline. Swimmer won the election.

Swimmer was quoted in 1977 as having said, "My first duty is to the bank I serve as president," but he did present a new constitution to the tribe during his first term as chief, and it was approved. Registration efforts were initiated. In 1977, there were twenty thousand registered Cherokees. A new management structure was devised, and tribal programs started to proliferate. Swimmer won reelection in 1979 and 1983. When he was appointed to the position of undersecretary of interior for Indian affairs by President Ronald Reagan in 1985, he resigned his position as chief. When Reagan left office, so did Swimmer.

T.

Tahachee, Chief

Born in Arkansas on March 4, 1904, Jeff Davis Tahchee Cypert appeared in his first film, *The Last of the Mohicans*, in 1921 at the age of sixteen. He was advised by director Rollin Sturgeon to call himself "Chief Tahachee" for his film career. In 1922, he played a cowboy in *North of the Rio Grande*, starring Jack Holt, and after that he never allowed himself to be typecast in just Indian roles. In a career that spanned more than forty years, he appeared in more than four hundred films, including *The Alamo* (with John Wayne), *Elmer Gantry; Psycho; Some Like It Hot;* and *Walk the Proud Land*. In addition, he was the author of four books, the most successful of which was *Poems of Dreams*. Tahachee died in California in 1978 at age seventy-four.

Tahchee, see "Dutch, Captain"

Tahlequah

Tahlequah was established following the Removal in 1838 as the capital city of the Cherokee Nation in what is now Oklahoma. The capital square was laid out, and a huge arbor built to accommodate large crowds. Two log cabins were built on the back side of the square to house government offices. Businesses were established on all four sides of the square as the town grew. In the early days, many people showed up from around the Cherokee Nation to attend National Council meetings, and they camped along what was then known as Wolf Creek, across the street from the back side of the square. A two-story brick capitol was constructed in 1873. With Oklahoma statehood in 1907, the building was taken over by the new Cherokee County for a courthouse. Under the administration of Chief Wilma Mankiller (1985–95),

Robert J. Conley

the building was returned to the Cherokee Nation. There are two legends about the naming of Tahlequah. One has it that three men were sent out to find a suitable spot to build the capital. Two of them met, and they waited a time for the third. At last, one of them said, "Tali eliqua," meaning, "Two is enough." The second version of the tale is similar. The men were sent out to find a place where three streams came together. They found a nice spot, but there were only two streams coming together. One of the men said, "Tali eliqua." The only problem with these stories is that they are probably not true. "Tahlequah" is almost surely a slightly different anglicization of the old Cherokee place-name from back east, "Tellico."

Tahlonteskee

Tahlonteskee was the brother-in-law of Doublehead. Both were former Chickamaugas. (See also "Dragging Canoe.") In the early part of the nineteenth century, the new U.S. government negotiated a treaty for land that was signed by Doublehead, James Vann, Tahlonteskee, and others, who were said to have accepted bribes for their signatures. The treaty was finalized in 1807, and Doublehead was executed by the Ridge (later known as Major Ridge) and Alex Saunders for his part in its development. In the spring of 1808, Tahlonteskee, fearing the same fate, voluntarily removed with his followers to the area around what is now Dardanelle, Arkansas. Three years later they were joined there by Bowles and his people, who had been living in Missouri. Tahlonteskee was elected chief of the Western Cherokees in 1818 in an election that was typical of them. The people gathered together, and nominating speeches were made. Those nominated then stepped out in front of the crowd, with some distance between them, and the people then moved to stand beside the man of their choice. The man with the most people standing by him became the chief. The Western Cherokees, because of their ongoing war with the Osages in this period, also elected a second chief and a third chief. Almost for sure, Tahlonteskee's main occupation as chief was the war. However, he permitted missionaries to establish Dwight Mission in the Cherokee Nation West. He died in office in 1819, and the Western Cherokees named their capital for him, Tahlonteskee.

Tahquette, John A.

John A. Tahquette owned a store and operated the post office in Cherokee, North Carolina. He was a half-blood Cherokee. He served as chief of the Eastern Band of Cherokees from 1927 to 1931.

Ta-ka-e-tuh

According to Cephas Washburn, Ta-ka-e-tuh, one of the Western Cherokees, was the uncle of Degadoga and was said to be more than a hundred years old. Washburn doubted that the old man was really older than a hundred, because of his appearance, although he said that Ta-ka-e-tuh could recall events dating back before the American Revolution (Washburn met him sometime after 1832). Washburn recalled Ta-ka-e-tuh as a "man of commanding eloquence." He apparently spent much time with the old man and repeated many of the old man's tales. They all sound like Bible tales retold as Cherokee stories, and they may represent stories told to the Cherokees by Christian Gottlieb Priber years earlier that some had learned as Cherokee stories.

Talmadge

Talmadge Davis, grandson of Sally Toney Davis and a descendant of Sequoyah, was born in McAlester, Oklahoma, in 1962. He spent his early years near Eufaula and went to school at Seneca Indian School. When the family relocated, Talmadge went to high school in Kerrville and Harper, Texas. A five-year hitch in the U.S. Army as a military policeman followed graduation. Talmadge said that he paints to educate and inspire generations of people about who the Cherokees are. The evidence of that can be seen clearly in his magnificent paintings. He has won major awards on a regular basis in such prestigious art competitions as the Tulsa Indian Art Festival, the Wichita Indian Center, the Five Civilized Tribes Museum's Competitive Art Show, Oklahoma City's Red Earth Celebration, and Tsalagi's Trail of Tears Art Show. Talmadge was living and working in Tulsa, Oklahoma, until his untimely and unexpected death from a heart attack in 2005. He had received a Cherokee Medal of Honor in 2004.

Tassel

Nothing seems to have been recorded regarding the ascendancy of Tassel (also known as Old Tassel and Onitositah) to the position of principal chief of the Cherokee Nation following the death of Ogan'sto' in 1785, but he emerges as chief in the histories. He came into the position during very troubled times. The Overhill towns in Tennessee were still trying to maintain peaceful relations with the Americans, whereas Dragging Canoe and the Chickamaugas (a faction that had separated from the Cherokee Nation just prior to the American Revolution and had relocated to Chickamauga

Robert J. Conley

Creek) were still fighting with them. Tassel did all he could to maintain peaceful relations with the United States. Indian-hater John Sevier had proclaimed the state of Franklin and in 1785 claimed that a treaty had been made between the Franklinites and some Cherokees. Tassel protested the treaty. He was invited to a meeting with some of Sevier's people, but he sent "Ancoo" of Echota in his place. "Ancoo" and the others with him signed a new treaty, giving up more land to the Franklinites. Tassel went to the governor of North Carolina to protest the "Treaty of Dumplin Creek," but with no results. On November 18, 1785, Tassel, other Cherokees, and representatives of the new United States met at Hopewell, South Carolina, on the Keowee River. Old Tassel's right-hand man was the war chief Hanging Maw.

The Treaty of Hopewell was the first treaty negotiated between the Cherokees and the United States. More than nine hundred Cherokees were present at the meeting. The first order of business was for the U.S. representatives to announce formally to the Cherokees that England was now out of the picture and that the United States was the new sovereign. The U.S. representatives then said they wanted nothing from the Cherokees and asked if the Cherokees had any complaints to make. Tassel presented a map of the Cherokee country that included the land (much of what is now Tennessee and Kentucky) that the Cherokees had sold illegally to the Transylvania Company, the sale that had precipitated the division between the Cherokees and the Chickamaugas. The United States maintained that the sale had been legal, so the Cherokees did not pursue the matter further.

Dragging Canoe, who was still fighting the Americans, was not present at this meeting. Nancy Ward, the famous Beloved Woman, was there, however, and Tassel asked her to speak. She said, "I have a pipe and a little tobacco to give to the commissioners to smoke in friendship. I have seen much trouble in the late war. I am now old, but hope yet to bear children who will grow up and people our Nation, as we are now under the protection of Congress and have no more disturbances. The talk that I give you is from myself."

Settlers continued to squat illegally on Cherokee land, and violence resulted. Congress forbade further incursions onto Cherokee land, but the squatters ignored what Congress said and continued to move farther in. The president issued a proclamation stating that the Cherokees had the right by treaty to deal with the squatters as they wished, and Dragging Canoe attacked the settlements at Muscle Shoals. John Donelson, surveyor, and Colonel William Christian were among the whites killed during the attack.

Governor Sevier called out the Franklin militia, which accused Tassel and Hanging Maw of the killings. Tassel answered the charge, "They are not my people that spilled the blood and spoiled the good talks. My town is not so; they will use you well whenever they see you. The men that did the murders are bad and no warriors. They live at Coyatee, at the mouth of the Holston River. They have done the murders. My brother Colonel Christian was a good man and took care of everybody. . . . I loved Colonel Christian and he loved me."

The Franklin militia went to Coyatee, found two Cherokees who were accused of the killings, and killed them. Then they claimed to Tassel that they had signed a treaty there at Coyatee giving them more Cherokee land. Bloody Fellow and the Fool Warrior then raided the Dumplin settlement, killing and taking prisoners. Even Hanging Maw could take no more. He attacked a crew of surveyors, who ran away to safety but left their equipment behind. Hanging Maw smashed their "land stealers" against trees.

In June 1788, Sevier led the Franklin militia to the Cherokee town of Hiwassee and burned it to the ground. Then he returned home, leaving Major James Hubbard in charge. Hubbard and the militiamen with him moved to Chilhowee, where they sent out an invitation to Tassel to come in for a talk. When Tassel and Hanging Maw showed up under a flag of truce, the Franklinites immediately grabbed their arms and held them while one young man stepped in behind them and bashed in their heads.

Taylor, Jonathan

Jonathan Taylor had been on the Eastern Band of Cherokees Tribal Council for sixteen years, serving as its chairman for several terms, before running for the office of principal chief in 1987. He had joined Chief Noah Powell in protesting the Tennessee Valley Authority's Tellico Dam project. He won the 1987 election for chief in a bitter runoff, becoming the youngest chief ever to serve the Eastern Band. As chief, he was instrumental in getting federal funding for new school buildings. He achieved a degree of notoriety when he appeared on the *Oprah Winfrey Show* and told the world that he did not object to the "tomahawk chop" of the Atlanta Braves. It just helped to sell more rubber tomahawks to tourists, he said.

After Taylor was defeated by Joyce C. Dugan in the 1995 election for principal chief, he was impeached by the Tribal Council for financial mismanagement. By a vote of twelve to zero, he was put out of office early and stripped of his title, retirement, and all tribal benefits.

Robert J. Conley

Teehee, Houston

Houston Benge Teehee was born in what is now Sequoyah County, Oklahoma, in 1874. He attended Cherokee Nation schools, the Cherokee Male Seminary, and Fort Worth University. He was a clerk in a merchandising store in Tahlequah, Indian Territory, for ten years and a cashier in the Cherokee National Bank there. He studied law and was admitted to the bar in 1907. He resigned his position at the bank and entered legal practice in 1908, specializing in probate oil and gas law. He was alderman of Tahlequah from 1902 to 1906 and its mayor from 1908 to 1910. In 1915, he went to Washington, D.C., as register of the U.S. Treasury. In 1919, he was hired as treasurer of the Seamans Oil Company, eventually becoming one of its vice presidents. He died in 1938 in Tahlequah.

Texas Cherokees

When agents of the U.S. government told the Cherokees in Arkansas that they were living on the wrong side of the Arkansas River and had to move, Bowles and his followers, angered, moved to near Spanish Fort (now Nacogdoches), Texas, in the winter of 1819-20. They formed a loose confederacy with other refugee Indians there: Shawnees, Delawares, Kickapoos, Choctaws, Biloxis, Alabamas, and Coushattas. They became known as the Texas Cherokees, and Bowles was recognized as their chief. He was soon replaced by Richard Fields, who worked diligently to acquire land title from Mexico City, but without success. Then Fields became involved in the ill-fated Fredonia Rebellion, a premature attempt at breaking Texas away from Mexico. Although the rebellion was put down without a shot being fired, Fields was killed after it was all over—it is thought because of his involvement. It is also believed that Bowles either killed him or had him killed. Bowles became chief again. In November 1835, a Texas provisional government was established and officers were elected. A treaty drawn up and signed later in Bowles's village promised perpetual friendship and guaranteed the Cherokees their land in Texas. After Texas independence, however, the new government refused to ratify the treaty, claiming that the provisional government was no government at all. In 1839, Mirabeau Lamar became president of Texas, and he ordered the Cherokees to leave, demanding that they surrender the gunlocks and be escorted to the border by Texas troops. Although Bowles refused, the Cherokees nevertheless left their homes and headed north for the Cherokee Nation in what is now Oklahoma. Along the way they were attacked by the Texans. Bowles, in his eighties, was killed in the bloody "battle of the Neches," along with more than one hundred Cherokees. Five Texans were killed. The remaining Texas Cherokees scattered, many making their way back to the Cherokee Nation. Mary Whatley Clarke says, "It is an ironic note to history that Chief Bowles of the Texas Cherokees may have been the single most important man in Texas' struggle for independence. Had he not kept his people neutral, the Battle of San Jacinto might have had a far different outcome." (See also "Bowles" and "Fields, Richard.")

Thomas, Colonel William Holland

A white man, William Holland Thomas was born in 1805 near Waynesville, North Carolina. His father died before he was born. At age twelve, he was put to work at an Indian trading store on Soco Creek. When the store was eventually closed for debt, Thomas had to accept a set of law books in lieu of his pay. While working at the store, Thomas was adopted by the Cherokee Yonaguska, or Bear Drowning Him, because he had no father or brother. He was known to the Cherokees as Wil-Usdi, or "Little Will." He learned to speak the Cherokee language, and after Sequoyah's syllabary became known, he learned to read and write it as well. Following the Removal in 1838, Thomas bought a home on the northern bank of the Tuckasegee River, above the present town of Whittier, North Carolina, the site of the old Cherokee town of Stekoa. He was the owner of five trading stores, was studying law, and was getting active in local politics.

About a thousand Cherokees under the leadership of Utsala, or Lichen, had managed to elude the soldiers rounding up Cherokees for removal and were hiding in the high mountains of North Carolina. James Mooney says that "the work of running down these fugitives proved to be so difficult an undertaking that when Charley [Tsali] and his sons made their bold stroke for freedom General [Winfield] Scott eagerly seized the incident as an opportunity for compromise. . . . He engaged the services of William H. Thomas . . . and authorized him to present to Utsala a proposition that if the latter would seize Charley and the others who had been concerned in the attack on the soldiers and surrender them for punishment, the pursuit would be called off and the fugitives allowed to stay unmolested." (See "Utsala.") Utsala consented. Thomas was taken to Tsali and convinced him to surrendered so that he would not have to be hunted down by his own people. Tsali and his sons, all but the youngest one, were tried, found guilty, and executed.

Thomas then went to Washington, D.C., and convinced the U.S. government to pay the Cherokee refugees their share of the money that had

Robert J. Conley

been appropriated for the Cherokee lands. He collected the money and purchased land for them in his name.

In 1848, Thomas was elected to the North Carolina state Senate, and in 1861 he voted for secession. In 1862, he organized the Thomas Confederate Legion of Cherokee Indians and Mountaineers, consisting of two regiments of infantry, a battalion of cavalry, a company of engineers, and a field battery. He commanded the legion as colonel, although he was nearly sixty years old. The Thomas Legion served largely as a frontier guard for the Confederacy. After the war, Thomas returned to his home and continued to work for the Cherokees. In spite of suffering from physical and mental collapse, he lived until 1893, dying at the age of eighty-eight.

Thomas Legion

When the Civil War broke out, William Holland Thomas organized for the Confederacy two regiments of infantry, a battalion of cavalry, a company of engineers, and a field battery and served as their colonel. Made up largely of Cherokees from the Qualla Boundary (Cherokee reservation) in North Carolina, they became known as the Thomas Confederate Legion of Cherokee Indians and Mountaineers, or simply as the Thomas Legion.

Thompson, Charles

Charles Thompson (Oochalata) was born in the old Cherokee country in the Southeast to a full-blood Cherokee father and a white mother. The family migrated west on the Trail of Tears and settled in what is now Delaware County, Oklahoma. Oochalata attended the Baptist Mission near Westville for a short time, where he came under the influence of Reverend Evan Jones. When the Civil War broke out, and after Chief John Ross announced for the Confederacy, Oochalata joined the First Regiment of Cherokee Mounted Rifles under Colonel John Drew. On July 11, 1862, just days before the arrest of Chief Ross by Union forces, he switched sides, joining the pro-Union Indian Home Guard under the command of Lieutenant Colonel Lewis Downing.

Following the war, Oochalata moved to Rattlesnake Creek, built a log cabin, and began farming, raising stock, and operating a trading post. Somewhere along the line, he also became a lawyer. He was serving his church as a deacon, but because he was a lawyer, the Baptist church refused to ordain him. In 1867, he was elected to the Cherokee Senate. Until that time, he had no English name. He selected "Thompson" because he was

Charles Thompson, c. 1875.
Public domain. Courtesy of the
Cherokee Honor Society.

replacing Dr. Jeter Lynch Thompson in the Senate. "Chala" was a short version of his Cherokee name, and "Charles" seemed a close equivalent. In 1875, Charles Thompson ran for the office of principal chief against W. P. Ross and won. Then the church ordained him. Thompson spoke no English, so he conducted all of his business and made all of his speeches in Cherokee.

During this time, white people were flooding into the Cherokee Nation in Indian Territory. Many white criminals were seeking refuge there as well, where they could not be touched except by the deputy U.S. marshals who roamed over the territory. This problem was one of Chief Thompson's major concerns during his term of office, and in 1878 he created a "citizenship court" to deal exclusively with it. When his term expired in 1879, he did not seek reelection, perhaps because he realized that he was representing only about three-fifths of the Cherokee population. Instead, he returned to ranching and trading and began preaching in the Euchee Baptist Church. Thompson was married to Rachel Sudee, a full-blood. In his last years, he was blind. He died at home on June 22, 1891.

Thompson, Sue

Edna Sue Girty Thompson received her education at Haskell Institute in Kansas, now Haskell Indian Nations University, graduating in 1960. She is presently a Cherokee cultural language specialist for the Cherokee Nation. She works with Cherokee youth in special projects such as the Youth Leadership Institute, the Cherokee Cultural Enrichment Program in the schools, the Cherokee Summer Institute, and the annual Cherokee Challenge Bowl and Cherokee Language Bowl. She has been a translator and an interpreter, and she has given Cherokee-language lessons in Georgia, Tennessee, North Carolina, and Oklahoma. She has taught basket-weaving classes as well. Thompson served as editor of the *Cherokee Nation News* from 1969 to 1971.

Thornton, Joe

Joe Thornton learned to shoot a bow at Chilocco Indian School in Oklahoma in 1933. He won the junior welterweight boxing championship at Fort Sill, and during World War II as a member of the Signal Corps, he received a Presidential Unit Citation. In 1956, when he learned that archery had become an organized sport, he began entering competition, and by 1960 he had become Oklahoma state champion. He went with the U.S. archery team to Oslo, Norway, in 1961, where he won the gold medal and set three new world records. In 1962, at the British International Trials in Windsor, England, he won the British National Championship. Both he and his soon-to-be wife, Helen, went to the U.S. Team Trials in Chicago in 1963, where they placed. From there they went to Helsinki, Finland, for the

Joe Thornton, 1961.
Courtesy of Joe Thornton.

world archery championships. Joe took the silver medal; Helen placed eighth and helped the U.S. women's team take the gold medal. In 1970, Joe won the U.S. National Championship in Oxford, Ohio. He served for three years on the board of governors of the National Archery Association. In 1972, archery was made an Olympic sport. Joe and Helen qualified for the first trials but failed to make the team. Joe was fifty-five years old. He was listed in *Who's Who in Oklahoma* in 1964 and inducted into the American Indian Athletic Hall of Fame in 1978 and the Chilocco Indian School Hall of Fame in 1985. He coaches young archers and competes in the annual Cherokee Holiday cornstalk shoot.

Threepersons Holster, see "Threepersons, Tom"

Threepersons, Tom

Tom Threepersons was born in Vinita, Indian Territory, on July 22, 1889, the son of John Threepersons, a rancher, and Bell Threepersons. Both of

Tom's parents were full-blood Cherokees. The following story has been told of Tom many times. A neighboring ranch was owned by Bill White, whose son, also named Bill, was Tom Threepersons's childhood friend. Possibly as a result of impending Oklahoma statehood, both families ended up moving to the Montana-Canadian border by 1907. Tom attended Carlisle Indian School in Pennsylvania. At home on the ranch, he became involved in the rodeo circuit in Wyoming, Oregon, and Washington. In the winter of 1907, both boys' fathers were killed by rustlers. Tom and Bill pursued the killers, but ran low on supplies before coming across them and had to return home. Then Tom learned that two of the men he was after had been arrested and were out on bond. He found them in a saloon and killed them. He stood trial and was acquitted.

Tom and his ever-present companion Bill White joined the Royal Canadian Mounted Police. Tracking a pair of smugglers and killers, Bill was killed in a gunfight. Tom continued on the trail for more than a week before he caught up to them and killed them. He later killed three bank robbers before deciding that he'd had enough of the Mounties. He returned to the ranch and the rodeo circuit and won the title of All-Around Champion Cowboy in Pendleton, Oregon, in 1912, after which he took a trip around the world.

The problem with the tale is that at least some of it is not true. Tom Threepersons has been confused with another Indian of nearly the same name, Tom Three Persons, a Blood Indian from Canada who was a rodeo bronc rider.

In 1916, however, Tom Threepersons did serve with General John (Blackjack) Pershing on the Mexican border, possibly as a horse wrangler, possibly as a scout, while Pershing was pursuing Pancho Villa, and in 1917 he joined the U.S. Army and was put to work breaking horses at the U.S. Army Remount Depot at Fort Bliss, Texas, near El Paso. A newspaper story from Douglas, Arizona, in 1916 referred to Tom as "a machine in the saddle and about the best in the southwest." Somewhere along the line he married a woman who is known to us only as Susie, but the marriage did not last long. Also during this time, Tom sustained a head injury, possibly from being kicked in the head by a horse. After World War I was over, and the army reduced its forces, Tom was let go in 1920.

Prohibition had become the law of the land, and illegal booze was flowing across the border from Mexico. Tom, at six feet tall and 180 pounds, wearing his trademark black Stetson hat, became a law enforcement officer in El Paso, Texas, serving as a city detective and later a deputy sheriff. In 1923, he returned to ranching and was foreman of several large ranches in

Robert J. Conley

the area. He was a federal prohibition officer for six months but quit to work for large ranchers in Mexico to reduce cattle rustling. In 1923, he was back in El Paso with the U.S. Customs Service. He and a partner caught some smugglers crossing the river with sacks of alcohol. Tom arrested and cuffed the first one to cross, but found that his partner had returned to the car. When others came across, Tom arrested them without help. Finally, an armed group came and started firing at Tom. He returned the fire. His partner, hearing the shots, called for help. Tom held off the smugglers for an hour, firing about forty shots. When he was down to three cartridges, he beat a retreat, taking his cuffed prisoner with him. Three police cars showed up to drive off the rest of the smugglers. On another occasion, Tom was run down by a smuggler's car.

In 1925, he resigned from the Customs Service, married Lorene Tritthart, a Cherokee, and moved with her to Safford, Arizona, where he became a rancher. The smugglers had put a bounty of $10,000 on his head. Later that year he was once again in El Paso as a deputy sheriff. He met writer Eugene Cunningham, who interviewed him in some depth and wrote a story about his life, incorporating some of the incidents of the life of the other Tom Three Persons. It is not known if Cunningham made the mistake on his own or if Tom, chuckling, allowed it to happen. In 1926, Tom quit the sheriff's department and went to work for the McElroy Ranch at Crane, but in 1927 he was back in El Paso as a police detective. He resigned from police work for good in 1929. He had been shot twice and run over, and his old head wound was bothering him. He sold his guns and moved to Silver City, New Mexico, where he worked on ranches. In 1962, he moved again to Safford, Arizona. Lorene died there in 1968. Tom did not stay single long. He married Rose Gould, but he did not stay married long this third time either. He died in 1969 of a heart attack, at the age of seventy-nine.

On December 10, 1964, the Kraft Suspense Theatre aired an episode called *Threepersons* in which Tom was played by John Gavin. But Tom is perhaps best remembered for the Threepersons holster. Designed by Tom and first made by Tio Sam Myers, a saddlemaker in El Paso, the holster fits close to the gun's cylinder, frame, and barrel and cuts away from the hammer and trigger guard for easy access. The gun's grips ride above the belt, and it hangs with a slight cant of the muzzle to the rear for a faster draw. The Threepersons holster is still sold under this name.

Thundercloud, Chief, see "Daniels, Victor"

Timmons, Alice

Alice Tyner Timmons was born in 1914 at Vinita, Oklahoma. She is the daughter of James Tyner and Grace Young Tyner, and the great-great-granddaughter of Betsy Snaketail, who walked the Trail of Tears at age sixty-eight from Hiwassee River, Tennessee. Alice attended school at Pawhuska, then at Chilocco Indian School in Chilocco, Oklahoma, then at Northeastern State College and the University of Oklahoma. She married Boyce Timmons of Pawhuska. She was a consultant to the Cherokee National Historical Society in their creation of the Cherokee Heritage Center, known as Tsalagi. In the 1970s, she and her brother James published the twelve-volume work *Our People and Where They Rest*, a compilation of maps and descriptions of cemeteries in Indian Territory, some of them long abandoned. With her husband, Boyce, she edited *The Cherokee Physician* (1975) by Richard Foreman. She has received the Phi Alpha Theta History Service Award, the American Association for State and Local History Distinguished Service Award, the Cherokee Nation Distinguished Service Award, and the National Indian Education Award. In addition, she was named Indian Mother of the Year in 1988 and was a recipient of the Cherokee Medal of Honor in 1999.

Tincup, Austin Ben

Ben Tincup was born in 1892 near Adair, Indian Territory (present-day Oklahoma). In 1914, he pitched for the Philadelphia Phillies of the National League. In 1917, he moved to the Little Rock Travelers in Arkansas, where he pitched a no-hit, no-run game in the Southern Association League. In 1928, he pitched for Chicago in the National League. He was inducted into the American Indian Athletic Hall of Fame in 1981. Tincup died in 1980.

Tindle, Jeff

In 1954, Chief Jim Pickup of the United Keetoowah Band of Cherokees in Oklahoma announced his resignation. His health and his ministry were the reasons he gave, and he recommended that the Keetoowah Band elect Jeff Tindle to replace him. They did so that same year, and he served until 1958. Tindle was born in 1900, the son of a full-blood Cherokee mother and a white father. He served in the U.S. Army and married a full-blood Cherokee woman, Betsy Smith. They had one child, a daughter, but when the child was four years old, Betsy died. Jeff left the child with her maternal grandmother.

Robert J. Conley

Tobacco

Tobacco (*tsola*) has been cultivated and used by the Cherokees and other Indian tribes for longer than anyone knows. Cherokees call their special tobacco *tsola-gayunli*, the "ancient tobacco." Because not much of the ancient tobacco is cultivated anymore, a medicine man or woman can remake any tobacco to be as effective as the ancient tobacco.

Using clay pipes, Cherokees smoked for pleasure, for ceremonies, and for medicinal purposes, and they still do. James Mooney says, "Tobacco was used as a sacred incense or as the guarantee of a solemn oath in nearly every important function—in binding the warrior to take up the hatchet against the enemy, in ratifying the treaty of peace, in confirming sales or other agreements, in seeking omens for the hunter, in driving away witches or evil spirits, and in regular medical practice." It might be smoked in a pipe or sprinkled on a fire.

In one old Cherokee tale recorded by Mooney, there is only one tobacco plant, used by all, and the geese steal it and carry it away. Various animals attempt to retrieve it, but all of them fail. At last, the hummingbird brings it back because he is so swift that the geese cannot see him fly.

Today the Cherokee Nation, like other Indian tribes, licenses "smoke shops" where tobacco products are sold at cut rates. Because the smoke shops are operated on Indian land, they are not required to pay state taxes. They have been controversial from time to time, with nearby non-Indian tobacco dealers screaming about unfair practice and sometimes even threatening violence.

Tobacco Will

Tobacco Will is said to have been the brother of Sequoyah. According to Reverend Cephas Washburn, he purchased a complete set of blacksmith's tools, opened a shop, and carried on the business well. He is listed as one of the "old settlers" present, along with Sequoyah, at the National Convention at Illinois Campground in 1839. He was one of the signers of the Act of Union between the Cherokee Nation and the Western Cherokees and of the constitution that the Cherokee Nation passed in 1839. He represented Skin Bayou (later Sequoyah) District on the Cherokee Nation Council in 1843.

Trail of Tears, see "Removal"

Treaties

In the late 1600s or early 1700s, some of the Cherokee Lower Towns supposedly signed a treaty with South Carolina, but if they did, the treaty does not
exist. But Cherokee treaties with the colonies came fast thereafter: Treaty
of 1721 with South Carolina; Treaty of 1730 with North Carolina; Treaty of
1755 with South Carolina; Treaty of 1756 with North Carolina; Treaty of 1760
with South Carolina; Treaty of 1761 with South Carolina; Treaty of 1768 with
the British Superintendent of Indian Affairs; Treaty of 1770 at Lochabar,
South Carolina; Treaty of 1772 with Virginia; Treaty of 1773 with the British
Superintendent of Indian Affairs; Treaty of 1775 with the Transylvania
Company; Treaty of 1777 with South Carolina and Georgia; Treaty of 1777
with North Carolina and Virginia; Treaty of 1783 with Georgia; and Treaties
of 1784 with the illegal state of Franklin. Each of these treaties involved the
Cherokees giving up land.

In 1785, the Cherokees negotiated their first treaty with the new United
States at Hopewell in South Carolina. Thereafter, the Cherokees signed a
total of eighteen more treaties with the United States, each one requiring
that they give up more land. The dates of the Cherokee-U.S. treaties are as
follows: 1791, 1794, 1798, 1804, 1805 (two), 1806, 1807, 1816 (two), 1817, 1819,
1828, 1833, 1835, 1846, 1866, and 1868.

Treaty Party

The faction of the Cherokee Nation led by Major Ridge, his son John, John's
cousin Elias Boudinot, and others who signed the Treaty of New Echota, or
the Removal Treaty, and then moved west before the Trail of Tears came
to be known as the Treaty Party. In Arkansas, they agreed to live under
the government of the Western Cherokees and thus were allied with the
Western Cherokees in opposition to the majority of Cherokees after the
Trail of Tears.

Tsali

In 1838, while the U.S. Army under the command of General Winfield Scott
was rounding up Cherokees to put them in stockades to await removal to
the West, Tsali (called "Charley" by the whites) and his sons resisted. One
soldier was killed, and the rest fled. Tsali and his family escaped into the
mountains. Frustrated at his inability to capture the fugitives, General
Scott, through William Holland Thomas, contacted Tsali and offered him
a deal. If Tsali and his sons would surrender, they would be punished,

but the rest of the refugees in the mountains of North Carolina would be ignored. Tsali and his sons surrendered and were tried, found guilty, and executed. Scott kept his word, and the remaining refugees were left alone, eventually to become the Eastern Band of Cherokee Indians. (See "Thomas, Colonel William Holland.")

U.

Uka Ulah

Cherokee family structure was a problem for the British in the early days of colonization. Cherokee family relationships are muddled in the records more often than not. Some historians have said that Uka Ulah was the son of Guhna-gadoga, others that he was the nephew. This confusion might arise from the fact that under the old clan structure, a Cherokee man looked after his sister's sons the way a European man would look after his own sons. It is likely, then, that Uka Ulah was the nephew of Guhna-gadoga, but the British took him to be the old man's son. However, we can't be sure. He is also sometimes called by his uncle's name, Standing Turkey.

Uka Ulah seems to have been involved in the assault on Fort Loudon, South Carolina, in 1760, but little else has been recorded about him. He did not last long enough in his position as the Cherokee "emperor" (one year, from 1760 to 1761)—another British attempt to understand and influence the Cherokees' government in their own terms—to have accomplished much of anything. During this time, the most influential men in the tribe were men other than the "emperor" anyway. For some years, Ada-gal'kala and Ogan'sto' had been the men most Cherokees listened to, and they seem to have completely overshadowed anything that Uka Ulah might have done. He died in 1761.

United Keetoowah Band of Cherokee Indians

In 1946, the U.S. Congress recognized the United Keetoowah Band of Cherokee Indians (UKB) in Oklahoma as an Indian group residing in Oklahoma within the meaning of the Oklahoma Indian General Welfare Act of 1936. At the time, the Cherokee Nation was in what might best be called a state of dormancy, with no elections, no council, and a

Robert J. Conley

presidentially appointed principal chief. It could not function as an Indian tribe. The UKB was organized so that tribal business could be conducted for Cherokees. It limited its membership to those with at least one-quarter Cherokee blood. Its corporate charter was approved by the U.S. Congress in 1950, and in that same year the UKB ratified its charter, constitution, and by-laws. At first, the UKB worked cooperatively with the Cherokee Nation, but when the Cherokee Nation began to revitalize with elections in the 1970s, the two split apart. In the years since, it has sometimes seemed as if a cold war has existed between the Cherokee Nation and the UKB, each one claiming to be the only valid government for Cherokees in Oklahoma. At this writing (2007), there is no end in sight to this feud. The chiefs of the UKB are listed here (for more information, see the individual listings under the chiefs' names):

 Jim Pickup, 1946–54
 Jeff Tindle, 1954–58
 Jim Pickup, 1958–68
 Bill Glory, 1968–79
 Jim Gordon, 1979–84
 John Hair, 1984–91
 John Ross, 1991–98
 Jim Henson, 1998–2001
 Dallas Proctor, 2001–5
 George Wickliffe, 2005–present

Uskwa-lena

Uskwa-lena, Big Head or Bull Head, is said to have led the Cherokees who defeated the Creeks in battle at Pine Island, Alabama (present-day Guntersville), in 1714. As a result, Pine Island was thereafter a Cherokee town called Creek Path, or Kusanunnehi.

Ustanali

Ustanali, near present-day Calhoun, Georgia, was the Cherokee capital in 1792. It had been destroyed by John Sevier in 1782 and rebuilt. It was the location of Tecumseh's speech to the Cherokees in 1812, where Major Ridge spoke in opposition to the speech and was attacked. According to James Mooney, the name "Ustanali" denotes a natural barrier of rocks across a stream.

Utsala

Utsala, or Lichen, was the leader of about half of the Cherokee refugees in the mountains of North Carolina during the roundup of Cherokees by the U.S. Army for removal to the West in 1838. When the army was seeking Tsali and his sons for killing U.S. soldiers, General Winfield Scott, through William Holland Thomas, contacted Utsala. Scott's proposition to Utsala was that if he and his men would capture Tsali and bring him in, the search for the refugees would be called off. Utsala agreed. Thomas went to see Tsali where he was hiding and told him of the proposal, to which Tsali replied that he would go in because he did want to be hunted down by his own people.

Robert J. Conley

V.

Vann, David

In 1801, David Vann, a prominent mixed-blood Cherokee, assisted the missionaries Reverend Abraham Steiner and Reverend Gottlieb Byhan to build the mission called Springplace in Georgia. His portrait was painted around 1845 and included in the McKenney-Hall Portrait Gallery.

David Vann, 1826. McKenney-Hall Portrait Gallery, Smithsonian Institution.

Vann, Donald

Donald Vann comes from Stilwell, Oklahoma. He is a full-blood Cherokee and a self-taught artist. In 1996, he was named Master Artist by the Five Civilized Tribes Museum in Muskogee, Oklahoma. He currently makes his home in Austin, Texas.

Vann, James

James Vann was a signer of the Treaty of 1806. He was selected in 1807, along with Ridge (later Major Ridge) and Alex Saunders, to execute Doublehead for treason for taking a bribe to sign a treaty turning over Cherokee lands to the United States. In the meantime, Doublehead shot and killed Bonepolisher. Vann supposedly became ill on the way to carry out the execution and dropped out, leaving the deed to Ridge and Saunders to finish up. Vann was killed in 1809.

Vann, Joseph (Rich Joe)

Joseph "Rich Joe" Vann signed the Cherokee Constitution of 1829. He built a two-story brick house at Springplace, Georgia, described by Harriet Gold Boudinot's father in a letter written in 1829. "Mr. Vann lives in a large elegant brick house, elegantly furnished. We stayed there overnight, and he would take nothing of us." After Rich Joe moved west, he had a duplicate of his Georgia home built near Webbers Falls (in what is now Oklahoma) by 1839. He cultivated between five and six thousand acres of rich bottomland with three to four hundred slaves. His racehorse Lucy Walker was known as the "fastest horse in the country," and her colts sold for as much as $5,000. He operated a mercantile business and a steam ferry across the Illinois River.

Rich Joe also had a steamboat that he named after his horse, the *Lucy Walker*. In 1844, he was racing another steamboat on the Ohio River, and in desperation because he was losing the race, he ordered the slave who was firing the boiler to throw on some slabs of bacon to make the fire hotter. The slave did so, and Rich Joe ordered him throw on some more slabs. The slave told Rich Joe that if he did, the boiler would explode. Rich Joe pulled out his pistol, aimed it at the slave, and repeated his order. The slave threw on the bacon and jumped into the river. The boiler exploded and blew the boat to pieces, killing Rich Joe and about fifty other people who were on board.

Vann, Wilson

Wilson Vann is originally from Sequoyah County, near Sallisaw, Oklahoma. He is a U.S. Navy veteran of World War II. He retired after thirty-seven years with Cessna Aircraft in Wichita, Kansas, and moved to Tahlequah, Oklahoma. He is one of the top teachers and practitioners of the martial arts in the United States, specializing in Tae Kwon Do and Kodokan Judo. He holds a black belt in Judo and a sixth-degree black belt in Tae Kwon Do. In more than thirty years of practicing the martial arts, he has won numerous trophies and medals in international competition. In Tahlequah, he opened his own school, the American Martial Arts Academy, and he

Wilson Vann, 2000.
Courtesy of photographer
David G. Fitzgerald.

Robert J. Conley

hosts his own martial arts tournament each year. Vann says that the study of martial arts is much more than a sport; "it is an art that is aimed toward improving the body, mind, and spirit. Some children might develop physical skills faster than others, but all are capable of self-improvement."

Viles, Philip

Philip Viles is the son of Philip Hubbard Viles and Mildred Elizabeth Milam, a daughter of Chief Jesse Bartley Milam. Viles received a bachelor's degree from the University of Virginia in 1968, a law degree from the University of Tulsa in 1975, a master's in business from the University of Tulsa in 1983, and a master's in library science from the University of Tulsa in 1998. He was appointed a justice on the Cherokee Nation's Judicial Appeals Tribunal in 1976 and served in that capacity until 1981, when he became chief justice. Between 1995 and 2001, he served as either justice or chief justice. In 1995, Viles dissented when the Judicial Appeals Tribunal ordered that the runoff election for principal chief go on as scheduled, with Joe Byrd and George Bearpaw on the ballot, even though no votes for George Bearpaw could be counted because he had to withdraw—a decision that in essence handed the election to Joe Byrd. In 2002, following the controversy between the Judicial Appeals Tribunal and the Chief Joe Byrd administration, and after Chad Smith defeated Byrd in the general election, Smith reappointed Viles to the tribunal, but the National Council denied him the appointment. Since 2002, Viles has been director of trust regulations, policies, and procedures for the Office of the Special Trustee for American Indians, Department of the Interior, in Washington, D.C.

In 1999, during the height of the Cherokee Nation's "constitutional crisis," Viles received a certain amount of publicity after Chief Byrd caused the court records to be seized and moved from the old capitol to the tribal headquarters. Viles notified the chief that he meant to retrieve the records. When he showed up at the headquarters to do so, Chief Byrd was not there, and the records were in a locked office. Viles hoisted Cherokee artist Virginia Stroud up to the ceiling so that she could remove a ceiling tile and crawl into that office. When Stroud opened the door, Viles had the records loaded onto a hand truck and taken outside to a waiting pickup. No one stopped them.

Viles is also the author of *National Statuary Hall: Guidebook for a Walking Tour* (1997), for which he was interviewed on national television a number of times. He wrote the foreword for *The Brainerd Journal: A Mission to the Cherokees, 1817–1823* (1998), transcribed by Joyce B. Phillips and Paul Gary Phillips; wrote the introduction to *The J. B. Milam Library: A Short-Title Catalog* (1993); and has authored essays on Jim Thorpe, Ross Swimmer, John Rollin Ridge, Stand Watie, and Elias Boudinot for *Notable Native Americans* (1994) and of essays for *American National Biography* (1998). In 2003, he received the Cherokee Medal of Patriotism.

For his service in the U.S. Air Force during the Vietnam War, Viles was decorated by both the United States and the Republic of Vietnam.

Robert J. Conley

W.

Walkabout, Billy

Billy Walkabout, a full-blood Cherokee, was the most decorated Native American Indian in the Vietnam War. He was a member of Company F, 58th Infantry, of the 101st Airborne Rangers. He received the Distinguished Service Cross, the second highest military award. When his ten-man patrol was ambushed, three men were killed and the rest wounded. Walkabout called in air support and mortar fire. Then he crawled around, firing from different positions to confuse the enemy and make them think that they had more than one soldier to deal with. When the helicopters at last arrived, Walkabout strapped the wounded men, one at a time, on the foldout struts to be hauled away to safety. In the book *Eye of the Eagle*, Gary Linderer, himself one of the wounded, wrote, "Indian [Walkabout] wrapped his arms around Conteros and the penetrator, lifted both clear of the ground, then carried his burden the necessary distance to place it directly under the hovering medevac." Walkabout died in 2007.

Walker, Dr. Jerald C.

Jerald C. Walker was born in Bixby, Oklahoma. He is a citizen of the Cherokee Nation. He attended Oklahoma City University, where he was president of the Student Association and a member of the Blue Key National Honor Fraternity. He graduated in 1960 with a bachelor's degree in sociology and went on to earn a bachelor's degree in divinity from the Divinity School at the University of Chicago and a doctorate in religion from the School of Theology in Claremont, California. He was named Distinguished Alumnus of Oklahoma City University in 1974.

Walker was chaplain and associate professor of religion at Nebraska Wesleyan University; president of John J. Pershing College in Beatrice,

Nebraska; vice president for university relations at Southwestern University in Georgetown, Texas; and president of Baker University in Baldwin City, Kansas. In June 1974, he was named the fourteenth president of Oklahoma City University, a position he held longer than any other president in the history of the university, more than twenty years.

Oklahoma City University made great strides under Dr. Walker's administration, increasing its enrollment and its budget, instituting new programs and adding to the physical plant. He built an especially meaningful and productive relationship with both the People's Republic of China and the Republic of China in Taiwan. In October 1997, he was named chancellor of the university and in 2000 chancellor emeritus. He retired to his hometown, Bixby.

Walker's publications include *The State of Sequoyah: An Impressionistic View of Eastern Oklahoma* (1985); "The Independent College and University President as Educational Leader," in *Courage in Mission: Presidential Leadership in the Church Related College* (1988); and "The Difficulty of Celebrating an Invasion," in *An Oklahoma I Had Never Seen Before: Alternate Views of Oklahoma History* (1994).

Walker, John, Jr.

John Walker Jr. was born around 1800 in Wachowee, located in present-day Polk County, Tennessee. His paternal great-grandmother was Nancy Ward, the Beloved Woman. His father, John Sr., was active in Cherokee politics and served in the 1813-14 Creek War under the command of Andrew Jackson. John Jr. was educated in New Jersey. He married a white woman, Emily Stanfield Meigs, daughter of Return J. Meigs, the onetime U.S. agent to the Cherokees, and moved her into a two-story log house in Tennessee. He also married Nannie Bushyhead, the sister of Reverend Jesse Bushyhead, but Nannie continued to live with her brother. Walker dressed like a frontier dandy. He served as a civil officer in the 1820s and on one occasion confiscated illegal whisky from James Foreman and some other men, knocking Foreman on the head and into the water in the process. When the activities of the state of Georgia grew intense against the Cherokees in the 1820s, Walker saw the Cherokee cause as hopeless. He became an advocate of removal to the West. He went to Washington, D.C., with delegates from the Western Cherokees in 1831 and again in 1833 and 1834 with David Vann. At the August 1834 meeting of the Cherokee National Council in Red Clay, Tennessee, Principal Chief John Ross gave his reasons for opposing removal. Tom Foreman spoke after Ross, accusing the proponents of removal of being traitors. Tempers flared, and John Walker Jr. decided to leave the council. Dick Jackson left with him, and they were followed shortly thereafter by James Foreman (the same James Foreman whom Walker had tossed in the water years earlier) and Anderson Springston. At Muskrat Springs on the old Spring Place Road, James Foreman shot Walker in the back. Walker fell from his horse, rose to his feet, and saw Foreman and Springston as they fled. Dick Jackson helped Walker get home, where he died in his own bed.

Walkingstick, Kay

Kay Walkingstick, of Cherokee descent, was born in 1935 in Syracuse, New York, where her mother had gone to escape an alcoholic husband, Kay's father. Kay was therefore raised away from Cherokee culture. She graduated from Beaver College in Glenside, Pennsylvania, with a bachelor's degree in fine arts in 1959. She became a respected painter of abstractions and a professor of art at Cornell University.

Ward, Nancy

Nancy Ward (Nanyehi, or One Who Goes About), a member of the Wolf Clan, was born in Echota in the part of the Cherokee Nation that coincided with Virginia. She was named Beloved Woman when she took the place in battle of her husband, Kingfisher, who had just been killed. She later married Bryan Ward, a white trader, and was known thereafter as Nancy Ward. She was a niece of Ada-gal'kala and a cousin of Dragging Canoe. In 1776, after the illegal sale of lands at Sycamore Shoals in Tennessee, Dragging Canoe was agitating for war against the settlers at Watauga, but Nancy Ward dissuaded him for a time. When Dragging Canoe finally made his plans of attack, Nancy sent runners to warn the whites of the approaching attacks. Dragging Canoe was wounded, and the three attacks were less than successful. This incident has led white historians to call Nancy Ward a friend of the white people, but many Cherokees call her a traitor. The truth is probably somewhere in between. It is possible Dragging Canoe should not have led the raids without the approval of Nancy Ward as representative of the women. Abram, who led one of the three parties in the attacks, came back with prisoners. One was killed, but one, Mrs. Bean, was rescued by Nancy Ward and later returned to her home.

At the negotiations for the Treaty of Hopewell in 1785, Nancy Ward accompanied Tassel and the other chiefs to South Carolina. Tassel requested that she speak for the Cherokees. She said, "I have a pipe and a little tobacco to give to the commissioners to smoke in friendship. I have seen much trouble in the late war. I am now old, but hope yet to bear children who will grow up and people our Nation, as we are now under the protection of Congress and have no more disturbance. The talk that I give you is from myself." In 1817, with some Cherokees wanting to make the move west, Nancy Ward wrote a letter to the "chiefs and warriors," urging them to sell no more land. She became the owner of a ferry and is said to have brought the first cattle into the Cherokee Nation and to have been the first Cherokee slave owner. She died around 1822.

Watie, Stand

Stand Watie was born December 12, 1806, near present-day Rome, Georgia, the son of Uweti, a full-blood Cherokee, and Susanna Reese, a half-blood. He was named Degadoga, a name meaning "two persons standing so close together as to form one body." Uweti was also sometimes known as David Uweti, but the surname was anglicized to "Watie." Degadoga was translated to English and shortened to "Stand."

Stand Watie grew up following many traditional Cherokee pursuits and speaking only Cherokee until the age of twelve, when he went to Brainerd Mission School in Tennessee. His older brother, Buck, had been born in 1802, went to school in Cornwall, Connecticut, and changed his name to Elias Boudinot in honor of his benefactor. At Cornwall, Elias met and married a white woman, Harriet Gold. He also published the first American Indian novel, *Poor Sarah; or, The Indian Woman*, in 1833. When Sequoyah presented the Cherokees with his syllabary and the Cherokee Nation began to publish a bilingual newspaper, the *Cherokee Phoenix*, he became its first editor.

His brother, Stand Watie, was a different sort, however—not a scholar but a man of action. Frank Cunningham writes, "In early manhood, Stand Watie had a close friendship with Sheriff Charles Hicks. When a notorious desperado murdered Hicks, Deputy Sheriff Watie hunted down the slayer and killed him." When pressures for Cherokee removal grew intense, Stand Watie resisted, along with the other tribal leaders, his uncle Major Ridge; his brother, Elias Boudinot; his cousin John Ridge; and Principal Chief John Ross. But when President Andrew Jackson refused to abide by the Supreme Court's ruling in favor of the Cherokees in *Worcester v. Georgia*, the Ridges, Boudinot, Watie, and others caved in. They saw no future in further resistance. At last, on December 29, 1835, they signed a treaty of total removal,

Stand Watie, c. 1840s.
Public domain. Courtesy of
the Cherokee Honor Society.

the Treaty of New Echota, with the U.S.
government. None of the signers were
legal representatives of the Cherokee
Nation, however.

The signers of the treaty and their
followers became known as the Treaty
Party. They moved themselves and
settled in with the Western Cherokee
Nation in Arkansas. After the Trail of
Tears, over which so many Cherokees died, some of those who had suffered that ordeal determined to kill the men who had signed the treaty.
After all, it had been Major Ridge himself who in 1829 had introduced to
the Cherokee Council at New Echota in Georgia a law calling for the death
of any Cherokee who signed a treaty giving out Cherokee land.

On June 22, 1839, John Ridge was dragged from his sickbed, stabbed
twenty times, and flung out into the yard. When his body thudded to the
ground, each of the assassins had their horses trample it and then rode
away. Mrs. Ridge and their young son, John Rollin Ridge, witnessed the
entire affair. Elias Boudinot was working at the home of Reverend Samuel
Worcester at Park Hill when some men came to ask him for medicine for
a sick person. As he walked down the lane with them, others came out of
the brush and hacked him to death with axes.

Major Ridge was riding down a road in Arkansas and was shot from
ambush and killed. Another group of men were on their way to the home
of Stand Watie, but a son of Reverend Worcester who had witnessed the
killing of Boudinot mounted his father's horse and rode to warn Watie.
Arriving in time, he gave the alarm, and Stand Watie fled. Watie gathered
armed men around himself for protection. Riding to his brother Elias's
home, he looked at the body and said, "I would give ten thousand dollars
for the names of the men who did this."

In response to Watie's band of armed men, another group of armed
Cherokees gathered around the home of Chief Ross. Watie went to
Washington, D.C., with a delegation of the Treaty Party to protest the kill-
ings and ask for federal protection. In 1841, back home, Stand Watie killed
James Foreman, a Ross supporter and supposedly one of the assassins of

members of the Treaty Party, in a fight at a tavern in Arkansas. He was tried for murder but acquitted. The violence escalated with killings on both sides. At last in 1846, it came to an end, at least for a time, and Watie seems to have forgotten his threats and thirst for revenge. He settled down to build his fortune.

When the Civil War broke out in the United States, the Confederacy began enlisting Indian tribes to its cause. Chief Ross intended to keep the Cherokee Nation neutral, but the Confederacy offered an attractive treaty, and the other four of the so-called Five Civilized Tribes ranged themselves with the Confederacy. At the same time, Watie put together a regiment and offered its services to the Confederacy. In reaction to Watie's Confederates, conservative full-blood Cherokees organized the Nighthawk Keetoowahs, who became known as the Pin Indians because of the identifying crossed pins they wore underneath their coat lapels. Fighting took place between the two groups of Cherokees. These two factions were basically the same division as before, just going under new names.

When help from the United States failed to materialize to quell the fighting, and Chief Ross began to fear that Watie would sign the Confederate treaty, he himself at last signed, making the Cherokee Nation Confederate, but then he left the Cherokee Nation and repudiated the treaty, establishing a Cherokee government in exile in Philadelphia. Stand Watie, now a colonel in the Confederate army, declared the Cherokee Nation Confederate, and in the absence of Chief Ross the new Southern Cherokees made Stand Watie principal chief. In 1861, Colonel Watie helped the Confederacy win the battle of Wilson's Creek in Missouri. He took part in the battle of Pea Ridge in Arkansas. Beyond that, Watie's troops roamed over Arkansas, Missouri, and what is now Oklahoma. In the Cherokee Nation, what the Pin Indians did not burn, Stand Watie's Confederates did. In 1864, President Jefferson Davis signed a commission making Stand Watie a brigadier general.

Stand Watie fought throughout the war, winning the admiration of the Confederacy and of his own troops. When Robert E. Lee surrendered at Appomattox on April 9, 1865, Watie was still holding out from his headquarters in the Choctaw Nation. He surrendered at last on June 23. His letter of surrender is signed, "Stand Watie, Principal Chief of the Cherokee Nation."

Watie fought for the best conditions for his people during the treaty negotiations at Fort Smith in Arkansas after the war, but when the majority of Cherokees returned to their homes, they reelected John Ross. Stand Watie spent his remaining years trying hard to rebuild his lost fortune. He died at his home on Honey Creek, September 9, 1871. He was sixty-five years old.

Robert J. Conley

Watts, John

John Watts was a follower of Dragging Canoe. Upon the death of Dragging Canoe, Watts became the principal leader of the Chickamaugas, a faction led by Dragging Canoe that had separated from the Cherokee Nation in protest against the sale of large amounts of Cherokee land to the Transylvania Company just prior to the American Revolution and that had sided with the British. In 1793, Watts led a large force of Creeks and Cherokees against Knoxville, Tennessee, but was sidetracked and instead attacked a small blockhouse called Cavitt's Station. The blockhouse was defended by three men and thirteen women and children. The men finally surrendered on Watts's promise that they would not be harmed, but instead held captive for exchange. When they came out of the blockhouse, however, Doublehead killed all of them except one boy whom Watts saved. Watts was disgusted at Doublehead's treachery and became an advocate of peace. It was he who signed the final treaty of peace between the Chickamaugas and the United States in 1794.

Weapons

The bow and arrow was the Cherokees' main weapon of war, with the war club being a close second. Charles Hudson says that the war club was the main symbol of war. Going into battle, a man carried a bow and arrows, a war club, and a knife. Some war clubs were solid wood and elaborately carved; some had copper celts mounted in carved wooden handles; and others had stone heads. The bow and arrow was also a main hunting weapon, the bow being made from black locust, ash, and Osage orangewood; the string from buckskin; and the arrow from cane, sometimes sharpened or sometimes tipped with flint or bone points.

Blowguns made of cane and darts made of hardwood and thistle down were used for hunting small game. Both short and long spears tipped with various kinds of projectile points were also used. By 1673, the Cherokees had acquired guns from the Spanish, so these handmade weapons were no longer used much.

Webber, Walter

Thomas Nuttall visited the home of Walter Webber in Arkansas in 1818 and described him as "a large, well-formed man." Webber had moved to Arkansas around 1809. He married a sister of Stand Watie. He was a merchant, but his store burned in 1824. That same year he became the third principal chief of the Western Cherokees. After the fire, he moved his operations to Nicksville in Lovely County in the Arkansas Territory in 1828. When the Arkansas Cherokees were moved across the Arkansas River into what is now Oklahoma, Webber moved again, this time to the place that would become known as Webbers Falls and is still known by that name today. He was a leader in at least one of the raids on the Osages during the long Osage-Cherokee war. However, he later accompanied Colonel Matthew Arbuckle of the U.S. Army on a peace mission to the Osages. He was a member of two different delegations to Washington, D.C., for the Western Cherokees. The second was in 1830 in which Webber, Sam Houston, and others dressed as conservative Cherokees, wearing turbans, leggings, breechcloths, and blankets.

Welch, John Goins

John Goins Welch was principal chief of the Eastern Band of Cherokees from 1907 to 1911.

Welch, Lloyd

Lloyd Welch (Dasigiyagi) was an educated mixed-blood from Cheowa on the Cherokee reservation in North Carolina. He defeated Flying Squirrel in the 1875 election for chief of the Eastern Band of Cherokees. He served one full term and was reelected to a second term, but died shortly thereafter in 1880. Various factions had grown up among the Eastern Band following the death of William Holland Thomas, and Welch worked hard at bringing them together. He consolidated his power and dominated the Tribal Council. The U.S. government recognized the constitution of the Eastern Band and the authority of the chief shortly before Welch died. He had resigned his position because of his failing health.

Western Cherokee Nation

When Bowles and his followers left the old Cherokee country in 1794, they settled for a time in Missouri before moving on into Arkansas. They were soon embroiled in a war with the Osage Indians and were dealing with the U.S. government as a nation separate from the Cherokee Nation. They became known as the Western Cherokees or the Western Cherokee Nation or the Cherokee Nation West. Following the Trail of Tears, they were reabsorbed into the Cherokee Nation through the Act of Union in 1839. The chiefs of the Western Cherokees were:

Robert J. Conley

Bowles, 1794–1813
Degadoga, 1813–18
Tahlonteskee, 1818–19
John Jolly, 1819–38
John (Captain Jack) Rogers, 1838–39
John Brown, 1839
John Looney, 1839

For more information, see individual entries under the names given here.

Whitepath

Whitepath (Nunna-tsunega), from Turniptown in Georgia, was a full-blood member of the Cherokee National Council in 1828. Echoing Tecumseh and William Weatherford of the Red Stick Creeks, he began to advocate a complete rejection of all white culture, including Christianity and the new written laws. He called for a return to old Cherokee ways. For a while, he had a large following. They were called Red Sticks by the whites, and his movement was called the Whitepath Rebellion. Whitepath was put off the council. With strong opposition from the more progressive tribal leaders such as John Ross and the Ridges, the "rebellion" soon faded away, and Whitepath was reinstated to his council position. He died on the Trail of Tears in 1838.

Whitepath Rebellion, see "Whitepath"

Wickliffe, Charlie

Charlie Wickliffe lived in the Delaware District of the Cherokee Nation, later Delaware County, Oklahoma. It is uncertain just when and why Charlie Wickliffe went afoul of the white man's law, but it seems that the only crime he was ever wanted for was the killing of some deputy U.S. marshals. Charlie was a member of the Nighthawk Keetoowahs, and the time was just before Oklahoma statehood. His reputation as an outlaw might have had something to do with that membership, or it might have been for some other reason altogether. Whatever the case, in 1906 Deputy Marshal I. L. Gilstrap was sent to bring him in. He and his posse of six men rode up on Charlie Wickliffe, his brothers John and Tom, and possibly a few more Cherokees. In the shooting that followed, Gilstrap was killed by a bullet between the eyes. His hound was also killed, another posse member was shot but escaped and survived, and the rest of the posse fled for their lives. Sometime later, John and Tom appeared before lawmen and said that Charlie was dead. They were not wanted by the law, just Charlie, so the lawmen went to the funeral. They asked that the casket be opened so they could identify the body, but they were told that it was badly mutilated. They accepted the story and left, closing the case against Charlie Wickliffe. Cherokees say that a hog was buried in the casket.

Wickliffe, George

George Wickliffe was born in Kenwood, Delaware County, Oklahoma, son of Ben Wickliffe and Rosa Blevins Wickliffe. He is a fluent Cherokee speaker. He attended Sequoyah Indian High School in Tahlequah, Oklahoma; Oklahoma Military Academy in Claremore; Northeastern State University in Tahlequah; the University of Tulsa; and Pittsburgh State University in Kansas. He holds associate's, bachelor's, and master's degrees in education and school administration. Wickliffe served on the Cherokee National Council from 1975 to 1979 and ran unsuccessfully for principal chief of the Cherokee Nation in 1995. He switched his allegiance to the United Keetoowah Band and in 2005 won election as its chief.

Wickliffe, John, see "Kaneega"

Wildcat, Tommy

Tommy Wildcat is a full-blood Cherokee from Oklahoma, raised in traditional ways. He has been called a "tradition bearer." As a young man, he spent much time teaching young Cherokees the old ways. He belongs to the Wolf Clan. Tommy launched a career by giving stomp dance demonstrations with his family. As the years went by, the family dropped out because of other interests, so Tommy started a one-man show, singing old songs and Cherokee hymns, playing the traditional flute, and telling old tales.

Tommy Wildcat. Courtesy of Tommy Wildcat.

Robert J. Conley

Wirt, William

William Wirt, a white man, was born November 8, 1772, in Bladensburg, Maryland, to a Swiss father and a German mother. He was privately educated and studied law. In 1792, he was admitted to the Virginia bar. He was clerk of the Virginia House of Delegates and chancellor of the Eastern District of Virginia. In 1807, he prosecuted the Aaron Burr treason trial and in 1817 became the ninth attorney general of the United States, holding the position until 1829.

In June 1830, on the recommendations of Senators Webster and Frelinghuysen, the Cherokee Nation, under the leadership of Principal Chief John Ross, selected Wirt to defend Cherokee rights before the U.S. Supreme Court. In the case *Cherokee Nation v. Georgia*, Wirt argued that the Cherokee Nation was a foreign nation and could not therefore be subject to the laws of Georgia. The Court refused to rule on the case, claiming that it did not have original jurisdiction.

On September 15, 1831, the state of Georgia sentenced two missionaries, Reverend Samuel Worcester and Reverend Elizur Butler to four years imprisonment at hard labor for violating one of its anti-Cherokee laws by refusing to sign a loyalty oath to the state of Georgia while living in the Cherokee Nation. Wirt once again took the case, *Worcester v. Georgia*, to the Supreme Court for the Cherokees, and this time he won. In the words of Elias Boudinot, "The laws of the state [of Georgia] are declared by the highest judicial tribunal in the country to be null and void." However, President Andrew Jackson refused to obey the Court's decision.

Wirt's feelings toward the Cherokees can be seen in an excerpt from his letter to Chief Ross in May 1831 in which he requested payment of $1,000: "But ... if you tell me ... that you are unable to pay fees, I shall solicit you no further on this subject, and you may continue to command my best services."

In 1832, having returned to Maryland, Wirt ran unsuccessfully as the Anti-Masonic Party's nominee for president against Jackson. He died in 1834. In addition to his distinguished legal career, Wirt was a successful writer. His titles include *The Letters of a British Spy*; *The Rainbow*; *The Old Bachelor*; and *The Life and Character of Patrick Henry*. As evidence of the respect Cherokees held for Wirt, a number of Cherokees carried his name, the most prominent among them being William Wirt Hastings.

Worcester, Reverend Samuel Austin

Reverend Samuel Austin Worcester was a white man born in 1798 and reared on a farm near Peacham, Vermont. His father, a preacher, taught him to farm and to set type. He graduated from the University of Vermont in 1818, where his uncle, Reverend Sam Worcester, was president. The elder Worcester was also one of the organizers of the American Board of Commissioners for Foreign Missions. Young Sam graduated from Andover Theological Seminary in 1825 and was ordained a minister of the Congregational Church. He and his wife immediately left for Brainerd Mission in Tennessee. After two weeks, he moved to New Echota, the capital of the Cherokee Nation (in Georgia), where he began work on translating the Bible into the Cherokee language. In 1831, Worcester was arrested by the Georgia Guard, according to Georgia's new anti-Cherokee laws, for living in the Cherokee country without having obtained a permit from the state of Georgia or having sworn an oath of allegiance to Georgia. His case, *Worcester v. Georgia*, eventually appeared before the U.S. Supreme Court, and it remains a landmark case in Indian law. Worcester spent sixteen months in prison, but won his case and was released. When members of the Treaty Party—those who signed the Treaty of New Echota, the Removal Treaty—began moving to the West, Reverend Worcester went with them, settling at Park Hill in what is now Oklahoma. He printed many Bibles, books, and religious tracts in his career. He died at Park Hill in 1859.

Worcester v. Georgia

In 1832, Reverend Samuel Worcester, Reverend Elizur Butler, and nine other white men were arrested in the Cherokee Nation by Georgia officials for having refused to sign the oath of allegiance to Georgia. Nine took the oath and were released, but Reverends Worcester and Butler refused. They were tried, found guilty, and sentenced to four years of hard labor in the penitentiary. Chief John Ross and the Cherokee Nation retained lawyer William Wirt to appeal the case to the U.S. Supreme Court. The Court ruled in favor of Worcester and ordered his release from prison. It ruled that in matters dealing with Indian nations, state law must give way to federal law. The Cherokees were ecstatic, but Georgia refused to release the two men, and President Andrew Jackson refused to enforce the Court's order—all leading up to the Cherokees' eventual removal to the West.

Worldview

According to the old Cherokee worldview, there are three worlds. There is the world we walk around on, a world up above, and a world below. The world above is on top of the Sky Vault. The world above and the world we

Robert J. Conley

walk on can be likened to a bowl turned upside down on a saucer. The Sun, a female, crawls along the underside of the Sky Vault, and when she reaches the bottom of the west side, the Sky Vault rotates a bit, and she goes under. It closes again, and she goes over the top. All the original life forms existed first on top of the Sky Vault. When it got too crowded up there, they came down, but they found only water. After several animals attempted to dive down under the water to locate some land, the little water beetle dived down and came up with mud, which they spread around, and then the great buzzard flew over it, flapping his wings to dry it. The world below is almost identical to this one, except that everything is opposite to this world, and it is chaotic. It is inhabited by great monsters, such as the ukitena, who can find his way to this world through the waterways. The world above and the world below are in opposition to one another, and our job on this world is to maintain balance between them.

In the old Cherokee world, there was an annual cycle of ceremonies designed to maintain this precarious balance. There were probably thirteen annual ceremonies. While a guest at the home of Principal Chief John Ross in the late 1830s, John Howard Payne interviewed old Cherokees and recorded the annual cycle in some detail. Anyone interested in the ceremonial cycle is encouraged to look for a copy of Payne's manuscript. For a much more thorough discussion of the Cherokee worldview, see Charles Hudson's *The Southeastern Indians*, chapter 3, "The Belief System."

Worm

Ujiya, or Worm, was one of the young men Sequoyah asked to accompany him in 1842 on what would become his last trip. Sequoyah did not tell the young men where they were going until they were well down into Texas, at which point he confided that they were headed for Mexico. Most of the men went back home, but the Worm and Sequoyah's son Teesee stayed with him. After much tribulation, they made it to Mexico, where they found the Mexican Cherokees. The Worm returned to Tahlequah, the new capital of the Cherokee Nation, with the news that Sequoyah had died there. He wrote the story of their trip, and it was printed in the *Cherokee Advocate* in 1844.

Woyi, Wili

Wili Woyi, also known as Bill or Billy Pigeon, was a highly respected Cherokee Indian doctor, or medicine man, of the last half of the nineteenth century. In 1886, he shot and killed a man who was trying to steal one of his hogs. He turned himself in to Cherokee authorities and was scheduled for trial. On his way to the courthouse on the day of the trial, he was met on the road by an acquaintance who told him that they had discovered that the man he had killed was not a Cherokee citizen, so the deputy U.S. marshals were waiting at the courthouse to arrest him and take him to the federal court for trial. Wili Woyi turned around and went back home. Shortly after that, he was arrested at his home by deputy marshals. While they were traveling to the federal courthouse, their prisoner somehow escaped. For the next eleven years, deputy marshals searched for him to no avail. At last, a badly decomposed body was discovered. The deputy marshals "identified" it as that of Bill Pigeon and closed the case. Most likely, the body was just a convenience. Cherokees believe that Wili Woyi could make himself invisible and could put himself into the body of an owl, and that is why the deputy marshals could never find him.

"Wrosetasetow"

In 1721, thirty-seven Cherokee chiefs met with Governor Francis Nicolson of South Carolina in Charlestown to protest the enslavement of their people. South Carolina had been deliberately starting wars between Indian tribes and collecting the prisoners from each side to sell into slavery in the West Indies. In addition, the chiefs set the boundary line between the Cherokee country and South Carolina, and discussed the South Carolina traders' bad treatment of the Cherokees. They made the first land cession to the white men in North America. They likely discussed other matters as well, but the lasting accomplishment of this meeting was the naming of a commissioner of trade by both sides. Governor Nicolson appointed Colonel George Chicken, and the Cherokee chiefs elected a man whose name has gone down in history as "Wrosetasetow." It has been suggested that his name as we know it was an attempt to spell the name "Outacity" and translated as "Mankiller."

"Wrosetasetow" seems to have served in his position of trade commissioner from 1721 until 1730. Little has been recorded concerning his activities during that time. The French were making inroads into the territory, and the tribes were dividing up according to their preference for the English or the French. The Chickasaws were strongly favorable to the British, and the Cherokees, although allied with the English, were leaning more and more toward the French. We know nothing more of "Wrosetasetow's" activities as trade commissioner or head chief. We do not even know if he lived beyond the year 1730. All we know is that in 1730 the English were once again looking for a new Cherokee chief to take charge.

Y.

Yonaguska

Soon after entering upon his duties at a store in Waynesville, North Carolina, young William Holland Thomas attracted the attention of Yonaguska (Bear Drowning Him), chief of all the Cherokees, living along the Tuckasegee and the Oconaluftee rivers. Upon learning that the white boy was an orphan, Yonaguska formally adopted him, and young Will became known to the Cherokees as Wil-Usdi (Little Will). When the Cherokee lands at Tuckasegee were sold in the 1819 treaty, Yonaguska and his people continued living on a 640-acre reservation on the site of the ancient town of Keetoowah in North Carolina. During the Removal in 1838, instead of moving west, he relocated his people to lands purchased for them by Thomas on Soco Creek, also in North Carolina. At around sixty years old, Yonaguska appeared to have died, but he revived after twenty-four hours and said that he had been to the spirit world. As a result, he quit drinking and encouraged them all to do the same. It was a message he brought from God, he said. When someone showed him a Cherokee translation of Matthew from the New Testament and read it to him, he said, "Well, it seems to be a good book—strange that the white people are not better, after having had it for so long." He was about eighty years old when, in 1839, he called his people together and recommended Will Thomas to them as their chief. Then he died.

Youngbird, Rebecca

Rebecca (Amanda) Youngbird was born on the Cherokee Reservation in North Carolina in 1890. She attended school at Cherokee and at Indian Industrial School at Carlisle, Pennsylvania. Around 1915, she began to make pots from clay found just outside her home near Cherokee. Entirely self-taught, Youngbird fashioned pots based on old Cherokee designs, but with her own individuality added. She also borrowed designs from the far west Pueblos. In 1934 at an Indian Fair in Atlanta, Georgia, Youngbird had the opportunity to observe the famous Pueblo potter Maria Martinez building pots over a period of a few days. She incorporated what she learned from Martinez into her own work. Over the years, she received numerous awards at the Cherokee Fair.

Youngdeer, Robert S.

Robert S. Youngdeer left Cherokee, North Carolina, as a young man and served eight years in the U.S. Marine Corps. He then went into the U.S. Army for twenty years. He was awarded the Purple Heart for his service in World War II. Returning to the reservation in 1975, he served as a law enforcement officer for the Bureau of Indian Affairs. In 1983, he won a hotly contested battle for chief of the Eastern Band of Cherokees by a mere seven votes. Although his stated priority was education, he attacked Cherokee bingo and was repudiated by the Tribal Council. He was an assimilationist, believing that the Cherokees needed to take their place in the larger American society. He was appointed by President Ronald Reagan to serve on the National Advisory Council on Indian Education, and he was instrumental in the first reunion of eastern and western Cherokees at Red Clay, Georgia, in 1984. He lost the election for chief of the Eastern Band in 1987.

Robert J. Conley

Z.

Za-wa-na-skie, Lewie, see "Downing, Lewis"

Bibliographic Essay

Discussions of the theory of American Indian migration from Asia across the Bering Strait can be found in any number of generic Indian books, including William Brandon, *The American Heritage Book of Indians* (n.p.: American Heritage, 1961); Colin F. Taylor, editorial consultant, *The Native Americans: The Indigenous People of North America* (New York: Smithmark, 1991); James A. Maxwell, ed., *America's Fascinating Indian Heritage* (Pleasantville, N.Y.: Reader's Digest Association, 1978); and Jules B. Billard, ed., *The World of the American Indian* (Washington, D.C.: National Geographic Society, 1974).

The migration story told to Alexander Long in 1717 has been reprinted in Russell Thornton, *The Cherokees: A Population History* (Lincoln: University of Nebraska Press, 1990). Two early attempts at chronicling the lives of the chiefs that are still somewhat useful are John P. Brown, "Eastern Cherokee Chiefs," *Chronicles of Oklahoma* 16, no. 1 (March 1938), and Gaston L. Litton, "The Principal Chiefs of the Cherokee Nation," *Chronicles of Oklahoma* 15, no. 3 (September 1937). Early Cherokee history and the lives of the early chiefs are covered in Grace Steele Woodward, *The Cherokees* (Norman: University of Oklahoma Press, 1963); R. S. Cotterill, *The Southern Indians: The Story of the Civilized Tribes before Removal* (Norman: University of Oklahoma Press, 1954); Peter Collier, *When Shall They Rest? The Cherokees' Long Struggle with America* (New York: Holt, Rinehart and Winston, 1973); Samuel Cole Williams, ed., *Adair's History of the American Indians* (New York: Promontory Press, 1930); James Mooney, *Myths of the Cherokee*, Nineteenth

Annual Report (Washington, D.C.: Bureau of American Ethnology, 1900); Emmet Starr, *History of the Cherokee Indians* (Oklahoma City: Warden Company, 1921); Tom Hatley, *The Dividing Paths: Cherokees and South Carolinians Through the Revolutionary Era* (New York: Oxford University Press, 1995); William G. McLoughlin, *Cherokee Renascence in the New Republic* (Princeton, N.J.: Princeton University Press, 1986); Dale Van Every, *Disinherited: The Lost Birthright of the American Indian* (New York: William Morrow, 1986); Charles C. Royce, *The Cherokee Nation of Indians: A Narrative of Their Official Relations with the Colonial and Federal Governments*, Fifth Annual Report (Washington, D.C.: Bureau of American Ethnology, 1887); Wilbur R. Jacobs, ed., *The Appalachian Indian Frontier: The Edmond Atkin Report and Plan of 1755* (Lincoln: University of Nebraska Press, 1967); and Patricia Dillon Woods, *French-Indian Relations on the Southern Frontier: 1699–1762* (Ann Arbor, Mich.: UMI Research Press, 1979).

Specific biographical material on early Cherokees is scarce, but a couple of works are valuable: James C. Kelley, "Oconostota," *Journal of Cherokee Studies* 3, no. 4 (1978); and James C. Kelley, "Notable Persons in Cherokee History: Attakullakulla," *Journal of Cherokee Studies* 3, no. 1 (1978). The only biography I have found of Charles Hicks is Rowena McClinton Ruff's "Notable Persons in Cherokee History: Charles Hicks," *Journal of Cherokee Studies* 17 (1996). Amazingly, it does not mention his son William. I have not been able to find a biography of William. In spite of the fact that William became principal chief, although for only one short year, historians apparently feel that his father played a much more significant role in Cherokee history. The elder Hicks did write "The Memoir of Charles Renatus," in *The United Brethren Missionary Intelligencer* (Winston-Salem, N.C.: Moravian Archives, 1827). Both Gary Moulton's *John Ross: Cherokee Chief* (Athens: University of Georgia Press, 1978) and Frank Cunningham's *General Stand Watie's Confederate Indians* (San Antonio: Naylor, 1959) are significant biographies. Moulton's slightly earlier and much shorter biography of Chief John Ross, "Chief John Ross: The Personal Dimension," *Red River Valley Historical Review* 2, no. 2 (Summer 1975), is still useful and interesting. Doug Tattershall has written an informative article on W. P. Ross, primarily as a journalist, called "Our Rights, Our Country, Our Race: W. P. Ross and the *Cherokee Advocate*, 1844–1848," *Chronicles of Oklahoma* 70, no. 3 (fall 1992). C. W. West's *Among the Cherokees* (Muskogee, Okla.: Muskogee Publishing, 1981) is primarily a compilation of many of West's newspaper articles. It includes a number of brief biographies, however, among them Bowles, Tahlonteskee, John Jolly, John Rogers, John Brown, John Looney, Richard Fields, Stand Watie, John Ross, William Potter Ross, Joel B. Mayes, Lewis

Downing, Charles Thompson, Dennis Bushyhead, O. H. P. Brewer Jr., Sam Houston Mayes, Colonel Johnson Harris, Thomas Mitchell Buffington, William Charles Rogers, W. W. Hastings, Jesse Bartley Milam, W. W. Keeler, and Ross Swimmer. The *Journal of Cherokee Studies* 10, no. 1, is a reprint of *An Illustrated Souvenir Catalog of the Cherokee National Female Seminary, Tahlequah, Indian Territory, 1850 to 1906*, printed at Chilocco, Oklahoma, no date given. It contains some useful information on Chief Dennis Bushyhead and a brief biography of O. H. P. Brewer Jr. There is much good material on William P. Ross and especially on Charles Thompson in Katja May's "The Cherokee Nation's Political and Cultural Struggle for Independence in the 1870s," *Journal of Cherokee Studies* 11, no. 1 (Spring 1986). Mrs. W. P. Ross had *Life and Times of Hon. William P. Ross, of the Cherokee Nation* printed in Fort Smith, Arkansas, by Weldon and Williams Printers in 1893.

The culmination of the 1887 election in Tahlequah, the capital of the Cherokee Nation, is retold by Janey B. Hendrix in "Humor and the Cherokee Spirit," *Journal of Cherokee Studies* 9, no. 2 (Fall 1984). John Bartley Meserve's "Chief Dennis Wolfe Bushyhead," *Chronicles of Oklahoma* 14, no. 3 (September 1936), is a very good brief biography, and his "Chief Thomas Mitchell Buffington and Chief William Charles Rogers," *Chronicles of Oklahoma* 17, no. 2 (June 1939), is an excellent treatment of the ways in which the last two chiefs before Oklahoma statehood dealt with the problems the Cherokee Nation was facing. John W. DeVine's interesting brief biography of Thomas Mitchell Buffington, "Last Chief of the Cherokees," *Frontier Times* 42, no. 3 (April–May 1968), claims to be based on an interview of five days with the old chief just weeks before his death at the age of eighty-three. Howard Meredith's *Bartley Milam: Principal Chief of the Cherokee Nation* (Muskogee, Okla.: Indian University Press, Bacone College, 1985) is both an excellent work on the life of Milam and just about the only book to deal with Cherokee history of that time period. A brief biography of Milam by Mildred Milam Viles appears simply under the family heading "Milam" in *History of Rogers County, Oklahoma* (Claremore, Okla.: Claremore College Foundation, 1979). There is also Grant Foreman's "Jesse Bartley Milam," *Chronicles of Oklahoma* 27, no. 3 (Autumn 1949). Brief biographies of W. W. Keeler and Ross Swimmer are in Dorothy Milligan, ed., *The Indian Way: Cherokees* (n.p.: Nortex Press, 1977). And then, of course, Wilma Mankiller and Mike Wallis's *Mankiller: A Chief and Her People* (New York: St. Martin's Press, 1993) is indispensable and thorough.

The best works on the jurisdictional conflicts in the Cherokee Nation during the days following the Civil War are Daniel Littlefield and Lonnie

Underhill's "Ezekial Proctor and the Problem of Judicial Jurisdiction," *Chronicles of Oklahoma* 48 (Autumn 1970), and Phillip W. Steele's *The Last Cherokee Warriors* (Gretna, La.: Pelican, 1993). Encroachments on Cherokee sovereignty, especially by the railroads and by the U.S. government regarding the Cherokee Outlet, are covered well in H. Craig Miner's "Cherokee Sovereignty," William W. Savage Jr.'s "Cattle and Corporations," and Alvin O. Turner's "Order and Disorder," all published in *Chronicles of Oklahoma* 71, no. 2 (Summer 1993). John Meserve's biography of Chief Harris, "Chief Colonel Johnson Harris," appears in *Chronicles of Oklahoma* 17, no. 1 (March 1939). A brief biography of A. B. Cunningham appears in "Necrology," *Chronicles of Oklahoma* 6, no. 4 (December 1928). Although Angie Debo's monumental work *And Still the Waters Run: The Betrayal of the Five Civilized Tribes* (Princeton, N.J.: Princeton University Press, 1940) contains very little information about any of the chiefs, it does have some information on two of the "chiefs for a day": E. M. Frye in his capacity as an Oklahoma state senator and W. W. Hastings in his capacity as a U.S. senator from Oklahoma.

Books on the Cherokees' involvement in the Civil War include W. Craig Gaines's *The Confederate Cherokees: John Drew's Regiment of Mounted Rifles* (Baton Rouge: Louisiana State University Press, 1989); Cunningham's aforementioned *Stand Watie*; Alvin M. Josephy Jr.'s *The Civil War in the American West* (New York: Alfred A. Knopf, 1991); and Vernon H. Crow's *Storm in the Mountains: Thomas' Confederate Legion of Cherokee Indians and Mountaineers* (Cherokee, N.C.: Press of the Museum of the Cherokee Indian, 1982).

The beginnings of the Eastern Band of Cherokees are covered admirably in John R. Finger's "The North Carolina Cherokees, 1838–1866: Traditionalism, Progressivism, and the Affirmation of State Citizenship," *Journal of Cherokee Studies* 5, no. 1 (1980). Duane H. King's "History of the Museum of the Cherokee Indian," *Journal of Cherokee Studies* 1, no. 1 (Summer 1976), makes mention of two of the Eastern Band chiefs. John R. Finger's *Cherokee Americans: The Eastern Band of Cherokees in the Twentieth Century* (Lincoln: University of Nebraska Press, 1991) and Sharlotte Neely's "Acculturation and Persistence among North Carolina's Eastern Band of Cherokee Indians," in *Southeastern Indians Since the Removal Era*, edited by Walter L. Williams (Athens: University of Georgia Press, 1979), are indispensable for information on the Eastern Band, as are Georgia Rae Leeds's *The United Keetoowah Band of Cherokee Indians in Oklahoma* (New York: Peter Lang, 1996) for the United Keetoowah Band of Cherokees and Mary Whatley Clarke's *Chief Bowles and the Texas Cherokees* (Norman: University of Oklahoma Press, 1971) for the Texas Cherokees.

Robert J. Conley

Other generally useful sources include Stan Hoig, *Sequoyah: The Cherokee Genius* (Oklahoma City: Oklahoma Historical Society, 1995); Morris L. Wardell, *A Political History of the Cherokee Nation, 1838–1907* (Norman: University of Oklahoma Press, 1938); Thurman Wilkins, *Cherokee Tragedy: The Story of the Ridge Family and of the Decimation of a People* (New York: Macmillan, 1970); William L. Anderson, ed., *Cherokee Removal: Before and After* (Athens: University of Georgia Press, 1991); Marion L. Starkey, *The Cherokee Nation* (New York: Alfred A. Knopf, 1946); Duane King, "The Day Tahlequah Burned," *Journal of Cherokee Studies* 13 (1988); Theda Purdue, *Nations Remembered: An Oral History of the Five Civilized Tribes, 1865–1907* (Westport, Conn.: Greenwood Press, 1980); Daniel F. Littlefield Jr., "Utopian Dreams of the Cherokee Fullbloods, 1890–1934," *Journal of the West* 10, no. 3 (July 1971); Marion E. Gridley, *Indians of Today*, 4th ed. (n.p.: ICFP, 1971); Barry T. Klein, *Reference Encyclopedia of the American Indian*, 10th ed. (Nyack, N.Y.: Todd, 2003); Carl Waldman, *Biographical Dictionary of American Indian History to 1900*, rev. ed. (New York: Facts on File, 2001); Bruce E. Johansen and Donald A. Grinde Jr., *The Encyclopedia of Native American Biography: Six Hundred Life Stories of Important People, from Powhatan to Wilma Mankiller* (New York: Henry Holt, 1997); *Biographical Dictionary of Indians of the Americas*, vol. 1 (Newport Beach, Calif.: American Indian Publishers, 1983); Frederick Webb Hodge, ed., *Handbook of American Indians North of Mexico*, parts 1 and 2 (New York: Rowman and Littlefield, 1971); John Parris, *The Cherokee Story* (Asheville, N.C.: Stephens Press, 1950). Information on Rebecca Youngbird came from Thomas J. Blumer, "Rebecca Youngbird: An Independent Cherokee Potter," *Journal of Cherokee Studies* 5, no. 1 (1980). The life of Stephen Foreman is dealt with admirably by E. Raymond Evans in "Notable Persons in Cherokee History: Stephen Foreman," *Journal of Cherokee Studies* 2, no. 2 (1977). Gaines's *The Confederate Cherokees* is an excellent source of information not only on John Drew, but also on the Civil War in the Cherokee Nation.

A detailed article on the work of Bill Glass and "Team Gadugi" by Dan Agent, editor of the *Cherokee Phoenix*, titled "Cherokee Monumental Art Returns to Origins," appeared in the July 2005 issue of that paper. And Lisa Hicks contributed a very informative article on Winnie Guess titled "Winnie Guess: Ballerina, Fancy Dancer, Ambassador, Athlete," in the September 2005 issue of the paper.

Information on James Mooney can be found in *Journal of Cherokee Studies* 7, no. 1 (1982). E. Raymond Evans's "Notable Persons in Cherokee History: Ostenaco," *Journal of Cherokee Studies* 1, no. 1 (1976), is very informative about the life of that interesting man. A biography of Arthur S. Junaluska appears in Marion Gridley's *Indians of Today*. The Sequoyah Indian Weavers Association is covered admirably in Cinda K. R. Baldwin's "The Sequoyah Indian Weavers Association," *Journal of Cherokee Studies* 9, no. 2 (fall 1984).

The Cherokee Historical Association, Cherokee, North Carolina, graciously provided me with information on the chiefs of the Eastern Band from 1947 in an article signed by J. Ed Sharpe and in additional unsigned brief biographies.

Finally, although Web research is frustrating, chancy, and often undependable, I did find useful information on several topics, including Gene Conley, Arthur Junaluska, Billy Walkabout, several of the chiefs, and other subjects.

www.ingramcontent.com/pod-product-compliance
Lightning Source LLC
Chambersburg PA
CBHW020536100426

42813CB00037B/3464/J